COLLEGEPREPGENIUS
THE NO BRAINER WAY TO SAT* SUCCESS

Jean Burk

Maven of Memory Publishing
Hurst, TX

I dedicate this book to Christ,
for He is the Hope of Glory.

ACKNOWLEDGMENTS

THANK YOU JIM, FOR insisting we home-educate Josh and Judah. You have held down the fort all these years so I could stay home to raise, teach and discipline our children. I am grateful for your total support of my dreams as our business has grown.

Josh and Judah, you've not only been my guinea pigs, you are the greatest blessings in my life. I appreciate your keen insight and wisdom in crystallizing this project. I thank you too, for your unbending desire to help make this book the best on the market so other families can benefit in the same way you did.

Thank you, Monica Brown, my dear friend. I appreciate your entrepreneurial spirit and your encouragement to make my acquired research and knowledge available for everyone's benefit.

Donna Boxerman, I thank you for your incredible input in the *Math* section. Invaluable.

And thank you, to all the tens of thousands of students who have gone through our program and achieved test success! Your inspirational testimonials of life-changes via raised scores and scholarship money are the reasons I continue to do this.

TABLE OF CONTENTS

PART IV: WRITING AND LANGUAGE

PART V: ESSAY SECTION

PART VI: SCHOLARSHIP SEARCH

PART VII: Journal for Test Success

HOW TO USE THIS BOOK

BEFORE YOU BEGIN A program to improve your *SAT* or PSAT/ NMSQT score, you need to know your starting place. Without that information, you won't be able to reliably check your progress. It's always a good idea to take a practice test in order to measure your strengths and weaknesses on the exam(s). To get a fair assessment, use the time constraints for each section. When taking a practice test, it is important to use official materials from The *College Board*, which writes the actual *SAT* and PSAT/NMSQT. Go to collegeprepgenius.com/ossgsat. More information on how to find official *College Board* material can be found on pages 53-54.

Once you've established your starting position, you should complete the *College Prep Genius* curriculum. Whether you are taking a live class/co-op or using it with the *College Prep Genius* online program, you should dedicate enough time to learn and understand all the strategies and information intended to help you better prepare for the *SAT*, *PSAT/NMSQT* and college itself. You may need to peruse this book two to three times to get a better understanding of the material.

As you learn the techniques and strategies for each section of the *SAT*, practice only on those sections in actual *College Board* materials (such as The Official *SAT* Study Guide). Start by practicing just one section at a time, then build up to two or three as you learn about different sections of the test. By the end of this program, you should be completing full tests. Always take practice exams in a similar testing environment to the actual test. If you use a page protector and wet erase pen or grease pencil, you can keep the practice tests clean for reuse, or for multiple students.

This book is full of **ACRONYMS** so you can easily recall the tips and tricks for answering questions correctly. During your practice sessions, always write the appropriate acronym at the top of the page to remind you of the recurring wrong answer patterns and traps that can be found on *College*

Start by practicing just one section at a time, then build up to two or three as you learn about different sections of the test.

Board tests. Take at least one test every week and spend the rest of the week correcting your mistakes. You can use the Journal for Success at the back of the book to help you keep track of your progress.

Learning lots of vocabulary words is not necessary for doing well on the test, but it can help you speak at a higher level and write better papers. You will need to learn the root words and negative and positive prefixes of the vocabulary words included in this text. It is essential to know and understand ALL the math definitions and how to apply them. Also, make sure you know the basic grammar concepts that have been supplied in the book.

Finally, take as many actual *SAT* practice tests as possible. When it is time to take the real test, you should be prepared and confident. Be sure to schedule more than one real test in a row, so that you will have multiple opportunities to do well.

TEST-TAKING TIMES

The *SAT* is offered 7 times a year from August-June. There are no penalties for taking the test as many times as you want and colleges generally take the highest score. They often take a composite score (Super Score) where the highest score from different sections on different tests is what comprises your end score. Colleges do not average the *SAT*-scores.

Find out which colleges participate:
    collegeprepgenius.com/SATSuperScore
    collegeprepgenius.com/SATScoreChoice

The *PSAT* can be taken multiple times but only counts for scholarships in the junior year. It is only offered once a year. Students should take the *PSAT 8/9* in the earlier grades for practice. Some schools offer the *PSAT8/9* in the spring and some offer it in the fall."

BEFORE YOU BEGIN...

The best way to gauge your success in this comprehensive program is to set a benchmark. By taking an actual *College Board* test before the *Master the SAT Class* program and the same one after, you can see immediate improvement as well as gain confidence and motivation to continue practicing. You will only retain a small percentage of what you hear the first time, so you will need to go over the program several times to really solidify the information to apply it appropriately. First there is introduction, then proficiency and then mastery.

Motivation is very important to help keep you on track.

1. Pre-test yourself
   Print and take test #1 at collegeprepgenius.com/ossgsat. The scan and score feature allows you to get your score in seconds at collegeprepgenius.com/SSS with the scoring sheets at collegeprepgenuis.com/answersheet. Make sure you have the *Daily Practice SAT* app on your smartphone. Record your baseline score, go through the *College Prep Genius* program and then retake the same or a similar test again. Notate your improvement. Always practice using pencil and paper rather than on the computer. It is best to rehearse answering questions in the same manner that is required of you in the real test. Useful Tip: *Keep the papers clean by storing them in a page protector and using either a grease pencil or wet erase marker to work the problems.*

2. Establish a *College Board* account at www.collegeboard.org. On this site, you can register for the SAT. This will give you the opportunity to print your registration ticket for the test and view your scores and your essay after it has been evaluated. You will have access to testing times, deadlines and testing facilities and a database of colleges and universities.

3. You can also get the *Daily Question* to practice from the website, Twitter or the mobile app. *Set up a separate email just for college and scholarship information.*

   Remember to work the *Daily Question* on paper. Print the screen, or copy, paste and print it. Work the problem like the real test by using your pencil to circle, underline and mark through certain words. Print these out and save them in a notebook, so you can practice with them many times. You can save the question of the day by archiving it on your phone. It will give you more test problems to practice with in the future and allow you to revisit the same questions.

4. Sign-up at www.fastweb.com, which will use your profile to send you scholarship offers and contests to enter.

5. Take the *My Motivation Test* at the back of the book on page 327 in Appendix C, or, if you have the ebook version, please find the pdf in the download section. Motivation is very important to help keep you on track. Discover what motivates you to succeed and use it to help you set goals for preparing for the *SAT* and *PSAT/NMSQT*.

6. Watch the book download tutorial video.

7. Watch the *Before You Start* video for an overview.

8. Follow the *Daily Homework Guide.*

PART I:

Introduction to the SAT

FUN TIP

The *SAT* has been renamed many times since its inception:

> 1924-1990-Scholastic Aptitude Test
> 1990-1993-Scholastic Assessment Test
> 1993-2004-*SAT* 1 Reasoning Test
> 2004- *SAT* Reasoning* Test

*The *College Board* trademarked this name.

WHAT IS THE SAT?

THE *SAT* IS A test used to evaluate students for college entrance and scholarships. The redesigned *SAT* is created by The *College Board* and is comprised of two sections: *Reading* and Writing (combined) and *Math*. The maximum score on each section is 800, with the highest possible score of 1600.

SAT is a Standardized Assessment Test. It is written by a group of people who make sure each question follows the same pattern, rules, standard, profile and criteria—year in, year out. You can rely on the testing format which is designed to be inherently the same, with the same types of questions for each exam. This design limitation is deliberate to level the playing field and by its nature it means the test can be figured out.

What is a standardized test? Because students come from a variety of educational backgrounds, colleges needed a way to measure a student's math and language skills without bias. It doesn't matter where or when you take the test. The *College Board* endeavours to create each test with the same level of difficulty and integrity, and every exam is independently graded on the same equal curve. The system allows you to take the test and compare your results to others' regardless of when you take the test.

It's reassuring the most fundamental aspect of the *SAT* (and other similar standardized tests for college) is its built-in objectivity. The same basic concepts are tested in each test by changing up the same question over and over again. Every type of question recurs on each test. If a student can learn how to correctly answer a certain type of question, he or she can answer the same question correctly each time it shows up on the test! The score you get is the sole component you will have in common with other students. Schools keep records of all students and their scores, so they can use them to assess college-

The *SAT* is created by The *College Board*, and is comprised of two sections: *Reading*/Writing and *Math*.

readiness of future applicants. This tracking of data helps colleges confirm the association between scores and achievement of students who were accepted.

All the standardized recurring test questions can be figured out through critical thinking.

The *SAT* is a test of *reasoning*, it is NOT *content-based* or a test of *subject matter*. Reasoning can be defined as "the use of reason/critical thinking to arrive at a conclusion." All standardized recurring test questions can be figured out through critical thinking, which is the mental process for evaluating information with discerning logic. The results give colleges a fair assessment of the student's reasoning and analytical abilities. To do well on this test you **do not** have to brush up on your classic literature or world history. Although students need a basic understanding of math and grammar, they do not need to have any specific knowledge about a certain topic. Students only need to learn how to answer the same basic questions that recur on every test.

By practicing and becoming very familiar with the patterns and question types, you can approach the test analytically and learn how to find the right answers automatically and easily.

I wrote this book to help familiarize you with the recurring question-types on the *SAT* and to give you the tools for the *right kind of practice*. When you practice answering the different questions correctly you'll feel confident and get better results because the right answers can become second nature to you.

If you want to raise your *SAT* and *PSAT/NMSQT* score—learn how to correctly answer the recurring question types and PRACTICE... PRACTICE...PRACTICE!

When Should Students Start Preparing?

It's never too early to begin preparing for your future.

Start now! Immediately! It's time to start preparing for the *SAT*. It's never too early to begin preparing for your future. Do not wait until you're a senior in high school—that's a HUGE MISTAKE! The more preparation-time you have, the more time you have to improve. You can never get back the time you lost, so go ahead and start!

Rule of thumb: The earlier you start the better—as early as the sixth or seventh grade is possible. I strongly believe that you need to have started *SAT*-preparation by the ninth grade, at the latest. You can start as early as the seventh grade. Younger students have the luxury of putting more time on their sides and iron out just about every problem they could encounter. We even have numerous students who start in sixth grade to gain test-taking maturity. With more time to learn the format and secrets of test-success, you will be able to achieve your ideal score way before the deadlines of college and scholarship applications. Remember, you can't rewind the clock!

IMPORTANT TIP

Young students can take the *SAT* for practice and talent searches but it only starts counting for college in 9th grade.

FUN TIP

The *SAT* determines where you get to go to college and who's going to pay!

If, however, you wait until somewhere in 11th or 12th grade to start your test-prep, then you really need to make acing the *SAT* a high priority. You'll need to practice as much as possible at home before it's time to take the actual test. Years of experience have proven to me time and again, you should schedule as many real tests as possible—especially seniors where only a few opportunities remain to take the test before graduation. There is no age limit on the test so even adults who have graduated can still take the test.

Learn to treat this test as a game. By learning to get in the mindset of the *College Board* (understanding how they write the questions and how they answer them), you can win at their game. Winning can mean higher test scores, entrance into the college of your choice, scholarships, etc. Colleges go up in their rankings nationally so the higher the score, the better a college looks, the more money they have and the more money you get!

Understanding the logic behind the questions is the key to test success.

Why Do Some Students Get Low Scores?

What's the big deal? I hear you ask. It's just another exam. That belief can be your biggest downfall. Many smart students do poorly on the *SAT* because they simply don't understand it. They approach it like a standard high school exam. They try to cram a bunch of information from school; advanced vocabulary words and math formulas. Although to know these things will be advantageous in life or other subjects, it may be fruitless on the *SAT*.

The *SAT* is a reasoning test and not content-based. Outside of knowing your basic math and grammar, every correct answer can be found without prior knowledge of the subject matter. It's great news for you. Instead of studying content, you need to study how the tests themselves are set up and how the questions are written. That knowledge is key to determine how to answer each question-type correctly. The *SAT* tests mental ability and how to answer questions under pressure. It takes a different skill-set to ace the test.

Some students are naturally logic-minded, and these types of tests come easily. This doesn't mean that those who are not won't be able to do well on the *SAT*. It simply means they will have to retrain themselves on how to look at these tests in a logical manner and spot all the hidden clues. Perfect practice makes perfect. Athletes practice and train to excel at their particular sport. The *SAT* is no different.

Part of my job is as an *SAT* myth-buster. With specialized experience since the early 2000s I'm pretty good at it now! You do not have to be a left-brained to do well on the *SAT Math*! You do not have to be right-brained to do well on the *Reading* sections! The *SAT* does not test how good you are at math or how proficient your language skills are; it tests your ability to use critical thinking and reasoning. Its vehicles are basic math and verbal concepts. When you learn how to address the test with a logical perspective, you will unlock your abilities to do well on this test! Remember, the questions are standardized, which means the same types of questions occur over and over again.

Tests like the SAT, PSAT and ACT are mental marathons and students can learn to know why the right answers are right and why the wrong answers are wrong. By learning to eliminate the trick answers first, it will protect students from encountering decision fatigue.

The key to test success is to understand the logic behind the questions.

TEST OBJECTIVITY

YOUR OPINION DOESN'T MATTER

The questions on the *SAT* are ALWAYS objective and NEVER subjective. You should find this reassuring as it means that no question is left up to personal opinion or interpretation. There is only one right answer and it can be found logically from the given information.

> Subjective—One's own opinion; no concrete basis of definition; perceived
>
> Objective—Factual without prejudices; truth can be derived from information

It is important not to be tempted to bring in your own opinion, read between the lines or look for any hidden agendas/meanings. Take every word literally. Students who understand this truth learn how to avoid subjective answer choices and correctly pick the right objective answers over and over again.

Don't justify why an answer should be right or wrong. There is no need to rationalize every answer choice; look for the obvious right one. If you are torn between two answer choices with similar meanings, they are probably both wrong since the test leaves no room for subjectivity. For example: A question asks you to define the meaning of a certain word, and the answer choices include happy, joyous and mirthful. You can be guaranteed that none of these three would be correct because they all have very similar meanings, which means if one of these is correct, you could argue the validity of the other two. This is what it means to be subjective.

ONLY ONE CORRECT ANSWER

There is only ONE correct answer for each question among the four multiple-choice answers in the *Reading* and *Writing* sections. If a question appears to have more than one answer, you need to double-check your work. Remember, the test is never subjective. *(Important exception to note:*

The questions on the *SAT* are ALWAYS objective and NEVER subjective.

It is important to not be tempted to bring in your own opinion, read between the lines or look for any hidden agendas/meanings.

Mathematical Student-Response questions may have more than one correct answer since there are no answer choices.)

Keep your concentration sharp so you can find the wrong answers which will undoubtedly follow The *College Board* patterns. If you find a problem in an answer choice, mark it off immediately and don't waste time. You will need practice to get out of your habit to second-guess yourself or overthink the question. Make it your goal to quickly eliminate all the wrong answers first which will generally leave you with the one right answer.

More than anything, the *SAT* is a test of managing time.

TIME MANAGEMENT

More than anything, the *SAT* is a test of managing time. How fast and how well can you answer the questions in the allotted amount of time? Most students do NOT finish answering all the questions in each section. A failure of many students is to approach each question long-hand. They get caught in the trap where they try to answer it in the conventional way. This standard approach will usually take much longer than the allotted time. The *College Board* designs most questions to be answered in 30 seconds or less. They construct the questions with predictable patterns that—if you know what to look for—will quickly point you to the answers. There is usually a long way to work the problems, and then there is a shorter and more logical way to approach and attack each question type. It is the goal of this book to teach you how to approach problems the short way!

MAINTAIN MOMENTUM

If you do not know how to answer a question, it is better to skip the question and go work the ones you do know. Your subconscious mind may continue to work out the problem so, if you get time at the end, you can come back and rework it. Be diligent and clearly mark the missed question with a star and you'll find it again quickly if you get an opportunity. My students are taught to examine the question; glance quickly to see if they can answer it quickly, if not, they move on. Most people won't finish all the questions, so don't waste time erring over the workings of a question that you may or may not be able to work out. Move on!

All questions are worth one point regardless of their difficulty level.

SAT STRUCTURE

The *SAT* is a three hour and 50-minute test (including optional essay) administered by the *College Board*. The format and structure of the test is standardized, and it generally keeps the same patterns. The questions are not sequenced in order of difficulty. You are required to look at each problem with a critical eye, regardless of where it is found in the section. The *Reading, Math* and *Writing* sections are all divided into parts.

The *Reading* section has one section and three parts:

- Passage-Based *Reading*
    1. Long Passage
    2. Passage with Chart or Table
    3. Dual Passage

You have 65 minutes to take the *Reading* test. It is comprised of six passages and fifty-two questions.

The *Math* section has two sections:

- *Math* with Calculator
- *Math* without Calculator
    1. Multiple Choice
    2. Student-Response

Some of the types of problems include: Algebra 1 and 2; arithmetic and word problems; factoring and functions; geometry; measuring; number lines; statistics; probability and data analysis; interpreting scatter plots; trigonometric functions; radian measure; linear and exponential growth and so on.

You have 80 minutes to take the *Math* test. It is divided into two sections: one 55-minute part and one 25-minute part.

The *SAT* is a three hour and 50-minute test.

There will be a total of four sections on the actual SAT.

The *Writing and Language* section has several passages with:
- Grammar Errors
- Style Errors
- Included graphs

You have 35 minutes to take the Writing test. There is one section of four passages each with eleven questions.

The optional essay section (I recommend my students take it) is 50-minutes long. It is not counted in with the *Writing* grade. There are a total of four sections on the actual *SAT*.

SAT ANSWER SHEET

When you take the *SAT*, you are given two items: A *test booklet* (with all the questions) and a separate *answer sheet* with a *bubble grid*.

It's very common to be told you are not permitted to write in your test booklet, but this is not true. Copy and print the *College Board* official tweet about the allowance of writing in the test booklet at collegeprepgenius.com/ testdayrule. Take it to the test.

The *SAT* booklet is yours to work out your problems in. Nobody will grade your test booklet, nor will it be sent to you in the mail, so feel free to mark it up. If you skip a question in the test booklet, be sure to put a star by it. If you circle back for another try, you can identify the question easily, but more importantly it will help you keep your place on the answer grid to bubble-in your answers correctly.

The answer sheet is read and graded by a machine. For answers to be counted, they must be marked in the bubble grid. I recommend you work several problems, circle your choices, and then transfer answers to the bubble in sheet in blocks.

Make sure your grid is bubbled-in neatly and dark. If you skip a question, double-check to see if the darkened ovals line up and correspond to the question numbers in your test booklet.

You <u>cannot</u> go back and forth between sections, return to earlier sections, or spend more than the time allowed on any given section. You may move around a given section or just flip through it to see what's ahead.

WHEN TO BUBBLE-IN YOUR ANSWERS

1. *Reading:* After each passage.
2. *Writing:* After each passage.
3. *Math:*
    a.) Multiple choice—after every two pages
    b.) Student-response—after each question

EXPERIMENTAL SECTION

At some testing facilities, students may encounter an unexpected 20-minute experimental fifth section with unpredictable subject matter. This will be for those who have opted-out of the essay and don't have accommodations (which may come in the form of extra time for students with special needs). The *Advising and Admission Handbook* given to counselors contains these instructions: "Any section of the *SAT* may contain both operational and pre-test items."

Operational—test questions that count toward a student's score.
Pre-test—test questions that are neither scored nor factored in.

HOW TO PREP FOR THE EXPERIMENTAL SECTION

The chance you may be the recipient of an extra 20-minute experimental section is completely unpredictable. Here are some guidelines to consider:

1. Expect the unexpected. Your test site may be chosen so if given a fifth section, don't sweat it.

2. Assume these extra questions count; don't disregard them. Treat the *operational* and *pre-test* items with the seriousness of the rest of the test.

3. You may find the items are a repeat of questions found in an earlier section so answer them the same way. This tactic is used to detect cheating on the test.

4. If the question appears weird, more than likely it is being used to gauge difficulty level for a future test and probably won't be scored.

5. During preparation, when getting close to an actual test date, add another 20 minutes of questions from another practice test to help with endurance. It can be math, reading or writing.

FUN TIP

Besides the number 2 pencils you bring to the test, bring a big, fat, round pencil from the hardware store to use to bubble-in and save time.

SCORING THE SAT

Your *SAT* score is calculated in two ways: *Raw Score* and *Scaled Score*.

For every correct answer you receive one point. This is your *Raw Score*. There is no penalty if you skip questions.

In every section, *Raw Score*s are converted to *Scaled Score*s (from 200 – 800). An equating process—based on statistical evaluation—is used to ensure each edition of the test is treated equally. The whole college entry system needs to rely on consistency, in order that an overall score of 1300 on one test is equivalent to a score of 1300 on a different edition of the test. This equating process, or "*SAT* curve," ensures **the same level of ability and opportunity no matter when you take the *SAT*.**

The essay is scored separately from the potential 1600.

SUB-SCORES

The *College Board* has also added two more detailed explanations for score-evaluation:

1. The cross-test scores show your strengths and weaknesses in analytical thinking in history, social studies and science and are reported on a 10-40-point scale.

2. The test sub-scores are a more thorough examination of each section.

For example:

Reading
- Command of Evidence
- Words in context

Writing and Language
- Exploring Ideas
- Standard Written English

Math
- Algebra
- Problem Solving and Data Analysis
- Advanced math

These scores are reported on a 1-15 range.

These additional scores help break down specific areas of weaknesses and are NOT factored into the overall maximum score of 1600.

For more information about scoring, visit:
www.collegeboard.com/student/testing/SAT/scores/understanding/howscored.html.

The average *SAT* score is around 1007 out of 1600. The minimum score for college entrance varies from college to college.

USEFUL SCORE FACTS

- The average *SAT* score is around 1007 out of 1600.
- The minimum score for college entrance varies from college to college.
- The average starting score for scholarships is around 1250.
- Full scholarships can be obtained with scores around 1400 and above.
- Always check with websites of individual colleges for more information.
- The fastest way to get your *SAT* results is to create an account at www.collegeboard.org. You can view your scores on the website around two weeks after the test date, and you can view your essay, too.

THE LANDSCAPE PROGRAM

The *SAT* Landscape Program provides data about a student's school and neighborhood for college admissions officers so they can have a more consistent background about the student; they use it to fairly consider every student, no matter where they live and learn. There is no score attached and no personal questions are asked of the student.

DETAILED SAT FEEDBACK

There is a way to discover the details of the *SAT* you took and use the feedback to enhance your college chances. For a small fee, you can order *The Question and Answer Service* by the *College Board*. You will receive a copy of a clean unmarked test booklet of the exam you sat; an answer sheet; a copy of your answers and the difficulty level of each question. This service is only available for tests taken in October, March and May and CPG highly recommends it.

Several factors can affect your score:

- How well you know and understand the test.
- The effectiveness of your test-taking strategies.
- How well you have practiced.
- How adequately you prepared the day before the test.

SENDING SAT SCORES TO COLLEGES

When you sign up online for the *SAT*, you can request four of your scores be sent to the college or colleges of your choice, at no charge. For a small fee, you can have your scores sent to additional colleges. For more information, visit http://www.collegeboard.com/student/testing/sat/scores.html. Some schools require scores to be received by a certain deadline. They refer to this as *Early Decision* or *Early Action*.

You could be worried you might send bad test score to colleges. The *College Board* offers *Score Choice*, which allows you choose to send only certain scores to select colleges. Sometimes a school wants to see ALL your scores, but the good news is that most colleges only want to know your highest score. There is no penalty for taking the test many times. Colleges don't average the scores, and many schools will take the highest scores from different sections on different tests to get you the best score. This amalgamation of best section-scores is referred to as your *Super Score*. Therefore, it behoves you to take the test many times. The *College Board* will save *SAT* scores for up to one year and then archive them indefinitely.

CANCELING TEST SCORES

After taking the test you feel like you really messed up, you can cancel your scores. There is a limited time frame that this can be done. A *Test Cancellation* form can be found at the testing facility, or you can contact the *College Board*. If you do cancel, your score report will be noted as "Absent or Scores Delayed."

When you sign up online for the SAT, you can request that your scores be sent to four colleges of your choice at no charge.

The ACT® (American College Test) is a test and also used for college entrance.

THE SAT VS. OTHER TESTS

ACT

The ACT® (*American College Test*) is another standardized test and is also used for college entrance. It tests four areas: English, *Math*, *Reading* and Science. It also contains an optional Writing section. The ACT is offered seven times a year: September, October, December, February, April, June and July. It can be taken twelve times. Basically, every college will take either the *SAT* or ACT, and if they prefer one over the other, they will usually convert the score.

FUN TIP

You don't have to have any scientific knowledge to do well on the science section on the ACT—it is very similar to the *Reading* section on the *SAT*.

In the fall of 2021, students can retake one section at a time on the ACT.

Both the *SAT* and ACT are extremely similar tests and strategies for one test can work on the other since there is a crossover of information. Students should take both tests since some schools may give more money on one test over the other.

Sign up for the *ACT Question of the Day* at www.act.org.

Most colleges will *Super Score* the ACT from different tests. For a list of colleges that do this, please visit collegeprepgenius.com/ACTSuperScore

SAT, ACT AND CLT CONVERSION CHART

CLT	ACT	SAT
120	N/A	N/A
118	N/A	N/A
116	N/A	N/A
114	36	1600
112	36	1580
110	35	1560
108	35	1540
106	34	1520
104	34	1500
102	33	1480
100	33	1460
98	32	1430
96	31	1410
94	31	1390
92	30	1370
90	29	1340
88	28	1320
86	28	1300
84	27	1260
82	26	1240
80	25	1220
78	25	1200
76	24	1160
74	23	1130
72	22	1100
70	21	1080
68	21	1060
66	20	1030
64	19	990
62	18	970
60	17	950
58	17	930
56	16	900
54	15	870
52	15	830
50	14	800
48	13	770
46	13	730
44	12	700
42	11	670
40	11	650
38	10	630

FUN TIP

The CLT has partnered with *College Prep Genius* as their test prep of choice. Use partner ID code: CPG18 for half off registration for the actual test and practice

The *SAT* is NOT like a normal school test. It is not an IQ test but a test of logic and critical thinking.

NORMAL SCHOOL TESTS

If you approach the *SAT* like a normal test, you are not likely to receive the score you deserve. This is because the *SAT* is NOT similar to a normal school test. It is not an IQ test but a test of logic and critical thinking, and takes a different skill-set to beat it.

Normal School Test	SAT
No more than an hour long	Nearly four hours long
Harder questions receive more credit	All questions worth one point
Partial credit for correct parts	Only one right answer
Use long calculations for math (show work)	30 seconds or less for the math
Deeply examining passage content	Skimming passages
Essays that have been through several drafts	50-minute optional essay
Rewriting correct grammar	Choosing from answer choices
Subjective answers	Objective answers

SAT II

The *SAT II* is a subject-specific test that measures your logic skills and mastery and knowledge in a specific subject area, but similar *SAT* strategies still work. You may have to take one or more of these tests if it is a requirement by the college of your choice. Certain colleges use them along with a student's transcript and *SAT* scores to help determine college preparedness. There are five categories of *SAT II* Subject Tests: English, *Math*, History, Science and Languages.

AP TESTS

AP (Advanced Placement) classes are college-level courses taken in high school. Students who complete AP courses are eligible to take AP exams designed by the *College Board*. These tests are scored on a scale of 1 to 5. A score between 3-5 may qualify a student for college credit at most colleges and universities.

CLEP TESTS

CLEP (College Level Examination Program) allows you to earn college credit by taking qualified *CLEP* tests in a particular subject. The tests are designed to correspond to a one-semester class; they can sometimes cover up to a two-year course. The exams are generally 90 minutes long and cover specific information on knowledge and skills acquired about a certain subject. Be careful not to study too many CLEP classes before starting college; it could cost you scholarships. It is usually better to do most CLEP tests after you are enrolled in college but check with the school first. If you receive too many incoming hours, colleges may consider you a transfer student, disqualifying you for some scholarships.

FUN TIP

Strategies learned in this guide can also be used on other tests such as AP, CLEP, GRE, L*SAT*, ACCUPLACER ... so since the *College Board* makes most of these tests, take similar ones. E.g. if you are taking an AP History test then take the corresponding *SAT* II History test and get credit for both.

THE CLT

The *CLT (Classic Learning Test)* is an alternative to the *SAT* and *ACT*. It is offered five times a year and taken on a device such as a laptop or tablet. New colleges are adopting it almost weekly and it is used for entrance and scholarship money. It contains 120 questions and is two hours long. The essay is optional and is unscored. The best possible score is 120. More information at www.cltexam.com

The *CLT 10* has partnered with the *NAS (National Association of Scholars)* so sophomores who take the test, and score in the top 1% of test-takers, can be eligible for scholarships. Sophomores can take all three CLT10s and the highest score is taken for scholarships! In 2018, approximately 1600 took the *CLT 10* which makes this vehicle very attractive because at the moment the competition is very low.

When taking a *CLT*, under the Partner ID section, use the code: CPG18 for prize eligibility and half-price registration.

WHAT IS THE PSAT/NMSQT?

PSAT/NMSQT stands for Preliminary SAT/National Merit Scholarship Qualifying Test.

*P*SAT/NMSQT STANDS FOR *PRELIMINARY SAT/National Merit Scholarship Qualifying Test*. Students in their freshman, sophomore and junior years of high school qualify to take this exam. Juniors who score in the top percentile can compete in the *National Merit Scholarship Competition* which may qualify them for numerous scholarship opportunities that can include full tuition, room and board, graduate school money, study abroad stipends and more!

There are also 1,700 Special Scholarships that are awarded to high-scoring applicants who do not qualify to compete in the scholarship competitions, but who meet other specific criteria designated by scholarship sponsors (businesses or corporations).

Registration for the *PSAT/NMSQT* must be done through a high school (not online). Parents should sign students up early to ensure a place, but you can sign up on the day of the test if there is room and they have enough booklets.

Because the *PSAT/NMSQT* is basically a scholarship test, you'll want to make practicing for it a priority.

Both the *SAT* and *PSAT/NMSQT* are written by the *College Board*. Since both tests have the same creators, the question types are similar. They both contain three sections: *Math*, *Reading* and Writing. However, the *PSAT/NMSQT* does not contain an essay and is shorter in time than the *SAT* (2:45). The *PSAT/NMSQT* is only offered in October (third Wednesday or Saturday) and the *SAT* is offered seven times a year (August, October, November, December, March, May and June). The *SAT* is used for college entrance as well as scholarship opportunities, but the *PSAT/NMSQT*'s sole purpose is to determine eligibility for the *National Merit Scholarship* program. Because the *PSAT/NMSQT* is basically a scholarship test, you'll want to make practicing for it a **priority**.

Colleges covet students with high *PSAT* scores because it is a bragging right to have *National Merit Scholars* in their marketing information. Schools are looking for a minimum number of these students. Please reference page 21 at www.collegeprepgenius.com/NationalMeritSchools

The *PSAT* is an important test and should not be ignored. Perks for students with high *PSAT* scores can include full-ride, free tuition, free room and board, study-abroad stipends, graduate school money, spending cash, new computer…

Both tests are important, and when you study test-taking techniques for one test, essentially, you're also studying for the other test. Similar to the *SAT*, the *PSAT/NMSQT* is <u>not</u> a test of how much you really know. It is a test of reasoning skills and critical thinking. The key to doing well on the *PSAT/NMSQT* is to become familiar with the test patterns, learn test-taking strategies and then practice with *College Board* materials. Students should take both tests since they have different purposes.

> **Like the SAT, the *PSAT/NMSQT* is NOT a test of how much you really know. It is a test of reasoning skills and critical thinking.**

NATIONAL MERIT SELECTION PROCESS

Since 1971, the *National Merit Scholarship Program* has offered scholarships through the *PSAT/NMSQT*. Although the test is offered to freshmen, sophomores and juniors, you will only qualify for the scholarship competition if you label yourself as a junior on the test. The *National Merit Corporation* receives all the *PSAT/NMSQT* scores of juniors—of which there are approximately 3½ million per year—and the competition begins.

Even though your scores will not count for the competition, you should strongly consider taking the *PSAT/NMSQT* as many times as possible before the junior year. Younger students should take the *PSAT 8/9* which is usually administered twice: September-January or February-April on various days.

There are two benefits for taking the test early. The first is the ability to gauge your score capability as a younger student and set realistic goals for future tests. The second is you will receive your actual test booklet back, so you can go through it to pinpoint your strengths and weaknesses. You'll get your score in

> **There are benefits for taking the test early.**

> **IMPORTANT TIP**
>
> Students can now only get the Wednesday test date *PSAT/NMSQT* booklet back.

about a month and can also be accessed online sooner. In order to view the score report, you will need to set up an account at *www.collegeboard.org*.

Score reports and test booklets will be sent back according to the school code on the test. Just be sure to write your correct school code on the booklet. Homeschoolers will need to check the appropriate boxes. "No, I am homeschooled" and the correct code will be applied based on the home address. Instead of going to the school, the test booklets and scores will be returned to the student's home, and his or her score will not be counted in the calculation of the testing facility's average. To find the home school code for each state go to http://www.collegeboard.com/student/testing/psat/reg/homeschool/state-codes.html.

The qualifying score for the *National Merit Scholarship Competition* varies year-to-year and is dependent on where a student lives and takes the test. The first step in the *National Merit* selection process is qualifying as a semi-finalist. The *Selection Index* score is the determining factor in qualifying as a semi-finalist. This score is the sum of the two scores from the *Math* and *Reading*/*Writing* sections of the test. To qualify, your score must be in approximately the top 2% of the state—in the 97th- 99th percentile. Each state varies in its cut-off score. The range is from 320-1520. Collegeprepgenius.com/predictedPSATscores

Although the test is in October, it's not until late August of the following year when *The National Merit Corporation* notifies the 16,000 students who have achieved semi-finalist standing. Around 50,000 students will be recognized (34,000 *Commended Letters* and 16,000 *Merit Semi-finalists*). They will also send a list of the semi-finalists to four-year colleges and universities all over the United States. Local newspapers will get the same list to print the winners' names in their paper. Only students who opt to be added to the *Student Search Service* will be included in this list. This authorizes colleges to mail pertinent information to certain students they are interested in recruiting. The *College Board* does not report specific test scores. Students should check the box for the *Student Search Service* option on the *PSAT/NMSQT* exam only in their junior year. (This keeps unsolicited mail from coming in a student's freshman or sophomore year.) For many colleges, having students with National Merit recognition is a bragging right because semi-finalists represent the top one percent of the nation. A semi-finalist's mailbox will start filling up with college offers and information. Some of the perks that will be offered may include full tuition, room and board, study abroad stipends, graduate money, honours dorms, a computer, cash and more.

The next step in the process is the *Finalist* stage. To become a finalist, the semi-finalists must complete the *National Merit Scholarship* application and submit it online on time. The application must include a high school transcript, show volunteer work, leadership skills and any awards received, letters of recommendation (principal, counselor, or parent) and a self-descriptive essay. It is a good idea to get letters of recommendation early from everyone that you work and volunteer for. These letters play a big part when the scholarship committee reviews the applications. Give the principal or counselor at least a ninety-day lead time before the letter of recommendation is due.

Semi-finalists must also take the *SAT* within a certain amount of time and earn scores that confirm the *PSAT* performance. Generally *SAT* scores from a year before or year after the *PSAT* can be submitted. Students should take the November and possibly the December *SAT* right after the October *PSAT/NMSQT* since they should already be primed and practiced. Such timing, right before the *PSAT/NMSQT* can help a junior prepare for their *PSAT/NMSQT*.

If you become a finalist, I strongly recommend you make a follow-up phone call to the *National Merit Corporation* to make sure they have received it: (847) 866-5100. Numerous students lose out on *Finalist* status and are terminated from the competition because they do not submit all the information by the deadline or it got lost in cyberspace..

In February 15,000 out of 16,000 Semi-finalists will advance to Finalist standing. Each student will receive a Certificate of Merit, and out of those students, 7,900 Merit Scholars are chosen.

There are three types of *Merit Scholarship* awards: *National Merit* $2,500, corporate-sponsored and college-sponsored Merit Scholarships. All Finalists are considered for the National Merit $2,500 award, awarded to 2,500 students. The 1,200 corporate-sponsored awards have certain criteria Finalists must meet to be considered. There are also 4,200 college-sponsored awards for Finalists who plan to attend certain institutions that offer this scholarship.

There are three types of Merit Scholarship awards: National Merit $2,500 scholarships, corporate-sponsored Merit Scholarships and college-sponsored Merit Scholarships.

The $2,500 National Merit scholarships are chosen in late January by a committee of experienced college admissions officers and high school counselors. Finalists are evaluated on several criteria:

- transcript (course load and difficulty level, depth and breadth of subjects studied, and grades earned);
- *PSAT/NMSQT* and *SAT* scores;
- the student's essay (his or her accomplishments, goals and interests);
- leadership abilities, community service and volunteer work;
- and letters of recommendation.

The *National Merit Corporation* will notify students in March if they have been chosen for their Scholars program and the corporate-sponsored scholarship award. Those students chosen for the college-sponsored award will be notified from April through June.

HISPANIC RECOGNITION PROGAM

Hispanic/Latino juniors who take the PSAT/NMSQT can partake in the Hispanic Recognition Program. They are invited to apply for academic recognition as part of the National Hispanic Recognition Program (NHRP) that recognizes about 7,000 Hispanic/Latino juniors who take the PSAT/NMSQT.

This is a very prestigious academic honor—not a scholarship program—and can be included on college applications to identify academically exceptional Hispanic/ Latino students.

Students will need to be at least one-quarter Hispanic/Latino and notate it on the PSAT/NMSQT answer sheet under race and ethnicity.

UNITED NEGRO FUND

Black African American juniors who participate in The National Merit Scholarship Program may be eligible to receive awards from UNCF once they graduate from college.

There are three types of NMSC awards: National Achievement Scholarship ($2,500), corporate-sponsored Achievement Scholarships and college-sponsored Achievement Scholarships.

PSAT/NMSQT QUALIFYING SCORES

The qualifying score for the *National Merit Competition* varies annually. It is dependent on the 2-3 percent of test scores the year you took the test which varies from state to state. There are also scholarship opportunities for those who score at the National Merit *Commendable* level (a certain amount of points below semi-finalist status). To find out the score percentiles for the *PSAT*, go to: *collegeprepgenius.com/PSATscores*

PSAT/NMSQT STRUCTURE

The *Reading* section is sixty minutes long and has forty-seven questions. These include:

- Long passages
- Long passages with a chart/graph
- Dual passage

The *Math* section is seventy minutes long and has forty-eight questions. On one section a calculator is not permitted. These include:

- Multiple choice
- Student response

The *Writing and Language* section is thirty-five minutes long and has forty-four questions. These includes:

- Grammar errors
- Style errors
- Included graphs

The total time given for the *PSAT/NMSQT* is 2 hours and 45 minutes.

The total time given for the *PSAT/NMSQT* is 2 hours and 45 minutes.

Each correct answer receives one point. Skipped questions do not count for or against the raw score.

GRADING

Each correct answer receives one point. Skipped questions do not count for or against the raw score. No points are subtracted for wrong answers. The best possible score is 1520.

An asterisk by your Selection Index on your score sheet signifies you did not meet the requirements for entry in the *National Merit* contest.

ALTERNATE ENTRY TESTING

The student can take the *SAT* I in exchange for the PSAT/NMSQT, and the scaled *SAT* score will be converted to the scaled *PSAT/ NMSQT* score.

If you miss your *PSAT/NMSQT* as a junior, there is still an opportunity to qualify for the *National Merit* program. Even though the *PSAT/NMSQT* is only administered once a year in October, a student has up to eight months (after the Wednesday and Saturday October sittings have been administered) to retake the test through the *Alternate Entry Testing Method*. There also may be an alternative day held after the Wednesday and Saturday dates; all tests must be missed to participate in the AET. The student can take the *SAT* I in exchange for the *PSAT/NMSQT*, and the scaled score will be converted.

This process begins with contacting the *National Merit Corporation* by calling (847) 866-5100 or sending a letter before the first of April stating that you (or your student) did not take the test and you request the extension/alternative testing time. You may need to give a brief reason for missing the test. The *National Merit Corporation* will send information showing future *SAT* test dates and instruct you use their code (code 0085) on the test. The scores will then go directly to the *National Merit Scholarship Corporation* who will take the highest score, from a single test, to apply for the scholarship program. Students will still be eligible for scholarship opportunities. These scores can also count for their *SAT* as well. Besides the *National Merit* code, students will need to put down the codes for the colleges they want to receive their *SAT* score. Students can take the *SAT* I every time it is offered that year for *The National Merit Program*.

Here are the steps to sign up for the *Alternate Entry Testing Method*:

Letter Method
1. Write a letter to The National Merit Corporation (NMC) *(see example)
2. Print and FAX to NMC (847-866-5113)
3. Receive a packet in approximately 2 weeks

Contact Information
    National Merit Scholarship Corp.
    1560 Sherman Avenue Suite 200 Evanston, IL 60201-4897
    Phone: (847) 866-5100
    Fax: (847) 866-5115

Make sure you carry out these steps every time you take the *SAT* in lieu of the *PSAT/NMSQT*. Students can have up to eight months to retake the test (November through June). The *National Merit Corporation* will KEEP THE HIGHEST SCORE!

FUN TIP

Students must have their high school counselor sign-off on this or a parent if they are homeschooled.

This alternate path is a great alternative for juniors who missed their *PSAT/ NMSQT. If you can, it is best to take it since it is a shorter and easier test than the SAT. More information at* collegeprepgenius.com/AET

*Sample letter

Date:

To: The National Merit Corporation

Re: Info on Alternate Testing Entry into NMSC Programs

To Whom It May Concern:

I am a (parent, guardian, etc.) and my (son, daughter), who is a junior, was unable to take any regular or alternative dates for the *PSAT/NMSQT* in October [insert brief description]. I understand (he, she) is able to take the *SAT* 1 test in exchange for the *PSAT/NMSQT*.

Please send me all information concerning:

- Alternate testing entry into NMSC programs,
- *SAT* 1 testing dates and locations in (your city and county)

Student Contact information:
(Student's name)
Address
City, State, Zip
Parent/Guardian Contact Information:
Name
Address
Phone

Email

Thank you very much for your prompt response.

Sincerely,
Parent's name

HOW TO PRACTICE?

THE KEY TO DOING just about anything well is to practice. Someone who plays a sport or learns an instrument can't expect to win a game or perform their best concert without practice. The same applies with these standardized tests. After learning the test-taking strategies, you should practice with official *College Board* practice tests.

It's a good idea to work towards a goal score for your tests, to gauge your progress and success. High test-scores really are achievable if you set clear test goals, are committed and dedicated to the task, and are laser-focused. Make a daily/weekly schedule to practice as outlined below. Group-study is a great way to learn, improve and encourage each other to excel.

The more you practice with your aims in mind, the quicker you will find the recurring patterns and the faster you will answer questions. Depending on what grade a student starts test-prep, high scores are a result of those who make practice a priority. Those students who learn to incorporate a few hours a week throughout the year, who treat test-taking skills as if it were a marathon and not a sprint, succeed. Cramming is never a good idea. The longer one waits, the less time there is to improve and the more time a student will need to study. Here is a basic minimum time *guideline for students for each year of high school:

- Freshman—three to four hours per week
- Sophomore— four to five hours per week
- Junior— six to eight hours per week but more before the October PSAT/NMSQT
- Senior—eight to ten hours per week

The key to doing just about anything well is to practice.

FUN TIP

Khan Academy is a good resource for subject matter if you need to brush up on some basic classes. Their test prep, however, doesn't teach shortcuts, strategies and recurring patterns.

*Your heaviest studying should be *at least* three months before your chosen test date.

FUN TIP

Proper
Preparation
Prevents
Poor
Performance

As the test approaches, put at least two hours a day during the week (for study and practice) and ten hours on the weekend. *Keep in mind your desired test score and/or amazing scholarships.*

I highly recommend you use *College Board* practice tests and materials as both the prep materials and the *SAT* and *PSAT/NMSQT* are created by the *College Board*. Work each section separately with the correct time restrictions. Then try working the problems in less time. E.g. for a twenty-five-minute section, time yourself for twenty-three minutes, then twenty-one, etc. Also, try to do the problems with distractions such as a radio or at a public setting. This can help train your mind to concentrate under pressure.

There is no instant success. You will need to go over the *College Prep Genius* online eCourse many times to solidify the information and apply it appropriately. Speed comes after accuracy; the more you internalize the strategies, the more adept you become. First comes introduction, then proficiency and finally mastery.

In today's world, your attention is being directed in many ways through technology, social media and the internet. You have to be so careful of distractions even when you are researching. Store your technology away from your study space. Don't wear earbuds and don't answer the phone. Success comes to those who make the tests a priority. Nothing will come of time spent time texting and watching funny videos. Schedule in your social time just as you do any other appointment. The results will be worth it.

You need to tackle test preparation with a clearly defined strategy.

PRACTICING STRATEGY

You need to tackle test preparation with a clearly defined strategy. First, you must master test-taking techniques, learn to answer the questions quickly and correctly and then finish the test on time. The best way to help lessen test anxiety is to gradually expose yourself to the real test environment; this will help to condition you for this mental marathon on test day. Your level of success depends primarily on your preparedness. Here's a workable practice strategy.

1. Go through each section (*Reading, Math* and *Writing*) of *College Prep Genius* one at a time.
   a. Learn all about the hidden strategies and recurring patterns.
   b. Memorize the acronyms for each section
2. Set aside adequate time to practice sections from the real test.
   a. Use only *College Board* materials.
   b. Keep notes open while working the problems.
   c. Study at least an hour straight each time.
   d. Take breaks and a lunch.
3. Keep records of missed questions in *The Journal for Test Success*.
   a. Go back over them and rework them.
   b. Review them to make sure you have conquered that pattern.
4. Take a full-length practice test with no time constraints.
5. When you have become familiar with each section, start timing the tests like the real test. Time each section correctly!

Before you learn the all-important strategies of test-success, you must know basic concepts, otherwise the shortcuts won't help much. Anxiety on the math section is often just a fear of the unknown. To overcome this, make learning math (terms and strategies) a priority. The *SAT Math* generally consists of simple concepts that are not difficult to master. Identify your weaknesses but don't forget to work on your strengths. Concentrate on one section at a time and practice in long blocks to build up stamina.

LEARNING STRATEGIES

This book is full of strategies and techniques to answer questions correctly on the *SAT*. Most of the tips are put together in ACRONYM form, so you can remember them easily. A good idea is to use index cards. They help you memorize the acronyms. Across the top, write the name of the section. Along the left side, write the ACRONYM in large letters in a vertical line.

> **IMPORTANT TIP**
>
> Students should take between 15-25 full-length practice *SAT* tests.

The *SAT* math generally consists of simple concepts that are not difficult to master.

Next to each letter, write the full definition.

On the flipside, do the same but write a shorter version. In the beginning, refer to the longer side as you are learning the ACRONYM. Then switch to the shorter version. After you have memorized each ACRONYM, start writing the word(s) at the top of the appropriate page. There is a section on the *College Prep Genius* program that contains the ACRONYMS for easy memorization.

THE PENCIL IS VERY IMPORTANT

Once you've learned the strategies and shortcuts for answering test questions, it's simply applying the logical reasoning you've learned to real test questions.

Your pencil is your best tool on taking the *SAT* and *PSAT/NMSQT*. Writing in your test booklet is not only acceptable, it is an essential strategy to achieve high scores. You will use it to write acronyms, note the time each section starts, underline words, circle sentences, rewrite math equations, redraw math diagrams, draw arrows and mark out wrong answers. This is like thinking with your pencil by engaging several senses to figure out the problem (it adds a kinesthetic component to the visual processing and helps deepen your understanding). You will also use it to star questions that you skip so you don't forget to come back and work them. Very importantly, use your pencil to circle the correct answer that you've arrived at. This will make it easier to transfer the correct answer on to the answer sheet.

Keep your pencil in hand and moving at all times. Don't lay it down during the test. Our minds are limited to a few thoughts at a time so ALWAYS write important information down in the test booklet. This unclutters a clouded mind and allows you to freely move from one question to another. Students ARE allowed to use their test booklet for scratch paper. To minimize mistakes, NEVER work problems in your head.

Students should download and print the *College Board*'s response that notes the test booklet can be used as scratch paper and written in. Take it to the test in case told otherwise. *collegeprepgenius.com/testdayrule*

MARKING THE CORRECT ANSWER

Once you've learned the strategies and shortcuts for answering test questions, you will simply apply the logical reasoning you've learned to real test questions. Here's an acronym for answering questions correctly:

R ead all the answer choices
E liminate obvious wrong ones first
A dd each answer choice into the question
D etermine the right answer and mark it confidently

If you get "stuck" on a question, reread it and break it down. (Often, your first impression is correct.) Write down key elements from the question, eliminate obvious wrong answers and make sure your selected answer choice answers the question. Never change an answer UNLESS you are certain it is wrong.

GUESSING ON THE TEST

The *College Board* writes questions in a way that will have most students read and gloss over the key word(s). This usually entices you to fall for the wrong answer choices that "look" correct but are actually wrong; they purposely misguide students with trick answers. Students who don't know how to answer a question properly, often make "educated" guesses. Guessing when you don't understand the logic behind the question or how it is set up can lead to a lot of wrong answers. Even though there is now no penalty for guessing, it should not become a habit to guess first. Instead, skip these answers and come back later to them after you've spent a short time assessing if you know how to work it. Oftentimes our subconscious works out the problem behind the scenes, so when we come back to it, we see the answer. Students should make 3-4 passes through the test. First, give the questions a quick glance to find questions that can be answered quickly. Then, answer the ones that take a little more thought and finally answer the ones that take more thought.

There is only one right answer and The *College Board* usually leaves a way for you to figure it out as long as you can recognize the recurring patterns on the test.

The goal is to get as many right answers as possible since each question is worth one point regardless of difficulty level.. If you have done everything above and it is near the end of the test, you can apply the "Straight A" rule and mark every blank answer with an "A" to better your odds of getting some right. Don't do this if you have ordered the *Question and Answer Service* so you can have an accurate score when you review the answers.

The good news is that there is only one right answer. As long as you can recognize the recurring patterns on the test, you will succeed. If you don't know the answer, it is generally better to leave the problem blank and come back to it later. Make sure you put a mark next to the skipped questions as well as a mark on the grid-in so you can continue to keep answers correctly tracked to the correspond*ing questions.*

SKIPPING QUESTIONS

You could actually skip a few questions in each section (*Reading, Math and Writing*) and still achieve a perfect score if all of your other answers are correct.

Don't waste time on a question that you are "clueless" about or stuck making up your mind on. Move on to answer the ones you do know. Your subconscious may work it out in your head and if you get time, you can come back and answer it. All questions are worth one point regardless of difficulty. Make sure you note the ones that are skipped so you can attempt them later and/or appropriately skip them on the answer sheet. You can skip about one-twelfth of the questions and still receive a score of 700; if you skip one-fourth of the questions and were correct on all the others your score could be 600; skip one-third of the questions for a maximum score of 500.

You could actually skip a few questions in each section (*Reading*/Writing and *Math*) and still achieve a near perfect score if all of your other answers are correct. All questions are worth one point, so an occasional skip is totally acceptable.

PACE YOURSELF

Don't rush to finish the test early. Carefully read each question with a very critical eye and work it quickly but accurately. To maximize your time efficiency, double-check your answers only at the end of each section so you'll have a greater chance to finish the test.

GRADING PRACTICE TESTS

When you go back over your practice tests, it's a good idea to identify the types of errors you make. This can help you pinpoint your problem areas, so you can work on them.

The ABCs of Errors:

A: Asinine ☹ (Made a careless, dumb mistake)
      You didn't double-check your work
      You didn't circle what it was asking, or you misread the question

B-Blank ◯ (Drew a blank because you forgot how to work it)
      Memorize ACRONYMS to help you remember steps to success
      practice daily/weekly to keep you fresh on techniques

C-Clueless ❓ (Didn't know how to work this problem)
      Skip it (All questions are worth one point, so move on)
      Commit to learning how to work it
      Write the problem down in your journal and review it periodically

When you go over your practice questions, write an A, B or C next to your wrong answers. Analyze what type of errors you keep making over and over again. Make a plan to work on them until they are drastically reduced and hopefully eliminated altogether.

When you go back over your practice tests, it's a good idea to identify the types of errors that you are making.

KEEPING A JOURNAL

It's important to keep a record of your missed questions (in the *Journal for Success* in the back of this book or online) because this will allow you to conquer them. From doing your first practice test (without strategies) to learning short-cuts, taking the *Master the SAT Class*, to practicing with *College Board* material, you can learn to figure out your strongest and weakest parts of the test.

Analyze each practice test by keeping a journal of which questions you get wrong. On this list, make a note of the question and the date. Return to it in a week and then in a month. If you can now remember what you did wrong and how to correct it, you can remove it from your list.

If not, keep revisiting it until you fully understand the question, its pattern and how to solve it. For extra help, you could copy in full the wrong questions in your journal and review them before going to bed. This can help solidify them in your head and when you are faced with similar problems on the real test, it'll be old hat to you.

By spending more time on your weak areas, you can start to see more improvements.

Spend more time on your weak areas and you will start to see more improvements.

Take the practice tests over and over again (since you'll forget the questions) and then check your journal to see if you conquered the questions you answered incorrectly on a previous practice session.

It is important you understand and conquer the basic rules of math and grammar before learning strategies. Review the basics until you understand them. You may want to seek one-on-one help in a particular area. After this, your goal is to streamline your energy to work on your weak points of the test.

Don't neglect the stuff you know. Remember to always review your strong points, too. This keeps you fresh and will help boost confidence on your test-taking skills.

RIGHT FRAME OF MIND

As you practice, it is important to keep a few tips in mind:

- Don't fixate on your score.
- Your focus is to familiarize yourself with the test-taking strategies.
- Look for recurring patterns on how to answer questions quicker.
- Test-taking is a skill like golf or piano.
- First use your notes to internalize the strategies.
- Make a game plan of what time of day/week you will study.
- Pace yourself with your own watch.
- Get a study partner—someone to keep you accountable.
- Set a test score goal and then work to achieve it.
- Be prepared to put a lot of time in—success is not instant.
- Remember, you can't bypass the work or shortcut the shortcut.

ACTUAL PRACTICE SAT TESTS

When you practice taking the *SAT*, you should only use actual tests created by the *College Board*. Students can reuse the same practice tests over and over again. Download and print the free tests at collegeprepgenius.com/ossgsat or purchase the official book.

Here is a list of *College Board* tests and materials, most of which you can acquire from www.collegeboard.org:

1. T*aking the SAT Reasoning Test* booklet*
   (Available free at most high schools in the guidance counselor's office.)
2. The *Official SAT Study Guide* (2016, 2018 or 2020 Edition).
3. Free full-length tests online at collegeprepgenius.com/ossgsat (Same as OSSG) Use the Scan and Score feature at collegeprepgenius.com/SSS
4. The test booklets from the *Question and Answer Service* for the October, March and May tests.

When you practice taking the SAT, you should only use actual tests that were created by The *College Board***.**

Download the *Daily Practice SAT app* and use the scoring sheets at collegeprepgenuis.com/answersheet

Every year pick up a new free SAT and PSAT booklet from the guidance counselor; they can be reused as well.

ACTUAL PSAT/NMSQT TESTS

To practice for the PSAT/ NMSQT, you can still use the same SAT materials.

The main differences between the *PSAT/NMSQT* and *SAT* test is that it is shorter and there is no optional essay on the *PSAT/NMSQT*. To practice for the *PSAT/NMSQT*, you can still use the same *SAT* materials. There is no need for a separate program for the *PSAT*. You will want to cover *Math, Reading* and Writing. Some other *PSAT/NMSQT* resources are:

1. *Taking the PSAT/NMSQT* booklet*
   Available free at most high schools in the guidance counselor's office.
2. *The Official SAT Study Guide* (2016, 2018 and 2020 Edition)
   Studying for the *SAT* is overpreparing for the *PSAT*.
3. Free *PSAT* tests online at collegeprepgenius.com/ossgpsat
4. *PSAT/NMSQT* Test Booklets
   Returned after the student takes the actual test.

Every year pick up a new free SAT and PSAT booklet from the guidance counselor; they can be reused as well.

ADDITIONAL STUDY MATERIALS

LOGIC CURRICULUM

The *PSAT/NMSQT* tests require you to THINK and practice your logic skills. It behooves you to use material or games—such as crossword puzzles and brain teasers—that can stimulate your creative thinking. Treat the test as a challenging puzzle that can be figured out logically. The material on the test is somewhat limited but the deliberation behind the problems is very definitive. Even if you think you are not naturally logically-minded, you can train yourself to be a critical thinker. Problem-solving is an important aspect to being successful in college and beyond. Logic is not a personality trait but can be a learned skill.

CLASSIC LITERATURE

One way you can prepare for the *Reading* section of the *SAT* and *PSAT/NMSQT* is to read classic literature. It can help build and enhance your vocabulary. There are so many good books to choose from! Choose a well-known title, one that enlarges your knowledge, has lasting value, has withstood time, has a high standard and is unabridged. There is an exhaustive list in *High School Prep Genius* or type "classic books" in a search engine to get started.

SAT VOCABULARY WORDS

Learning a lot of vocabulary words before the test is not necessarily the key to scoring higher on the *Reading* Section since there are over 171K words in the dictionary. The *College Board* is the only one who knows what words will be on the test. You could learn 4,000 vocabulary words and not one of them might be on the test. Since the *SAT* is a logic test, there are ways to figure out the words without knowing them. However, having a good grasp of vocabulary will help you communicate more effectively and intelligently. Learning difficult vocabulary words that may be on the *SAT* can be painlessly mastered in a fun way by the new *VocabCafe Book Series*. Check these out at www.collegeprepgenius.com

TAKING THE REAL TEST

There are no penalties for taking the *SAT* many times.

The *SAT* is offered seven times a year, starting in August and ending in June. You can take the *SAT* as many times as you want. All your scores will be recorded; however, prospective colleges usually only consider your top scores. If you have any doubts, contact the admissions office at the college of your choice.

There are **no penalties** for taking the *SAT* many times. Most colleges just drop the lowest scores (they don't average them.) Many colleges will take the highest score from each section from different tests. Most colleges don't have cut-off dates to receive *SAT* scores, but some do, so please be sure to always check with the college of your choice. Since colleges go up on their rankings based on test scores, the higher the score-the more money you can get!

Tests are held on Saturday mornings. If you can't take a Saturday test due to religious obligations, you can take it on the Sunday. You will need a signed letter from your clergy person written on official letterhead to qualify. You will use the code 01000 when taking the test; all future tests will be administered on a Sunday.

Parents or students can sign-up by mail or on the official web site, www. collegeboard.org. Please sign up early because deadlines and late fees may apply. There is a fee to sign up for the test, but waivers are available for individuals that may find this fee a financial burden. You can receive up to four free *SAT* tests in your junior and senior year. Check with the high school's guidance counselor for the criteria. Homeschoolers can also apply for fee waivers at the local high school.

The *PSAT/NMSQT* can only be registered for at your local high school up until the day of the test, if there is room. There is a nominal fee to take it, but waivers are available at local guidance counselor offices.

CHOOSING A TEST LOCATION

To find the schools that are administering the *SAT* or *PSAT*, go to collegeboard.org and search for test locations with your zip code.

It is very important to know the reputation of the school/test site before deciding where to take your test. There are horror stories of proctors who have cut the test-taking time short or forgotten to set the timer altogether!

There are other stories of proctors who have totally humiliated outside students by standing over them or isolating them in the hallway. Make sure to talk to others about their personal experience at the local schools where they took their tests. *You do not have to take the test at the school you attend, and homeschoolers should be able to take it at any scheduled testing facility.*

Practice Right Before the Real Test

It is best to prepare well for your first real test because this will help boost your confidence. If you are not happy with your score, don't get discouraged, but refine your study plan. Besides, using ONLY practice tests from the *College Board*, is great preparation for when you take the real test. In the same vein as the live test, you should take a practice test in its entirety with only a five-minute break between sections.

You should also take it at the same time as the real test (this is usually around 9:00am). Always use the same watch and calculator (not cell phone) in practice that you plan to use during the real test. To save time and frustration, be familiar with the rules for each section before taking the real test. Don't waste time reading the rules when you open the test booklet. They don't change, so know them ahead of time.

Memorize the essay templates and make them your own. As you will see in the essay section, old essays will come in handy for the real test so read over them ahead of time. The optional essay is last and offered at the end of the *SAT* for those who have opted in to take it.

It is best to prepare well for your first actual test because this will help boost your confidence.

The DAY Before the Test

Do not do any *SAT* work the day before the actual test.

Do not do any *SAT* work the day before sit the real test. Relax and go to bed ON TIME. Make sure you have the correct driving directions, gas in the tank and all your supplies ready. Know the time you should arrive on test day—that time will be on your printed ticket.

The Morning of the Test

- Wake up with enough time that you will not be rushed. You do not need any added pressure.
- Eat a light breakfast.
- Leave early.

What to Bring

Bring three to four **sharpened** #2 pencils with good erasers. Mechanical pencils are banned! Also bring a manual pencil sharpener; this can keep you out of the long pencil sharpener line if all your pencils break. Highlighters are also banned from the test. It is a good idea not to use them on your practice tests since you want to work them like the real test.

It is always good to use the same calculator that you have been practicing with at home.

It is always good to use the same calculator that you have been practicing with at home. Always bring one to the test just in case, and make sure it has fresh batteries. Simple functions are all that are needed, so don't waste your money on expensive calculators. One with exponents and square roots are allowed. *You are only allowed to use it during one math section. Sharing your calculator is cause for dismissal from the test.*

Acceptable calculators include graphing calculators, scientific calculators and four-function calculators (although this option is not recommended). BE WARNED—students may be seated away from other students (at the test proctor's discretion) if their calculator has characters that are one inch or bigger or if it has a raised display where others may see it. If needed, students should bring one that has exponents and square roots on it.

Unacceptable calculators include laptops and portable/handheld computers; any calculator that has a (typewriter-like) keypad, uses an electrical outlet, makes noise or has a paper tape; electronic writing pad or pen-input/stylus-driven devices; pocket organizers; and cell phone calculators.

Bring a watch with either a second hand (set 12:00 at each section) or a chronometer. Please try to use this same watch when you're practicing for the *SAT*. Timers and alarms are not allowed.

Dress in layers or bring a sweater. Schools like to keep the rooms cold since there are usually a lot of people taking the test. Dress comfortably.

Food is normally not allowed, but you may be able to bring snacks to eat during the breaks. If you bring a water bottle, it cannot have a label.

No cell phones or backpacks are allowed in the test.

If you are easily distracted, you may want to bring earplugs.

You will need your picture I.D. (driver's license, passport, school I.D., military I.D.) and the ticket you received when registering for the test (It can be printed off the *College Board* website); and names must match on both.

Print the *College Board* statement about writing in your test booklet: collegeprepgenius.com/testdayrule

*Students who do not have a driver's license or who are homeschooled and do not have a school I.D. can get a State issued ID for non-drivers, which costs around $18. It takes 2 to 3 weeks to process from your state's *Department of Public Safety* or *Motor Vehicles*. Homeschoolers can also get an ID form from their public school, with the school's letterhead, and then attach a passport photo. For more information, visit http://www.collegeboard.com/student/testing/sat/testday/id.html.

AT THE TEST

Stay calm and trust in the fact that you have been preparing for this day. Take deep slow breaths to help clear your mind if you feel anxious. Treat it as a game that can be beat. Relax! Do your best. Remember, you can always take the test again as many times as you want, and you are not penalized.

You will want to pace yourself just like you've done during your practice tests. Use the same watch during all tests. If the watch has a count-up timer, start it at the beginning before each test and occasionally glance at it to see how much time you have left. Start the watch when the proctor starts the test. Depending on the length of the test, you can keep an eye on how much time you have left.

Watch the time. Don't rely on the proctor to give you a warning.

Watch the time. Don't rely on the proctor to give you a warning. Use your own chronometer watch or set your second-hand watch at 12:00 for each section. (*This keeps you from having to calculate how much time is left.*) Use your breaks to recharge your thinking. Concentrate on the test; don't waste time on thinking about the score results.

If at first glance, the question seems to be "B" (draw a blank) or "C" (clueless), then skip it and move on. Put a star by it and come back to it if you have time. Remember, every question is worth one point so there is no need to waste time on questions that you know you can't answer.

Always double-check your work. Work it backwards to catch any mistakes made the first time or check each step in math after you do it so you can catch errors immediately. This only takes a few seconds but could save you points.

Don't ever change an answer unless you know for certain it is wrong!

QUESTION-ANSWERING STRATEGIES

When you sit the test, you should go through the test 3-4 times to maximize the score. Follow these steps both as you practice and on test day:

1. Give the question a ten-second look. If you can answer quickly then go ahead and work the problem. If not, put a star on it and move on to the next question.

2. Return to the skipped questions to answer them. Very often, your subconscious continues to work out the problem in the back of the mind; so, answer the ones that you can easily solve.

3. Go back and answer the problems that take a little more thought.

4. Do another pass and answer the questions that take more thought.

5. After doing all of the above and there is a couple of minutes left, then employ the "Straight A Rule". (Mark empty bubbles all with an A, or B...)

All questions are worth one point regardless of difficulty; since they are not in order of difficulty, students can encounter easier ones towards the end if they go through the test more than once. Once you learn to answer questions in 30 seconds or less, you will free up time to work on problems that you were not able to answer quickly. Accuracy before speed.

EVALUATING YOUR PERFORMANCE

Ifyou would like to thoroughly evaluate your test results, the *Question and Answer Service* is available for three *SAT* tests (October, March and May). If you take any of these three tests, you will have up to five months to purchase the service for a fee. The *ACT* has a similar program called the *TIR* and is available December, April and June. I highly recommend using these services to help students pinpoint their weaknesses.

They will receive in the mail:

- A clean copy of the test booklet
- A record of their answers and the correct answers
- Information on question difficulty levels

Having this test booklet will also allow you to use it again for practice.

A FAIR TEST FOR EVERYONE

The *College Board* strives to make sure the *SAT* and *PSAT/NMSQT* are unbiased and offer a fair testing experience for everyone who takes them. The *SAT* is available for all high school students, regardless of race, religion or economic standing. If you can't afford the test, fee waivers (up to four) are available for juniors and seniors at most local high schools. You will need to contact a local guidance counselor for more information. They will give you a form with a waiver number. You will need to find out your correct code by calling (212) 713-8000 or (609) 771-7600. Then go to www.collegeboard. org, register and add those codes to the form. Some *PSAT/NMSQT* waivers are available through the coordinators at most local high schools. (Apply early!) Qualifying students can receive up to 4 waivers in the last two years of high school: *SAT II* test waivers can be used in ninth through twelfth grade. These students may also have their college application fees waived. Waivers CANNOT be used for late registrations. *Homeschoolers can also apply for test waivers.*

GRADING MISTAKES

If you think your test has been unfairly graded, you can request your test be hand-scored for a small fee. Call (609) 771-7600 for more information.

If you think your test has been unfairly graded, you can request that your test be hand scored for a small fee.

UNFAIR TESTING ENVIRONMENT

Sometimes, there can be major distractions that may hinder your success on the test. If this occurs, lodge a complaint with the *College Board*. Encourage any other person who had a similar experience to do the same as this will add credibility. You may get a new test or other compensation. Here are the contact details.

> Contact: Fair Test
> Phone: (617) 864-4810
> Fax: (617) 497-2224
> www.fairtest.org

TEST-OPTIONAL SCHOOLS

Around fifteen percent of colleges are considered test-optional or test-flexible as a part of their application process. Most of these are specialized schools and often still have their own entrance exam. To apply for scholarships, a student will still need to submit an *SAT* or *ACT* score.

DYSLEXIA, DISABILITIES AND SPECIAL NEEDS

Accommodations can be made for students with special needs, and time constraints can be lessened. However, going through the process of obtaining special accommodations could take many months. Parents will need to schedule a battery of tests, obtain the diagnostician's report for their student, arrange for and implement accommodations at school and have these accommodations in use in the school setting for a minimum of four months (a *College Board* rule). When applying for special accommodations please keep in mind the time it takes for the *College Board* to process and grant or deny the request. Families may be limited to working with the school's calendar or timetable for testing (ARD meetings and creating IEPs). Ideally, the process of preparing for standardized tests should start in the student's freshman or sophomore year, to allow time for accommodations to be in place before the *PSAT/NMSQT* in the student's junior year. For more

When applying for special accommodations please keep in mind the time it takes for The *College Board* to process and grant or deny the request.

information about forms, eligibility and documentation, visit http://www.collegeboard.com/ssd/prof/physical-disabilities.html. Phone: 212-713-8333. Fax: 866-360-0114.

The *504 Plan* specifies that no one with a disability can be excluded from federally funded programming, and that all should be given the opportunity to perform at a level equal to their peers. In this case, disability could include physical impairments, injury, disease or chronic conditions.

ADULTS AND THE SAT

Adults can take the *SAT* if desired. However, many colleges do not require it for older applicants. Please check with the school of your choice. There is no age limit on taking the *SAT* even if a student has graduated from high school.

Many students take a gap year after high school to study for the *SAT* so they can receive scholarship money.

HOMESCHOOLERS

For the homeschooler, many colleges weigh *SAT* scores heavily because they are an unbiased evaluation of academic prowess. This is why homeschooled students should make this test a priority. Homeschoolers are at no disadvantage when taking the test. The material is not an exclusive curriculum found only at public or private schools. The test is a critical reasoning or logic test, and the key to doing well is to learn the hidden strategies and recurring patterns that are usually found on these tests.

PSAT/NMSQT scores will automatically be sent to the high school code placed in the grid on the test. To ensure that scores and test booklet are sent to your home, check the appropriate home school code boxes. Tests with the home school code will not affect the average scores of the testing facility. The home school code for your state can be found at: http://www.collegeboard.com/student/testing/psat/reg/homeschool/state-codes.html.

PLAN FOR TEST SUCCESS

1. Read this *College Prep Genius* textbook—hard copy or digital.
   Follow the daily homework guide and learn all the good information about test strategies, the college interview process and how to get scholarships. Take the *Master the SAT Class* in person or via the online *e*Course.

2. Learn the ACRONYMS for each section.
   After you memorize these, you can write them in your test booklets to help you remember what to do in each section. While notes are NOT allowed at the test, you can write all over your test booklet.

3. Practice with *College Board* tests.
   These can be found in bookstores, guidance counselors' offices and at www.collegeboard.org. If you start preparing as a freshman or earlier, you should spend at least one to two hours per week practicing. Sophomores starting out should spend two to four hours, and juniors new to the test need to spend four to six hours per week taking practice SATs. If you've waited until you're a senior, it's a good idea to spend at least six to ten hours a week preparing. Your minimum studying should begin at least three months before you take the test.

4. Know the rules for each section ahead of time.
   The rules for each section of these tests always stay the same, so learn them long before you take the real *SAT* and *PSAT/NMSQT*. This not only saves you time, but you will already know what to expect in each section.

5. Create a similar test environment.
   Many students don't realize that these tests are very long and require mental endurance to finish them without running out of steam. The *SAT* itself is three hours long plus an optional fifty-minute essay. One way to prepare for this academic marathon is to practice as if you were sitting the real test. Create a test environment and you will eliminate any surprises and help with test success.

Practice like this:

    a.   Start the practice test around 9:00 a.m.

    b.   Take only a five-minute break in between sections.

    c.   Use the same watch and calculator that you will use at the real test.

    d.   Make sure the testing area is free of distractions.

    e.   Time each section correctly.

    f.   Use a watch with a chronometer or set a second-hand watch set at 12:00 for each section.

    g.   Keep several sharpened pencils nearby.

6.   Take *PSAT 8/9* for practice in eight and ninth grade and the *PSAT 10* in tenth grade. The score won't count, but it will help familiarize you with the test, and you'll also get your test booklet back in the mail. The test score arrives later in the mail or can be viewed online at your *College Board* account. When you receive it, go over your mistakes and find the patterns of the questions you missed. You can also use the booklet to retake the test later and see how much you have improved. (*Retaking it can be beneficial since most will forget the questions.*)

7.   Take the *PSAT/NMSQT* in your junior year when it counts.
This test will not only measure how well you might do on the SAT, but it's also an opportunity for amazing scholarship offers from colleges all over the nation.

Students who score in the semi-finalist range can get a full-ride to numerous colleges because they are in the top 1-2% of the nation. This test only counts in their junior year.

8.   Take several *SAT** tests in a row and take it many times.
Take two to three tests in a row, since you will already be studied up. There are no penalties for taking the *SAT* many times, so you should take it until you get your desired score. Colleges do not average the tests but generally take the highest scores. Many colleges will even take the highest score from each section from different tests to get the student's best overall score. Every college is different

when it comes to their desired entrance score as well as entry level for starting scholarships, so make sure you check with the college(s) of your choice.

9. Record your scores in your *Journal for Test Success*. This will help you track your progress.

* 85% of colleges admit and hand out scholarship money based on the *SAT* score.

Download the *Roadmap for College Prep Success* at www.collegeprepgenius.com/roadmap

The *SAT* determines where you get to go to college and who's going to pay!

FUN TIP

Learning the strategies first is the introduction, then going back over the information brings proficiency and practicing the correct way brings mastery.

IMPORTANT TIP

If you are unsure of attending college, still take the *SAT* in high school while math is fresh on your mind because if you change your mind later, the *College Board* holds your *SAT* scores for a year and then archives them and they can be retrieved indefinitely.

PART II:

READING
SECTION

READING SECTION

Most students cringe at the thought of the *Reading* section on the *SAT* and *PSAT/NMSQT*. Having to read six passages and answer 52 questions in 65 minutes is frightening! Yes, you only have just over one minute per question, and you also have to figure in the time it takes to read the passages. It's practically impossible to finish this section on time if you try to tackle it the normal way.

For school exams, you are taught to read all the questions first, then the passage and then all the questions again. Naturally, this is the same approach most students take for standardized tests like the *SAT* and *PSAT/NMSQT*. Of course, if you do this, you are likely to run out of time, end up with a lot of blank answers and an unsatisfactory score.

To add to the incredible time constraints, you could be dumbfounded by questions that seem to have more than one correct answer. It seems like not only do you need a supernatural speed-reading ability, but also psychic powers! Fortunately, many mortal students have aced both the *SAT* and *PSAT/NMSQT*. They key to doing well on the *Reading* section is to learn the different types of questions and how to answer them quickly and correctly.

It's not about how fast you read the passages but how to distinguish one right answer from the three wrong ones. Years of experience teaching exam strategies to people like you proves time and again, you just have to learn how to find them.

This is an objective test, so *Reading* questions can only have one right answer. The correct answer MUST be derived from the key words and clues from the sentence, but not necessarily what you think the answer should be. The *College Board* writes answer choices intended to trap test-takers; but once you learn how to recognize these traps, you can answer the questions quickly and accurately. You must justify every answer from the passage, or it is not the correct answer.

Most students cringe at the thought of the *Reading* section on the *SAT* and PSAT/NMSQT.

It's not about how fast you can read the passages but knowing how to distinguish the one right answer from the four wrong ones.

Steps to Reading Success

1. Learn the strategy ACRONYMS*.
2. Memorize the root words and positive and negative prefixes found in the back of this book.
3. Read and understand the rules for this section before taking the real test.
4. Practice taking the *Reading* section in *College Board* exams.

The ACRONYMS are designed to help you remember the specific strategies for each section.

*I designed the ACRONYMS to help you remember the specific strategies for each section. While you learn the ACRONYMS, keep your notes open for easy referral as you work practice problems. When you take a practice exam, get in the habit of writing the ACRONYM at the top of the paper to jar your memory on what to do.

When you sit the actual exam, you are not allowed to bring in any notes, but you are permitted to write in the booklet. (Do not write on the grid-in paper.) This is why it's important to memorize the ACRONYMS!

PASSAGE-BASED READING

THE PASSAGE-BASED READINGS SECTION discuss a particular topic which is followed by several questions that relate to the passage. You do not need previous knowledge of the topics in the reading passages. Even if you're clueless about the subject at hand, don't worry! Every correct answer is located within the text and you'll always find the direct evidence from the passage.

There are three types of passages:
- Long Passage
- Long Passage with a Chart/Graph
- Dual Passage

For each passage type, there are generally five types of questions you will be given:
- Vocabulary Use
- Line Citation
- Command of Evidence
- Chart Analysis
- Overall Passage

You will learn to first skim the answer choices and notate which question category they fall under. Then you'll put them in the right order.

All five types of questions are answered using different processes all of which will be discussed in this chapter. Do NOT read all the questions first, then read the passage and then go back and read each question! This will waste time and confuse you. It may surprise you but you do not need to read the whole passage. You will have a basic understanding of it, not be an expert. Most of the information inside the reading passages is irrelevant to answering the questions. You cannot study for the test, since it is not content-based. What you must study are the patterns of the test.

It is not necessary to have a previous knowledge about the topics in the reading passages.

Take every word literally rather than analyze or interpret the passage. Instead of reading the question and looking for the right answer, eliminate the three wrong answers first. The correct answer must be justified by the passage. It will restate a concept or demonstrate an idea from the given text.

RECURRING PATTERNS AND STRATEGIES

OPINIONATED ANSWER CHOICES

If a question seems to ask your opinion, it is a trap. The questions are 100% objective which leaves no room for personal opinions. The right answers are ALWAYS objective—never subjective. There is ONLY one right answer and it is found in the text.

If an answer is too strong, too opinionated or negative toward a person/ group of people, it is wrong. If an answer choice expresses a radical idea with no room for exceptions, this answer choice is wrong. You always want to avoid statements that seem to exclude all possibilities. Only choose answer choices that leave room for exceptions. Avoid answer choices with words like exactly, always, all, every, must, no, none and never.

Avoid answers that contain S.O.N.

> S trong
> O pinionated
> N egative

To be politically correct, the good answer choices will usually contain words that cover all possibilities such as often, if, mostly, usually, may, can, almost, sometimes and some. For example:

> **Wrong Answer Choices:**
>> It is <u>never</u> cold in December.
>> Post-Modernism paintings are <u>always</u> confusing.
>> <u>Everyone</u> in the military during the sixties needed psychological help.

If a question seems to ask your opinion, it is a trap. The questions are 100% objective which leaves no room for personal opinions.

<u>None</u> of the teachers liked their job.

Money <u>only</u> appeals to the rich.

Good Answer Choices:

Boys are <u>usually</u> tougher than girls.

It <u>sometimes</u> rains in the big city.

Eating too much fat will <u>probably</u> result in weight gain.

<u>Most</u> adult Americans own a car.

Women <u>often</u> work outside the home to supplement the family income.

The *College Board* will never express a negative opinion about a certain people group, ethnicity or world region. Any answer choice that puts a general population in a negative light will be incorrect.

Passages will always be positive that reference a people group. NO answer choice will be correct if it puts a negative light on people. In Example 1-1 you can automatically mark off the negative answers (A) and (C) because these are negative toward a group of people.

This leaves only two answers (positive) to choose from; the correct one can be found in the key parts of the text. The correct answer may not seem perfect to you, but it is always the choice with the least wrong information and no hidden meanings or secret agendas. Only the correct answers can be defended by the *College Board*.

WATCH OUT FOR EXCEPTIONS

If a question has the word "except" in it, as in Example 1-2, immediately circle the word. The word "except" means you are looking for any answer that does not appear in the passage.

> ## EXAMPLE 1-1
> In the passage, how did the people of the village view the foreign missionaries?
>
> (A) intrusive
> (B) helpful
> (C) needy
> (D) loving

> ## EXAMPLE 1-2
> The passage suggests all of the following **<u>except</u>**

Find all the answer choices that appropriately reference the text; then **mark them out!** These are obviously wrong. Choose the answer choice that isn't eliminated. There will only be one.

ANSWERS WITH THE SAME MEANING

Remember, the test is objective and there can never be two correct answers. If two answers have the same meaning, they are both wrong.

In Example 1-3 if when you look at the answer choices you will notice two synonyms: (B) Irate and (D) Wrathful. They both mean being full of anger. Neither of these answers could be correct because they have the same meaning. Since the test is objective, there can ONLY be one answer. They are both wrong. Mark them off! The answer needs to be negative because of "critical reviews" and (A) is neutral so the correct answer is (C) Cheeky.

It is a good idea to jot a quick definition next to each word to help you identify its meaning. To minimize mistakes, NEVER work problems in your head.

EXAMPLE 1-3

Line 16: The reporter was surprised by the (brazen) attitude the author had toward the critical reviews of his most recent novel.

8. What does the word "brazen" most nearly mean in Line 16?
   (A) Nonchalant
   (B) Irate
   (C) Cheeky
   (D) Wrathful

FUN TIP

Sometimes when there are two answer choices that are opposites, one of them will usually be the correct answer.

ANSWER CHOICES THAT DON'T ANSWER THE QUESTION

An answer choice may be correct, but it may not appropriately answer the question.

For the above Example 1-4 you may have an answer choice like "(A) Siberian Huskies can withstand severe bitter cold so they often thrive

EXAMPLE 1-4

The author mentions the trainer he met at the dog show in order to show that...

in Canada as pets." This statement may be true and may be found in another part of the passage, but it does not answer the question. The right choice

MUST answer the question.

LINE CITATION QUESTIONS

The *Line Citation Question* type is when a question asks about a particular line in the reading passage and then gives you five answer choices. See Example 1-5.

Citation questions are usually in order of the passage; they are easy to locate without having to read the entire passage first.

EXAMPLE 1-5
The author refers to "my favorite place" in lines 21–22 in order to…

READ or SKIM?

It is NOT necessary to read the whole passage. Go directly to the cited part of the passage as the answer should be there. (*Always circle the citation.*) If you need a little more information, you can dig a little deeper by reading a few lines above or below the cited line. Remember, this is not a test about knowledge, but how well you can reason and get the correct answer.

Some students like to read the whole passage, while others only get confused by doing so. This is strictly a personal choice of what works best for you. Since most of the information in the passage is irrelevant to answer the questions, it is **NOT** necessary to read the entire passage; 75% of the passage can be skipped. You will only feel comfortable with this approach if you get lots of pre-test practice. You'll be able to sniff out the patterns and approach the section efficiently. Without practice, you'll be tempted to read everything. The *SAT* usually gives you the most important parts they want you to know from the line citation questions and they are generally in relevant order.

WHAT TO LOOK FOR

Look for the answer that restates the citation, not a direct quote. The correct answer usually does not have the exact words but gives more of a general idea. If you do not find the correct information in the citation, think logically and look above and below the circled citation.

WORK THE PENCIL

Use the pencil to circle the citation in the passage as your very first step. Then, circle the nouns and verbs in the citation. Next, circle the nouns and verbs in the answer choices. The one that has the most matching nouns and verbs is usually the correct answer.

FIRST WORDS

Always circle the first word in the answer choices. Very often it will point you to the right answer or help eliminate the wrong answers.

Look at Example 1-6. You can see the first word in every choice has a very different meaning. Many first words do not even come close to fitting the meaning of the example sentence. "Celebrating" and "Instilling" do not fit the context and "Preserving" contradicts the example, so mark them off without even reading the full answer choices. Therefore **(D)** is the correct answer choice.

EXAMPLE 1-6

Line 48: At the well as I sat meditating on what had just happened, I felt like I finally rid myself of all those fears that encompassed my childhood.

3. The narrator refers to "all those fears" in line 48 primarily in order to show that he was
   (A) celebrating his upbringing
   (B) instilling a truth about deep thoughts
   (C) recreating a joyous memory from school
   (D) shedding the trepidation that preoccupied him

COATED WRONG ANSWERS

Your job is to look for *Goldilocks answers*: ones that are just right! Look for answers that don't contain too much, too little information or information that is different from the original citation. The *College Board* likes to **C.O.A.T.** the wrong answers with four hidden patterns:

C ompletely irrelevant
O bscure information
A dditional information
T otally contradictory information

FUN TIP

Write a C. O. A. or T. by each answer so you don't go back to the answer and second guess yourself.

Don't look for the right answer but look for the wrong ones that fall under the COAT acronym and mark them off first. This should leave the right answer that doesn't break any of these rules.

Usually you can find the **ONE CORRECT ANSWER** by marking off the three incorrect answers. Always circle what the question is asking! When approaching a test-question, circle the citation, circle the first words of the answer choices and then circle the nouns and verbs. As you go through the answer choices, write a "C," "O," "A," or "T" next to each incorrect answer choice, whichever applies. Read questions carefully and critically so that you don't fall for these four traps.

EXAMPLE 1-7

Line 48: At the well as I sat meditating on what had just happened, I felt like I finally rid myself of all those fears that encompassed my childhood.

(D) shedding the trepidation that preoccupied him

IMPORTANT TIP

Scrutinize every answer looking for COAT answers first with the mind set of finding what is wrong with each answer choice.

Look at same Example 1-7. By simply circling the nouns and verbs in the citation and answer choices, it is much easier to find the correct answer. Notice how "rid," "fears," and "encompassed" almost perfectly mirror "shedding," "trepidation," and "preoccupied" in the correct answer choice.

If you are overthinking the question or second-guessing yourself, you are probably falling for a *COAT*ed answer. Do not read anything additional into the information. The passage has all the information you need to answer the question. Nothing added—nothing subtracted. Make sure ALL words in your answer choice coincide with the line citation.   If the passage states the sentence below:

> **EXAMPLE 1-8**
> Previous studies have shown that many professional athletes file for bankruptcy within five years of retirement.

"Previous studies have shown that many professional athletes file for bankruptcy within five years of retirement." [Example 1-8]
A wrong answer might be: like Example 1-9

This choice reads too much into the citation and adds to the text. The second statement may be true, but it is not supported by the original sentence. The original sentence says professional athletes (not former football players) file for bankruptcy (not necessarily because of their lifestyle) within five years (which may or may not be long after retirement). Always justify the answer from the information found in the text so you can confidently mark it as correct.

> **EXAMPLE 1-9**
> (A) Most former football players have created a lifestyle that is hard to maintain long after retirement.

SIMPLIFY BIG WORDS

Advanced vocabulary words are often used to confuse the meaning of the answer choices. One strategy for helping you find the right answer is to simplify the big word to something easier to understand. Substitute everyday normal words for hard words and write them above the given options. You may also want to rewrite the answer choice to make more sense.

> **EXAMPLE 1-10**
> The author's main purpose for mentioning Ken's apathy when David forgot his backpack was to emphasize the
> (A) erratic way school supplies are used
> (B) dualistic personality of Ken
> (C) zeal that David felt
> (D) foretelling of a recurring event
> *(E) comparison of Ken's effervescence to David's amazement

Let's simplify these answer choices in Example 1-10 by rewriting them. You only need to mark out the big words and write the easier word next to them.

(A) **erratic** way school supplies are used
Changing the use of the backpack—C, this is totally irrelevant.

(B) **dualistic** personality of Ken
Ken has **two** personalities—O, this is obscure information.

(C) **zeal** that David felt
David was **passionate**—A, this adds additional information.

(D) **foretelling** of a recurring event
Predicting a usual act—CORRECT, fits the sentence because the event was no surprise.

(E) comparison of Ken's **effervescence** to David's amazement

Comparing Ken's **light-heartedness** to David's excitement—T, this contradicts the sentence.

Reword the sentence and it may make finding the correct answer much easier.

* Five answer choices used to signify all four *COAT* answers

APPOSITIVES (RENAMING THE NOUN)

An appositive sets off a nonessential part of the sentence and renames the noun.

My brother, Bill, is a doctor.

Bill and doctor describe the same person. By understanding this in a passage question, it will be easier to answer it. See Example 1-11

Your goal in this question is to find a phrase that restates "made a mistake." From the answer choices, notice that (**D**) restates this idea, and it is the correct answer.

> ## EXAMPLE 1-11
> She made a mistake, a slip of the tongue, when it was her turn.
>
> The phrase "slip of the tongue" refers to which of the following?
> (A) a political misunderstanding
> (B) a discerned comment
> (C) a failed attempt to adapt
> (D) a faux pas utterance

LINE CITATION EXAMPLE

To Below is an example (1-12) of how to properly work a *Line Citation* question using the *COAT* strategy:

Start, find the cited part of the passage (e.g., line 23) and **circle** it. Then read it and **circle** the nouns and verbs. Proceed to the answer choices and circle all the nouns and verbs. If the question asks about a particular line and it is in the middle of a sentence, go to the beginning and read the sentence in its entirety. If the citation starts with a pronoun like *they, it, those*, etc., go back to identify who or what the pronoun represents.

In this example you would circle these nouns and verbs: *girl, sat, church, praying, God* and *politics*. You find the correct answer choice with the words "religion, God, political interest".

> ## EXAMPLE 1-12
> In line 23, what was the author describing?
> *Line 23* The girl sat at the church praying to God about politics.
> (A) The priest had strict policies about mixing religion and politics.
> (B) Praying in the church about politics is prohibited during the week.
> (C) The beautiful stained-glass windows help inspire a more thoughtful praying time for the people.
> (D) The girl's religion and political interests were often in her prayers to God.

If you haven't found the right answer yet, try to eliminate the wrong answer choices—those that have been *COAT*ed with hidden tricks. When you find one, cross it out and write a **"C," "O," "A,"** or **"T"** by it. This might seem like overkill, but there will be times when you accidentally cross out all four answer choices. If this happens, go back and read the lines around the citation. Any answer choice that has an **A** (for **Additional Information**) marked by it, could be the correct answer. The correct answer should restate the main points in the citation. In 1-12, (D) has similar nouns and verbs and is correct.

The *Line Citation* questions are generally in a row. The answer is usually found in the line or 2-3 lines above or below it so ALWAYS read around it. Write a "C" by this type of question.

Read carefully, critically and conscientiously.

Here's an ACRONYM to help you remember the process for answering *Line Citation* questions:

> **C** ircle the citation in the passage
> **I** dentify nouns/verbs—circle them
> **T** erminate wrong answers first
> **A** dditional information
> **T** otally contradictory information
> **I** rrelevant information
> **O** bscure information
> **N** ote the one that restates

Write CITATION at the top of your test page during practice and on the actual test booklet.

The correct answer will restate the important elements of the line citation. Read each answer with a critical eye and with great scrutiny to find direct evidence from the text. Every answer MUST be justified from the passage!

Nothing Added—Nothing Omitted! No Addition—No Subtraction!

USE OF VOCABULARY QUESTIONS

This question-type asks you to define the use of a vocabulary word in a sentence. You'll usually be given the most common definition as a choice. However, it is usually the WRONG answer. The correct answer will fit grammatically, make the most sense and go with the context of the sentence.

In the above Example 1-13, when one thinks about "charges," the definition "costs" comes to mind first. As mentioned above, this is a trap. Mark it off because it doesn't fit this sentence. The way to find the correct answer is by **U**nderline key elements and **S**ubstitute **E**ach answer choice in the sentence. Write the acronym **USE** at the top of the test page and write a "U" next to this type of questions.

U nderline key elements
S ubstitute
E ach answer choice in the sentence

If you insert each answer choice into the example sentence, you find B and D do not fit. C is the correct answer because it makes the most sense and fits grammatically.

When approaching vocab questions, the word "and" connects (same flow) and "or" contradicts (changes flow).

EXAMPLE 1-13

The word "charges" in line 27 most nearly means...

Line 27 The shop foreman had heavy charges put upon him with the new load of responsibilities.

  (A) costs
  (B) minds
  (C) burdens
  (D) innocence

FUN TIP

If there are two answer choices that are similar in meaning, then they are both wrong because the test leaves no room for subjectivity.

KEY ELEMENTS

There are often key elements in the sentence that can help define the vocabulary word. Always underline them to help you pinpoint the answer.

REVERSE WORDS:

EXAMPLE 1-14

16. Despite the singer's perplexing use of lyrics, her overall tone was actually lucid. What does the word "lucid" most nearly mean in Line 16?

(A) Baggy
(B) Clear
(C) Difficult
(D) Troublesome

EXAMPLE 1-15

23. Doctors proclaim that a person's brain is remarkably plastic the nerve cells change as a person's situation changes.

As used in *line 23*, "plastic" most nearly means?
(A) Cheap
(B) Artificial
(C) Unbreakable
(D) Pliable

This category of words reverse the direction of the sentence, i.e., change the flow from negative to positive or vice-versa.

Be on the lookout for reverse words like: not, unlike, although, but, while, rather, in spite, however, despite, nonetheless, whereas, instead, nevertheless, by contrast, yet ...

COLONS, SEMICOLONS AND COMMAS

The correct vocabulary word will mimic information found in the other part of the sentence that doesn't contain the vocabulary word. The clue will be before or after the colon, semicolon or comma when a sentence doesn't have a word. The correct answer will be a descriptive word that restates the other part of the sentence that doesn't contain the vocabulary word.

Magnify them by circling the colon or comma and then cut the sentence in half with your pencil. Underline the key elements in the sentence.

Then draw an arrow from the vocabulary word(s) it should describe.

CAUSE AND EFFECT WORDS:

Cause and effect words can be found in sentences that don't change direction. They show the result in the correct answer choice by showing the cause-and-effect and indicate that the word in context is similar to the key word in the sentence.

Hence, therefore, so, then, consequently, accordingly, when, because, thus

These words signify continuous flow of a sentence. They show the result of the previous statement and continue the logic of it. Magnify the vocabulary word by circling it and underline the key elements in the sentence.

> ## EXAMPLE 1-16
>
> 32. Samantha decided to stay home and watch a movie rather than socialize with her cousins <u>because</u> she was primarily (mousy.)
>
> What does the word "mousy" most closely mean in *line 32*?
> (A) Outgoing
> (B) Varmint
> (C) Pest
> (D) Shy

OVERALL PASSAGE QUESTIONS

This question type asks about the entire passage. *Overall Passage Questions* include five main types of problems:

Tone—determine the predominant mood of the passage—whether it's positive or negative, mysterious, neutral (*What tone does the author take? How did the villagers feel?*).

Main Idea—discover the important thought or main purpose from the author (*What is the author's primary thought? What is the passage's main purpose?*).

Inferences—decide what is implied by the author and draw inferences by taking every word literally and derive a correct conclusion from the given details (*What is the author suggesting? What is the author implying?*).

Details—detect and identify specific information from the given text/citations (*In Line 4, what is she describing? Who is responsible (in Line 16) for...?*).

Comparison—determine the difference between two points of view (*How would the author of Passage 2 respond to the last sentence in Passage 1? Which statement would best fit Passage 2 and not Passage 1?*).

The *Overall Passage* question type is usually the first question in the passage section. This is because most students answer questions in a row starting with question one. But on these tests, this can waste a ton of time because they cause you to read through the passage several times in order to try and answer it. **PASS** these questions up <u>until</u> you have answered all the other question types first. Put a "P" by them so you can remember to come back and answer them. You'll have the main points already under your belt because of all the questions you've answered before you attempt the *Overall Passage* questions. This overview of the passage will most likely mean you won't even have to read the entire passage.

When you come across an overall passage question, go back and do the essential reading: underline the italicized introduction, and both the opening and closing sentences of each paragraph and review all the circled citations. By going over these parts, you should be able to infer the answer to the question. If the question is about tone, this simple exercise should show you whether the overall tone is either positive or negative. Even if there are parts with negative information, if the overall passage is positive, then your answer will be positive and generally found in the first and last lines so always underline and read first.

Notate a brief description of the main idea. E.g. If the passage is about a young girl growing up poor in 1920, you can draw a stick figure of a girl, the money sign in a circle with a line through it and "1920" next to it.

Use basic reasoning to mark off the wrong answers and pick the one that alludes to the right answer. Every single word in the correct answer will match the tone and will be right! It will usually be politically correct, contain no harsh words and will not distort the truth. Avoid **S.O.N.** (**S**trong, **O**pinionated, **N**egative) choices.

Write the acronym PASSAGE at the top of your page:

P
A } these questions up until the end
S
S
A dd the essential reading
G o over the circled portions/answers
E very word is nice and politically correct in the correct answer

COMMAND OF EVIDENCE QUESTION

There will be (at least) two questions that interrelate. A Command of Evidence question usually asks you to consider evidence in a previous question. To make matters more difficult, often these related questions are printed on different pages or columns.

One way we recommend you catch these related questions is to label every passage question but start with the very last question and work backwards. Command of Evidence questions usually comprise of two questions about the same passage that require a unique way to resolve them.

Here are the basic steps followed by a detailed explanation of each point:

Start at the last questions and work backwards. Write COE for command of evidence questions Since it asks about providing the best evidence for a previous question, know there is usually key information in that question. Don't try and answer the previous question first or you will waste a lot of time.

Next, don't read the second question; it says the same thing each time so it is unnecessary to read. Mark it out. It says, "Which choice provides the best evidence for the previous question".

Carefully read the first question and circle matching keywords in both questions.

Eliminate obvious wrong answers simultaneously in both questions.

Now, read remaining lines in the second questions and you'll discover the answer to <u>both</u> questions, so now mark the correct answers on both.

In example 1-17, circle "Carolyn" in the first question 7. Notice that "annoying" in (B) and

EXAMPLE 1-17

7. The passage indicates that Carolyn found the new classmate to be
   (A) Silly
   (B) Annoying
   (C) Quiet
   (D) Fun

8. Which choice provides the best evidence for the answer to the previous question?
   (A) Lines 3-5 (He...home)
   (B) Lines 16-18 (Once...again)
   (C) Lines 22-28 (She...bothered)
   (D) Lines 33-35 (Today...quickly)

"bothered" in (C) in question 8 are matching keywords; and question 8 also has "she" which matches with "Carolyn." This is the place to start. Read lines 22-28 in (C). It does answer question 7 so (B) is correct for 7. And (C) is correct for 8. Both answered simultaneously.

Lines 3-5 He knew school was extremely boring to her and she would rather study at home.

Lines 16-18 Once the new school year started, her dad would have to fight Carolyn to attend once again.

Lines 22-28 She had no tolerance for Julia's goofy attitude toward shirking her homework responsibilities which left her bothered.

Lines 22-25 Today was a relief from the monotony since the emergency phone call allowed her to bow out quickly.

Even if you didn't notice any matching key words right away, you could circle "Carolyn" and "new classmate" in the first question. Then read the lines and circle "Julia's" and "goofy" in answer (C) in 8. and notice it works with (B) in 7. The location of the first question is found in the second one.

Here's an ACRONYM to help you remember the process for answering Command of Evidence questions:

C ircle both questions together
O mit reading the 2nd question
M eticulously read the first question
M ark matching keywords in both
A bolish obvious wrong answers
N ow read remaining lines in 2nd question
D iscover answers for both questions

THE LONG READING PASSAGES

The Long Passage and the Long Passage with a Chart or Graph are very similar to one another. They both contain the five main question types: Line Citation, Vocabulary Use, Command of Evidence and Overall Passage but add the Chart Analysis question. You can use all the same strategies for answering the questions on both.

The key is to identify each question type and put it in the correct order. The best way to remember this is to think *small* to *large* for the order to answer the labeled questions.

Vocabulary Use (a word)
Line /Citation (a line)
3. Command of Evidence (2 questions)
4. Chart Analysis (1-2 questions and a chart)
5. Overall Passage (entire passage)

FUN TIP

Before answering questions, start backwards at the last question working to the first one and annotate the correct letter type next to the question. E.g. "C" for Citation.

CHART ANALYSIS QUESTION

This type of question asks about information from a chart, graph or table found within a long passage. Write a "CH" next to these question types.

First, scan the chart/graph/table to get a good idea of the given information. Next, read the title, description and the horizontal and vertical data. Then read all around the chart: sub-titles, text with asterisk and italicized parts. Finally, decipher one complete row, bar, slice or column depending on the type of diagram.

Read the question carefully, you can grab at least one or two data points they are asking for each time. You'll simply circle the two or so points that the question asks for and with that you'll have an exact cross reference to the answer you need.

EXAMPLE 1-18

1992-2012 Friday Nights in Springtown	# of Calls	Avg. Yearly % of ALL 911 Calls
Noise	543	23%
Curfew	442	19%
Domestic	326	14%
Animal	256	11%
Theft	186	8%

The partial table above displays information pertaining to the amount and type of 911 calls in Springtown which doubled every decade.

Identify the data points and circle where those points are on the chart. Determine where the two points intersect. The information which correlates on the chart and in the question/answer will be correct.

This strategy works in the math section as well!

Example 1-18.

It can be reasonably inferred from the chart that

A. a large majority of calls involve animal issues
B. domestic situations make up half of the calls
C. the ten-year total of noise complaints is almost equal to the total amount of theft problems represented on the chart
D. approximately 25% of calls are emergency health related

In example 1-18 the first thing to do is cross out "it can reasonably inferred" because you know this test is objective.

Second, connect key data points in the answers to the chart.

A—circle "large majority" and "animal issues" and circle them on the chart. There were only 11% so not the majority, eliminate this answer.

B—Circle "domestic" and "half" in the question and on the chart. Only 14%, so eliminate this one too.

C—This one seems to take more thought, so skip it (put a star next to it) to see if you can eliminate D.

D—Circle 25% and "emergency health." There is no "emergency health" category; but add up all the yearly averages, it comes to 75%. Be careful, you can't assume the other 25% comes from emergency, so it is also wrong. C is correct but there is no need to read it since there is only one right answer.

To double check it, you can circle "ten year" and "equal." Notice the table info says it doubled "every decade" and the table shows the chart is from 1992-2012 (20 years), so the total of noise complaints in 20 years was 543. If you divide it by 3, it would equal 181 for the first 10 years, which is close to the existing theft complaints of 186, so C is correct.

Here is our Chart Acronym:

C arefully read the question
H ighlight/circle data requirements
A nalyze points on the chart plane
R eview crossing points of the circles
T he intersecting point is the answer

DUAL READING PASSAGE

This section contains two separate passages followed by several questions. The two passages are usually connected by the same common topic. They may give opposing or harmonious points of view. Always note (write in the booklet) whether the passages agree, disagree or complement one another. This can often be reflected in the italicized part. <u>Always read and underline the italicized portion of both passages first.</u> Very often, an answer or two can be found in the italicized section.

As a general rule, if two passages appear to have different subject matter, they probably agree on a unifying theme. If they both speak on the same subject, they probably disagree.

Passage 1 and Passage 2 are next to each other expressly for you to read them both together and then answer the questions. *This is a trap!* Don't fall for the way they have set up this section. Skim the first passage and answer just its questions, and <u>then</u> do the second passage and its questions. Circle the citations and look for the answers in or near them. PASS up the Overall Passage questions about <u>both</u> passages until the end.

Read and underline the main theme of each passage—found in the first couple of lines. Notate a brief description about the main idea next to each passage. E.g. If Passage 1 is about how terrible global warming is, you could put "GW" and a sad face next to it. If Passage 2 contends that there is no such thing as global warming, you could write "GW" in a circle and draw a line through it. This will help to keep the two passages straight. Read the circled citations, first and last sentences of each paragraph, and the italicized opening. Now you can answer the overall passage questions.

Just like the other passages, skim the questions first, notate the type of question alongside and then answer in the correct order:

1. **Use of Vocabulary Questions (U)** which ask about the particular use of a vocabulary word in context.
2. **Citation Questions (C)** which cite specific lines from the text.
3. **Command of Evidence Questions (COE)** ask about which choice provides the best evidence for the previous question.
4. **Chart Questions (CH)** ask about information from the passage that relates to a chart, graph or table.
5. **Overall Passage Questions (P)** which ask about information about the entire passage's purpose.

For the Dual Passage Overall Passage Questions, Write P1, P2 and then PP.

Always start backwards when you label the questions.

DUAL PASSAGE TRAPS

1. Watch out for answers that neglect one passage altogether (where an answer choice only gives information from one passage and not both).
2. Sometimes the answer choices swap passages. An answer choice gives information from the other passage or changes person from the other passage.

EXAMPLE 1-19

What negative feature does each passage stress?

(A) Passage 1 discusses political harmony and Passage 2 discusses critical analysis.
(B) Passage 1 discusses dissension in the ranks and Passage 2 discusses peaceful unity.
(C) Passage 1 discusses discord among brotherhood and Passage 2 discusses harsh judgment.
(D) Passage 1 discusses deliberate strife and Passage 2 discusses severe ranking.

Always circle what the question is asking! Often, the question has several criteria that need to be answered, and by knowing these, wrong answers can be immediately spotted.

In Example 1-19 when you circle the two criteria (negative and each), you can quickly eliminate answers with the wrong patterns. If any answer choice contains any positive words, mark them out. (A and B have a positive word so cross out.) With the remaining answers, make sure that the information in the correct answer is found in each passage. Remember that the answer choices often switch passages or ignore one passage altogether.

Here's an acronym to help you memorize the process for doing DUAL Passage questions:

Do each passage and questions one at a time
Underline main themes in each passage
Answers must match correct passage
Leave both passage questions till the end

Write DUAL at the top of your page, on the Dual Passage section.

THE POSITIVE/NEGATIVE TEST

Many unknown words can be figured out if you apply the Positive / Negative Test. What is your first impression of the unknown word? Say the word and listen to the sound of it. If it seems to have a good meaning, then it is probably a **positive** word with a good connotation. When you listen to the sound of the word and it seems to have a "bad" meaning, then it is probably a **negative** word with a poor connotation.

See if you can figure out by the sound of these words whether they're positive or negative. What is your first thought on the word? After you take this test, look up the actual definitions in the dictionary and see if your first impression was correct.

Word	Positive	Negative
Sycophant	✓	
Tedium		✓
Decorous	✓	
Timorous		✓
Expunge		✓
Florid		✓
Lurid	✓	
Pacificator	✓	
Querulous		✓
Pinion	✓	
Quintessential	✓	
Ribald		✓
Licentious		✓

When you take the test, predict if the word in the blank is positive or negative. Write a P (positive) or N (negative) in the blank. Above the P or N, write a word that might fit. Then find answer choices that give the sentence the same pattern of negatives and positives. See if the words are closely related to the word(s) you wrote. Try this for yourself in Example 1-20.

This question was for illustration since Sentence Completion questions have been omitted. The above sentence is negative, and there's no change in direction, so both answers will be negative. One strategy is to predict the missing words; in this case you would probably substitute something along the lines of "stormed" and "hurriedly." Now look at the answer choices and find the two words that are negative and have a close meaning to "stormed" and "hurriedly."

In (A), both words are positive. In (B) and (C), the second word is positive. In (D), both words are negative and close to the predicted words. Therefore, answer (D) is correct.

EXAMPLE 1-20

*The angry man _____ out of the store as he _____ grabbed his bag of groceries.

(A) walked ... carefully
(B) marched ... sympathetically
(C) ambulated ... tenderly
(D) stamped ... aggressively

Answers from the positive/negative test on page 98 (N, N, P, N, N, P, N, P, N, N, P, N, N)

Roots and Prefixes are Important!

Latin roots, cognates and derivatives are useful tools for deriving the meaning of an unknown word. Another way to apply the positive/negative test is to learn prefixes, because many of them are either positive or negative. Sometimes just the beginning or ending of a word can point you to the correct answer.

EXAMPLE 1-21

Line 10. Frankfort resumed direct control of North Brussels after just six weeks of self-rule.

What does the word "self-rule" mean in *line 10?*

(A) serendipity
(B) waspishness
(C) autonomy
(D) ignobility

Although Example 1-21 appears difficult, it's actually just testing your reasoning skills as usual. Understanding prefixes as well as the positive/negative test, is the key to answering this question. By the context, you know you need a word that is not negative and means "self-rule." (A) sounds positive; (B) sounds negative -like a wasp; (C) auto means self; (D) the prefix means "not" so it's negative. Answer (C) is correct. Autonomy means independence and self-governed.

Learn the positive and negative prefixes, root words and suffixes found in appendix A (page 277). Mark down when you know them and then write and learn several new words that use them.

PART III:

MATH SECTION

MATH SECTION

THE *MATH* SECTION OF the *SAT* and PSAT / NMSQT is not a math test. *Math* is only the vehicle being used to test a student's reasoning skills. This section requires students to think. Sometimes you are thinking in extremes—large, small, opposite, backward—but you must think the questions all the way through, in order to get them correct.

The test can be defined as a test of math terms, definitions and properties. I have provided you with a glossary of math terms that you must know. Find these in Appendix B (page 293)

While this section may be challenging, you don't have to be a math genius! Each math question can be answered quickly, and the key is to find the easy solution to each problem. All you have to do is learn to look at the questions logically and understand how to set up the problems to find the correct answer. Most questions are more simple than you think.

The *SAT Math* doesn't test unknown or tough concepts. However difficulty exists because the questions are designed to trick the students. If a student knows the basic math concepts, then the key to answering the questions is memorizing how to work each problem type. Most mistakes come from these areas:

- Carelessness—don't rush. Work out what the question is really asking
- Incorrect Problem Solving—missing a step/s or doing it in your head
- Falling for the Tricks—read with a critical eye so you can recognize the question-type
- Separating Question and Answer—treat the Q&A as one entity
- Relying on Calculators—use your pencil to solve the problem, not your calculator

The math section of the *SAT* and *PSAT/ NMSQT* is NOT a math test.

The *SAT* math tests unknown or tough concepts, but it can be difficult because the questions are designed to trick the students.

IMPORTANT TIP

Keep the book open when practicing the math until you have internalized the strategies.

If you are taking a long time to work each problem, you are probably doing it the wrong way.

If you take a long time to work each problem, you are probably doing it the wrong way. Every math question can be solved two ways: in a long, tedious way or a short, direct way. There are shortcuts for every type of math problem on the *SAT*. There is no need to show all your work: It will take too long and they only want to see your answer. It's a good idea to familiarize yourself with all the shortcuts outlined in this section. Not only can you cut your time in half with shortcuts, you can also avoid dumb mistakes with less work. Always give the question a quick glance-over and if you don't understand how to work it, skip it and come back to it at the end. Don't be determined to finish a question. You only have about a minute per question so use it wisely.

FUN TIP

Questions can be answered quickly but speed must come after you understand how to answer correctly. I.e. Accuracy Before Speed or:

PRECISE PRECEDES PRONTO
EXACT ERE EXPEDITED
ACCURATE AHEAD ACCELERATION
RIGHT RANKS RAPIDNESS

Read all questions with a critical eye. This is fundamental to your success. You will be presented with problems purposely written to challenge your understanding. You must learn to decode the questions. Even though each question contains all the necessary information, many times you will have to be a detective to locate it. Solving a hard problem may not involve working the math. It can simply be a matter of working several easy steps to get the answer.

Never try to do them in your head—always work them in your booklet. Do your thinking with your pencil. Even shortcuts should be written out to help you derive the correct answer. Rewrite confusing problems to make them clearer.

Understanding the language is imperative to doing well on this section.

Understanding the language is imperative to doing well on this section. *Math* vocabulary is very important to know; otherwise, it will be difficult to answer many of the questions correctly. For example: The word "positive" does not mean "even only," and zero is never positive.

You will find geometry formulas used in this section (for area, circumference, volume) at the beginning of the real test. These may be useful for problems that involve cubes, prisms, cylinders, cones, spheres, pyramids, rectangular solids, etc. If you forget how to work a certain problem, check the formulas and try again.

Solving math questions requires five steps:

Decide —What are they telling you in the question? It probably needs to be rephrased if the language is obscure.

Decode —What is the bottom line? Circle what is really being asked of you so you stay on track.

Disguised —What answer do they want you to fall for? They have cleverly hidden the real answer and try to throw you off-track with "dummy" answers.

Declare —What should you really be thinking? To understand the recurring patterns, PRACTICE is essential.

Double-Check —What did you miss or mess up? Check each step along the way as you do them. I.e. If a problem has several steps, check them separately.

> **FUN TIP**
>
> Learn to SEE the math and not do the math.

Remember, the *SAT* and *PSAT/ NMSQT* are tests of logic and reasoning.

STEPS TO MATH SUCCESS

1. Learn the CPG Acronyms.
2. Know the 300+ *Math Terms*. You'll find them at the back of this book.
3. Read and understand the rules for this section before taking the real test.
4. Practice the *Math* Section in genuine *College Board* Tests.

Remember, the *SAT* and *PSAT* are tests of logic and reasoning. The math formulas are printed on the test booklet and you are permitted to use a calculator. It is EXTREMELY IMPORTANT that you know the meaning of the math terminology and how to apply basic math concepts. At the back of this book you will find more than 300 math vocabulary words and their definitions. Make sure you review and know ALL of them. Check them off if you know them and continue to revise those you do not know and they are committed to memory. ^make sure

Learn to look at each math problem logically. Learn the shortcuts and unique strategies that can unravel the hidden patterns on the math section.

Memorize the CPG Acronyms to help you remember these steps. While you are learning the CPG Acronyms, keep your notes open to remind yourself of what each letter stands for. Get in the habit of writing the CPG Acronyms at the top of your paper. When you sit the *SAT* test, you are not allowed to bring any notes, but you are allowed to write in the booklet—but NOT on the grid-in paper. This is why it is important to memorize the CPG Acronyms.

THERE ARE TWO SECTIONS:

- Multiple Choice
- Student Response

The *SAT* math problems are often a combination of more than one concept.

There are two math sections: one 25-minute section in which a calculator is not permitted; and one 55-minute section. You have 80 minutes in total. Both sections contain Multiple Choice and Student-Response questions.

MULTIPLE CHOICE:

The multiple choice section contains questions followed by four answer choices.

The *SAT* math problems often combine more than one concept. You need to understand the basic math as well as the math terms, definitions and properties. Below are the types of problems that can be found on the actual test:

- Arithmetic and Word Problems
- Algebra 1 & 2, Factoring & Functions
- Geometry, Measurement & the Number Line
- Statistics, Probability & Data Analysis
- Unit Conversions
- Range and Standard Deviation of Data
- Interpreting Scatter Plots
- Linear vs. Exponential Growth
- Frequency
- Conditional Probability

- Chords
- Equations of Circles
- Trigonometric Functions Applied to Right Triangles and Complementary Angles
- Trigonometric Functions with Radian Measure
- Quadratics
- Exponents
- Proportions
- Radicals
- Graphs and Tables
- Inequalities

IMPORTANT TIP

Factoring In—There are four basic operations in math that factor in to solve equations: addition, subtraction, multiplication and division.

TRAIN YOUR MATH BRAIN

1. Read the question and answers together and treat them as one entity because the answer is often evident by doing so.
2. Analyze the question to see if you can answer it in 30 seconds or less.
3. If you cannot answer it quickly, star and skip it.
4. Repeat process on every question.
5. Return to answer ones that require some thinking.
6. Save the ones you are unsure of until the end.
7. Repeat process so that you will have gone through the test 3-4 times—efficiently and with minimal time-loss.

Do not be determined to finish a problem by spending a lot of time on it. Points are gained by more right questions so give yourself permission to use your time wisely.

FUN TIP

SAT math is often a combination of simple concepts presented in a strange way.

BASIC STRATEGIES

NO CALCUATOR NEEDED

Always bring your calculator to the *SAT* and PSAT/NMSQT.

ALWAYS BRING YOUR CALCULATOR to the *SAT* and PSAT / NMSQT. Make sure it has square root and exponent functions, and bring a set of fresh batteries. However, most questions on the *SAT* should never need a calculator. Often, these devices only slow down the answering process. Your goal is to find the fastest way to answer the question. In my experiences, I have found that calculator use tends to increase the more chances of making a mistake. My aim is to teach you how to answer math problems without the use of a calculator so you can eliminate steps and save time. Try for yourself in Example 2-1.

EXAMPLE 2-1

The area of each shaded square is 12. What is the total area of the non-shaded circles?

(A) $12\pi - 12$

(B) $24 - 12$

(C) $3\pi - 36$

(D) $18\pi - 36$

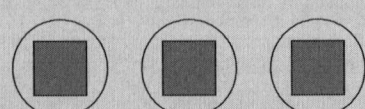

Let's look at what the question is really saying. The answer will be the area of the shaded squares subtracted from the non-shaded circles. In other words, the correct answer will have a – 36 in it. Because 12 times 3 equals 36.

You can mark off (A) and (B) right away. This leaves us with (C) and (D). Don't be too quick to pick (D). Pi is only 3.14, and that would make the answer a negative number, which is impossible. (9.42 - 36 = -26.58) therefore, the correct answer is (D) $18\pi - 36$.

WHAT'S THE QUESTION REALLY ASKING?

The questions are designed to throw you off, so you must CIRCLE what the question is asking. This will help keep you from getting the question wrong.

Look at Example 2-2. At first glance, most students would think to add 7 + 11 = 18 and divide by 2 to get the average of 9, which is answer (D). This is a wrong answer choice. If you circle all the key elements in the question (p, q and r), you will find you need to divide by 3 instead. The correct answer is (B) 6. Always circle what the question is asking.

Another example of how careful one needs to be is shown in Example 2-3.

Another illustration to show why you need to read carefully can be found in example (2-?) Convert 6/16 to 3/8 and 1/4 to 2/8. 3/8 – 2/8 = 1/8 But 1/8 is NOT the answer. Remember to circle what the question is really asking!

How many 8ths? The correct answer is (D) 1.

Try looking at example 2-4. You can easily figure out that x could be equal to three (C). But remember these questions are designed for you to fall for the "dummy" answer. Always circle what the question is really asking. "How many" are the key words. The correct answer is (A) one, since there is only "one" integer that will make it true. This question was NOT asking you to work it out.

EXAMPLE 2-2

If $p + q = 7$ and $r = 11$, what is the average of the variables?
- (A) **5**
- (B) **6**
- (C) **7.5**
- (D) **9**

EXAMPLE 2-3

How many 8ths is 6/16 – 1/4?
- (A) 1/8
- (B) ¼
- (C) 7/16
- (D) 1

EXAMPLE 2-4

How many different integers for x will make the following statement to be true?

$$4 < 2x < 8$$

- (A) one
- (B) two
- (C) three
- (D) five

MAKE NEW DIAGRAMS

Beware when you see the words "Figure Not Drawn to Scale." It should really say: "Figure Drawn to Confuse You." The disclaimer lets the *College Board* off the hook for drawing an incorrect diagram, or one not correctly scaled. The drawing will not correctly reflect the question and if you try to work the problem using that figure, you will probably get it wrong. If it were drawn correctly, the answer would probably be easy to determine. So, redraw a new figure using the specifications from the question.

EXAMPLE 2-5

In the following figure, Point P is the center of the circle. If x=120°, what's the value of y? Note: Figure not drawn to scale.

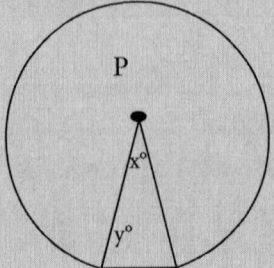 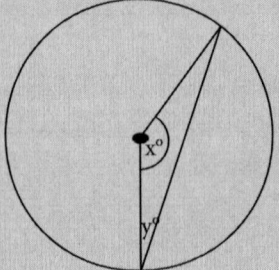

Redraw the figure correctly according to the question.

In the figure which accompanies Example 2-5, the angle drawn is not accurate and if relied upon, will mislead you. Redraw the diagram for a better representation.

DIAGRAMS/CHARTS & DRAWINGS

Don't take test diagrams or charts at face value. There is probably a better way to figure out the answer.

EXAMPLE 2-6

In the following figure, the circle is tangent to sides WX and YZ of the 12-by-18 rectangle. What is the area of the circle?

(A) 12π (B) 18π (C) 24π (D) 36π

Read the question once, then fix the drawing: i.e., redraw it correctly; fill in the missing information from the question; or make a different diagram to better reflect the question. Then re-read the question to confirm what it is really being asked of you.

ALWAYS draw a diagram or picture if there is not one and label all the information from the question. Exaggerate it so you can easily see it. By enlarging and overlabeling the diagrams, you can often see the answer much quicker.

FUN TIP

Sometimes the *SAT* figure is correct, but it's confusing and difficult to figure out the answer using it. In that case, draw a different diagram that will better reflect what the question is asking and give you a better visual on how to solve the problem.

ADD IN ALL GIVEN INFORMATION

> ### FUN TIP
> Write on answer choices by substituting variables with discernable numbers to find a quick answer.

Often the example diagram will leave out vital information that is contained in the question. Assume every drawing (whether to scale or not) is incomplete. They have purposely left out pertinent information in the drawing. Go to the question and get ALL the correct information and put it in the figure. Also, add in more information than given. E.g. If only the area is given, label it and the perimeter. This will help you to answer the question correctly.

Although the question in example 2-6 gives sufficient data to figure out this problem, the diagram leaves out some essential information. This is why students should always fill in the given information to the diagram in order to help them answer the question correctly. Remember, "tangent" means touching but not intersecting.

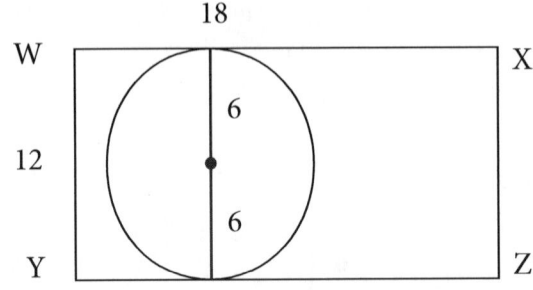

The circle's diameter is 12, and therefore its radius is 6. $\pi r^2 = 36\pi$ Answer (D).

ALWAYS DRAW A DIAGRAM

> ### EXAMPLE 2-7
> If a square with the area of 36 is inscribed in a circle, what is the area of the circle?
>
> (A) 4π (B) 6π (C) 10π (D) 18π

Note: There is no diagram in the question, so construct a clear one of your own. Look at Example 2-7.

Diagram A:

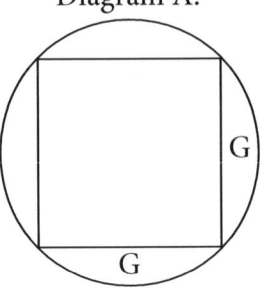

Make sure you know what "inscribed" means (enclosed inside another shape touching each side). Draw a line through the rectangle to find the radius of the right triangles. Now use the Pythagorean Theorem to find the diameter of the circle.

Pythagorean Theorem = a² + b² = c²

$6^2 + 6^2 = c^2$

$36 + 36 = c^2$

$c^2 = 72$

$c = \sqrt{72}$

Since the diameter is $\sqrt{72}$, the radius is $\frac{\sqrt{72}}{2}$. Now, to answer the question (what is the area of the circle), use the formula πr^2.

$\pi r^2 = \pi \left(\frac{\sqrt{72}^2}{2^2}\right)$ or 18π Answer **(D)**

Sometimes a problem doesn't illustrate a specific picture to draw.

However, it is always a good idea to write out an illustration of the problem, even if it doesn't contain any geometric shapes or figures. See Example 2-8.

If you write out the sum of all integers 201–300 (Group A), it would be 201 + 202 + 203 …

If you write out the sum of all integers 301–400 (Group B), it would be 301 + 302 + 303 …

Just by looking at it, you will notice that every number in Group A is exactly 100 less than the numbers in Group B. Therefore, the difference between each number is exactly 100.

  301 + 302 + 303…
 – 201 – 202 – 203…
  100 + 100 + 100…

EXAMPLE 2-8

If the sum of all integers from 201 to 300 is subtracted from the sum of all integers from 301 to 400, what would be the difference?

(A) 0 (B) 100 (C) 1,000 (D) 10,000

Diagram B:

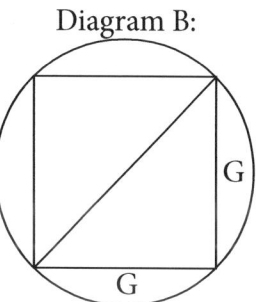

FUN TIP

Get in the habit of over-labeling math diagrams. E.g. If the perimeter is given, then notate the area.

Between 201–300 and 301–400, there are exactly 100 numbers. Therefore, 100 numbers have a difference of 100, so the correct answer would be 100 x 100—(D) 10,000.

ELIMINATE SOME ANSWERS RIGHT AWAY

EXAMPLE 2-9

Which of the following is divisible by 4 and 7, but not 5?

(A) 25 (B) 32 (C) 45 (D) 56

Most multiple-choice questions contain answer choices that are clearly wrong if a student looks at them logically. To find the correct answer you may not need you to work out the problem in the normal way. If you can eliminate all the wrong answers using logic, you may be able to find the right answer without ever doing a calculation. See Example 2-9.

You already know with basic math that only numbers divisible by 5 end in a 5 or 0. Therefore, you can eliminate (A) 25 and (C) 45 right off the bat. (B) 32 is clearly not divisible by 7, so the answer is (D) 56. No calculations needed!

EXAMPLE 2-10

The Clay Pottery's old kiln fired 20 cups an hour. They purchased a new model that fired 50 cups an hour. If they ran both machines at the same time, how many minutes would it take to fire a total of 100 cups?

(A) 45 (B) 55 (C) 90 (D) 160

In Example 2-10, instead of doing the long algebra equation, you can simply eliminate the obvious wrong answers. If the machines together fire 70 cups in one hour (60 minutes), mark off (A) and (B) because they are too low. Two hours (120 minutes) would result in 140 cups, so mark off (D). (C) is the correct answer.

FUN TIP

Always test answer (C) first to save time since answers are in ascending order.

THE M AND M RULE

To answer a question that calls for a range, first find the Maximum and then the Minimum and you can find the answer.

The Maximum outcome would be if every girl voted for themselves and every other girl: or 30 girls multiplied by 30 votes equals 900. So mark off (C) and (D) because they are too high.

> ## EXAMPLE 2-10B
> There are 30 girls in the sorority. They need to pick one to represent them in the homecoming court. How many different results can be decided by a ballot vote?
>
> (A) 820 (B) 870 (C) 909 (D) 930

The Minimum outcome occurs when you subtract one girl and where everyone voted for themselves and every other girl. This would be 29 x 29 = 841. So mark off (A) since it is too low and (B) is CORRECT.

COULD VS. MUST

Two math terms that are important to know:

Could means it is a possibility whereas Must means it absolutely has to be true. Always circle these terms dark because often you don't have to do any calculations by understanding their meanings.

See example 2-12.

MATH SHORTCUTS (FOR FASTER COMPUTING)

SUBSTITUTE

Sometimes a fast answer can be found by plugging in numbers to help you find the correct answer. This is usually necessary when there are variables that cannot be determined and have no values. See Example 2-11.

EXAMPLE 2-11

If w, x, y and z are four consecutive even integers, and $w < x < y < z$, then how much smaller is $w + x$ than $y + z$?

(A) 6
(B) 8
(C) 9
(D) 13

Circle the words four consecutive even integers and replace them with $2 + 4 + 6 + 8$.

First: (C) and (D) are odd numbers and can be marked off immediately, because this problem strictly deals with even numbers. Now substitute: $w + x$ (2 + 4) and $y + z$ (6 + 8) to get 6 and 14. Subtract 6 from 14 and the answer is 8 (B).

Six, Seven and Eight Work Great!

EXAMPLE 2-12

If x and y are both even integers, to get an odd number, which of the following answer MUST be true?

(A) $x + y$
(B) xy
(C) $xy + 3$
(D) $2xy$

Because numbers like 0, 1 or 2 have unique properties, it is always a good idea to use more regular numbers when using substitution. Note: when substituting numbers, don't use numbers that are in the equation. Some good numbers that work every time are 6, 7 and 8. Try this idea in Example in 2-12.

If you use 6 and 8 for the variables, (A), (B) and (D) come out even. (C) is correct ($6 \times 8 + 3 = 51$).

An even faster way to answer this type of question is to apply basic math principles. When you add or multiply any two even numbers, the result is always even. The answer must involve an odd integer. Therefore, (C) must be the answer.

FUN TIP

Adding

Even number added to an even number equals an even number $2 + 2 = 4$

Odd number added to an odd number equals an even number $3 + 3 = 6$

Even number added to an odd number equals an odd number $2 + 3 = 5$

Multiplying

Even number multiplied by an even number equals an even number $2 \times 2 = 4$

Even number multiplied by an odd number equals an even number $2 \times 3 = 6$

Odd number multiplied by an odd number equals an odd number $3 \times 3 = 9$

START SUBSTITUTION FROM ANSWER C

Save time!

The *College Board* puts the answer choices in ascending or descending order. This is important to know because you NEVER have to test four answers. By starting at answer (C), you will know whether you need to go higher or lower; and therefore, only test one of the remaining answers. If it is right, then pick it; and if it is wrong, then the other answer is correct!

Let's try this approach with Example 2-13 and plug answer choice (C) into the equation. Therefore, $47(99 + 1) = 4700$. Look for a result of 4747 which is greater than 4700. You can immediately

EXAMPLE 2-13
If $4747 = 47(x + 1)$, then x = ?
(A) **10**
(B) **11**
(C) **99**
(D) **100**

FUN TIP

When you are trying to get an equal number-you take a higher percent from the lower number.

mark off (A) and (B), because they would definitely be too small. This gives you **(D)** 100 as the correct answer.

Summary: If you start with answer choice (C), you can automatically eliminate up to 50% of the other choices by figuring out if the correct answer will be larger or smaller than (C).

If the answer needed to be smaller, you could pick either A or B. If one didn't work, then the other one is correct. You have saved time and only performed two calculations.

CONVERT

EXAMPLE 2-14
Which of these numbers are between 1/4 and 1/3?
  (A) .14
  (B) .21
  (C) .24
  (D) .29

Another way to find a quick answer to a math question is to convert. You can turn fractions into decimals. Try this in Example 2-14.

Instead of working on a long calculation, convert the 1/4 to 0.25 and 1/3 to 0.33. Make a new diagram to better reflect the question like our example below:

You can clearly see that our answer is **(D)** 29.

$$\overleftrightarrow{\quad\quad\quad\quad}$$
0.25   0.33

EXAMPLE 2-15
Paula's famous cinnamon rolls consist of 30 pounds of cream cheese and 5 pounds of butter. What is the minimum number of pounds of butter that she must add into the butter to come up with a batch that is 25% butter?
  (A) Three
  (B) Four
  (C) Five
  (D) Eight

PERCENTAGE CONVERSION

Always convert percentages to decimals. This will make computation easier and help limit the possibility of error. There is a very simple formula to convert percentages to decimals and vice versa.

Percent to Decimal = move decimal two places to the left (75% = .75)

Percent to Fraction = put number over 100 (75% = 75/100)

Fraction to Decimal = divide numerator by denominator (4/17 = 0.235)

When using a percentage in an equation, make sure to convert the number into either a fraction or decimal depending on the type of problem. To increase or decrease the percent, make sure the increase or decrease is converted to the same form as the original amount. See Example 2-15.

First, make sure you label 25% as 25/100 so you can use a ratio to solve for the answer. Add the parts, 5 + 30, to find the denominator. You could set up the equation as $\frac{x+5}{x+35} = \frac{25}{100}$, and then cross multiply. **(C) Five** is correct.

MONEY CONVERSION

If a question asks you to convert dollars into cents, you simply multiply by 100. If you are required to convert cents into dollars, simply divide by 100.

Look at Example 2-16. This question asks you to convert cents into dollars. If you purchase x pound of oranges, then the cost is $89x$ cents. Since there are 100 pennies in every dollar, you need to divide by 100. So, the answer is $\frac{89x}{100}$ **(C)**.

> ## EXAMPLE 2-16
> The corner fruit market has clementine oranges on sale for 89 cents per pound. How much, in dollars, would x pounds of oranges cost?
>
> $x + 89$　　(B)　$89x$　　(C)　$\frac{89x}{100}$　(D) $\frac{100x}{89}$

REDUCE

When you have a long equation that needs reducing, don't work it out first and then reduce. You can avoid steps and save time if you **reduce first** before multiplying. See Example 2-17.

> ## EXAMPLE 2-17
> $\frac{90}{50} \times \frac{200}{35}$　reduction process equals　$\frac{9}{5} \times \frac{40}{7}$

EXAMPLE 2-18

If x = 10, then $\dfrac{x^2 + 4x}{x}$ =

(A) 14   (B) 20   (C) 80   (D) 140

If you reduce the first fraction by 10 and the second fraction by 5, the equation is much easier to compute. Also keep in mind that you can reduce variables from equations as well. Try this in Example 2-18.

Skip working on the long calculation and just simplify the equation. Eliminate the "x" from $\dfrac{x\,(x+4)}{x}$, which makes it simply $x + 4$. And, if $x = 10$, then $10 + 4 = 14$, **answer (A)**.

CANCEL

EXAMPLE 2-19

A = {3/7, 2, 7/2, 5, 9/4, 9}

B = {3/7, 9/7, 5, 9}

If x belongs to both set A and B, which of the following must be true?

I. x is an integer

II. $3x$ is an integer

III. $x = 5$

(A) None
(B) I Only
(C) I and II
(D) III Only

Sometimes when you cancel first, you can find a quicker answer. See Example 2-19.

The first thing to do is to cancel out every number that only exists in one set but not the other. Here those values would be 2, 7/2, 9/4 and 9/7.

The meaning of the word "integer" is very important. (*It can be positive, negative or zero however not a fraction or decimal.*) Look at Roman numeral I ("x is an integer"). The statement is not true since there is a fraction in both sets.

Since Roman numeral I is not the answer, you can cancel all answers that have a Roman "I" in them: (B) and (C).

There is no need to work Roman numeral II ($3x$ is an integer), since Roman II is not left in the answer choices.

Roman III ($x = 5$) is also incorrect since x could also be 3/7 or 9 and the question says MUST be true. So, by canceling all the obvious wrong answers, the correct answer is **(A) None**.

ESTIMATE

Many times you can find an answer by just estimating. Now using this idea, try example 2-20.

EXAMPLE 2-20

If a square piece of matting with a perimeter of 48" was cut diagonally for a picture frame, what might roughly be the perimeter of the cut mat?

(A) 36   (B) 41   (C) 48   (D) 52

Draw a figure to represent the question. Then draw a diagonal line in the square.

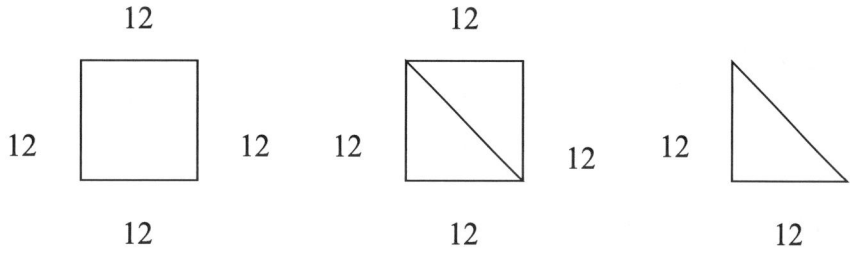

The square is to be cut down the middle diagonally, so you can automatically mark off (C) and (D) because they are equal to or larger than the total perimeter of 48". Mark off (A) because 36" is equal to three straight sides, and anytime you cut something diagonally, that side will be longer than the straight side. The answer is **(B) 41**.

EXAMPLE 2-21

A strobe light rotates on the disco ball and flashes its light on the DJ every 27 seconds. If the light maintains a constant rate of rotation, approximately how many times will the light flash the DJ every hour?

(A) 27
(B) 62
(C) 125
(D) 2343

Before working out the problem entirely, check to see if the answer can be easily derived through estimation. Mark off any answers that clearly fit outside the realm of possibilities for your estimated answer. Sometimes, only one answer will be close to the estimation.

Think this through and estimate to find a quick answer. If a light flashed every 30 seconds, then it would flash twice in a minute. That would be 120 flashes. Since the question said "approximately," you can confidently mark answer (C).

CHECK THE LAST DIGIT

EXAMPLE 2-22

Multiply these three numbers: 276, 103 and 61
  (A) 1,459,791
  (B) 1,563,987
  (C) 1,698,212
  (D) 1,734,108

Sometimes by just looking at the last digit of the answer choices, you can find the correct answer or at least eliminate a lot of wrong ones. Try this idea in Example 2-22.

Find a quick answer by looking at the last digits. When you multiply all three numbers, $[(6 \times 3 \times 1) = 18]$ the answer ends in 8, so (D) is the correct answer.

Notice that only ONE answer ends in an 8. This process also works for division.

EXAMPLE 2-23

Please find the correct answer. $\frac{64896}{208}$

(A) 311   (B) 312   (C) 313   (D) 314

In Example 2-23, look at the last digits (6, 8) to identify a quick answer. Division is the opposite of multiplication and from that you know 8 multiplied by an unknown number will end in a 6. Because $8 \times 2 = 16$, you will look for an answer choice that ends in a 2. (B) is correct. Again, notice that only ONE number ended in a 2.

THINK LOGICALLY

In a test like the *SAT*, where time is very important, being able to save a step or two is invaluable. Sometimes you can save a step by properly examining the question—thinking the opposite. See Example 2-24.

If you add 21% and 39% and multiply it by $30.00, you will get (B) $18.00—but that is not what the question is asking. It asks how much will be left over, so you have to subtract $18.00 from $30.00, which is **(A) $12.00**. For a quicker answer, THINK OPPOSITE. Naomi owes 21% and 39% for a total of 60% to her parents. This means that she will keep 40% of the money. You need to calculate 40% of $30.00, which is $12.00. It saves a step and seconds of your valuable time!

Sometimes you don't even have to work out the problem to find the correct answer. You may only need to look at the question logically. Let's try this approach with Example 2-25.

You could work this problem using an algebraic equation, but your goal is to save time by finding the fastest way. Let's use logic to answer this question. If the mixtures were even, the cost would be $5.50 a pound. Take the $3 and $8 per pound, add them together, and then calculate the average, which is $5.50. This is clearly more than $5 a pound, so the mixture is not made up of equal parts peanuts and walnuts. The given ratio is cheaper than $5.50, so there must be more peanuts than walnuts, as peanuts are the cheaper ingredient. If the new nut mix is 10 pounds and if the peanuts comprise more than half the mixture (more than 5 pounds), then the only answer larger than 5 is **(D) 6.**

> ## EXAMPLE 2-24
> Naomi has saved $30, but she owes her dad, John, 21% of this money and her mother, Lisa, another 39%. After Naomi repays everyone, how much of the $30 will she have leftover?
> (A) $12.00
> (B) $18.00
> (C) $22.00
> (D) $23.00

> ## EXAMPLE 2-25
> At the market, Savannah bought nuts for a trail mix that consisted of peanuts at $3 a pound and walnuts at $8 a pound. If the resulting mixture is now worth $5 a pound, how many pounds of the peanuts are needed to make 10 pounds of the nut mix?
>
> (A) 2.5   (B) 3   (C) 5   (D) 6

HIDDEN PATTERNS

IMPOSTER ANSWER CHOICES

Most math problems contain wrong answer choices that look similar to the correct answer. The *SAT* tries to confuse students by writing answer choices that look almost identical. It's important to be vigilant: Make sure you select the right answer choice and not an imposter!

(1) Opposites Attract:

EXAMPLE 2-26
(A) 1/3 (B) 5/7 (C) 7/5 (D) 1¼

Sometimes there will be an imposter answer that is the exact opposite of the correct one. For instance, if the correct answer is 5/7, one of the answer choices may be 7/5. See Example 2-26.

(2) Double or Nothing:

EXAMPLE 2-27
(A) 7 (B) 10 (C) 11 (D) 20

Sometimes the wrong answer choice will be double or half the correct answer choice.

FUN TIP

Another pattern involves a series of numbers in which usually the first and last number is not the answer. E.g. (1/2, 2, 8, 32) The answer is probably not 1/2 or 32.

In the Example 2-27 above, (B) and (D) are double or half of one another. If you're not careful, you could accidentally pick the wrong one.

(3) Clone Invasion:

Very often, multiple answer choices will look like the right answer. Often, the test-makers use the correct answer to come up with the wrong answer choices where the right answer probably

> **EXAMPLE 2-28**
> (A) -4/3 (B) 4/3 (C) 4/9 (D) 7/3

contains the most elements of all the other answer choices. These are clones.

Notice that in Example 2-28, 3 out of 4 are positive so eliminate (A); 3 out of 4 have four as the numerator, so you can eliminate (D); 3 out of 4 have three as a denominator, so you can eliminate (C); and B is our answer. If you weren't careful, it would be really easy to fall into The *College Board's* trap and to pick the wrong answer. Cloning happens a lot with variables.

MISSING STEPS

The *SAT* likes to propose answer choices that contain elements of the equation that are correct, but do not answer the question. Very often one of the answer choices will be the number you get after only working on one portion of the equation without finishing it. If you don't follow through all of the steps of the question, you could pick the wrong answer. Read the question carefully and always circle what the question is asking.

Some of the wrong answer patterns will be to include: an answer choice that contains the perimeter when the question is looking for area, numbers added where they should be multiplied, or the product of one or two steps when the question has three steps. Now try and work out Example 2-29.

> **EXAMPLE 2-29**
> If a = 3b and b = 2, what is the value of 2a?
> (A) 6
> (B) 8
> (C) 10
> (D) 12

When you substitute for *b*, you get: $3 \times 2 = 6$. You may be tempted to pick 6 as your final answer. However, this is missing a step. Don't forget what the question is asking! Always circle it. The value of $2a$ is 2×6, so **(D) 12** is correct.

CONFUSING ORGANIZATION

EXAMPLE 2-30

In five years, Jeremy will be twice the age that Heidi was three years ago. Heidi is twelve years old today. How old is Jeremy?

(A) 12 (B) 13 (C) 18 (D) 26

The *SAT* has questions that are written purposely to be confusing and out of order. You will have to rearrange the information to find the correct answer.

In Example 2-30, the time sequence is out of joint. First, rearrange the order to make more sense: Heidi is 12 today.

Three years ago, Heidi was half as old as Jeremy will be in five years. How old is Jeremy today?

If Heidi is 12 now, then she was 9 three years ago. Jeremy will be 18 (2 × 9) in five years. All you need to do is subtract 5 from 18 to get Jeremy's current age. Jeremy is now **(B) 13**.

OUT OF ORDER

EXAMPLE 2-31

The number of Business Majors, B, at a local liberal arts college is 30 more than twice the number of Music Majors, M. What is the best way to express this information?

(A) B = 2M x 2(30)
(B) 2B = M ÷ 30
(C) M = 30 + 2B
(D) B = 2M + 30

Here, you must take the math terms and translate them into math equations. You'll need to pull out the information, write it down and translate it correctly. You'll then be able to see how to work out the equation. [See Example 2-31]

The number of Business Majors, B, at a local liberal arts college is 30 more than twice the number of Music Majors, M.

So the answer is **(D) B = 2M + 30**.

The number of Business Majors, B, at a local liberal arts college is 30 more than twice the number of M.

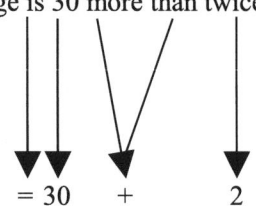

B   = 30   +   2   M

SPECIFIC RULES

GEOMETRY PROBLEMS

Generally the information needed to answer most geometry problems can be found in the question when combined with basic principles. [See Example 2-32]

EXAMPLE 2-32

In $\triangle$ XYZ, what is the value of m?

(A) 25°
(B) 35°
(C) 40°
(D) 80°

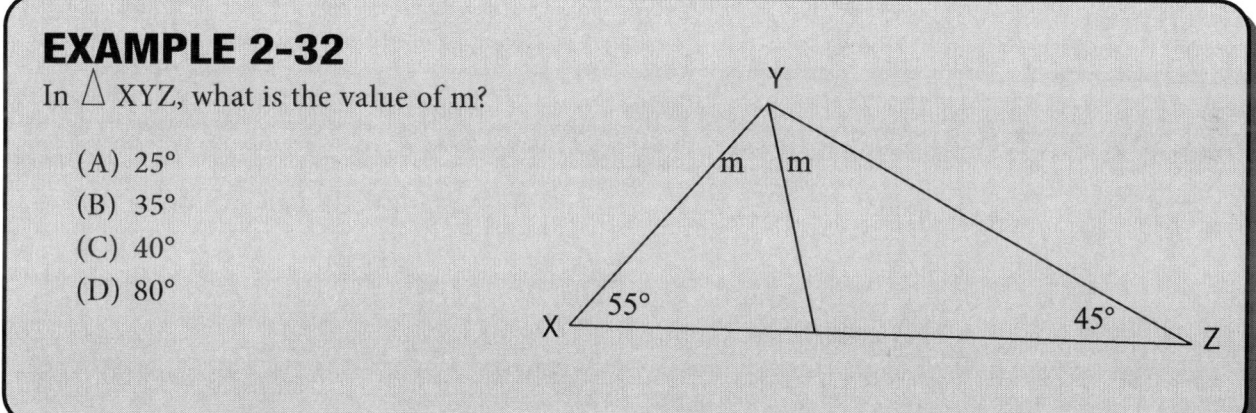

The sum of all three angles of a triangle always equals 180 degrees. When you add the two given angles (55 and 45), the result is 100. Subtract this number from 180 to get 80 degrees which would be answer (D) but be careful of the *SAT* traps and look what the question is really asking.

It is NOT asking for the measure of the third angle but what m equals. This is half, so (C) 40 is correct. Notice C and D are "double or nothing" answer choices.

Even if a problem seems to be missing certain key elements, there is always enough information to solve it with the given information. Now look at Example 2-33.

EXAMPLE 2-33
In △ ABC, x =

(A) 20°
(B) 25°
(C) 30°
(D) 60°

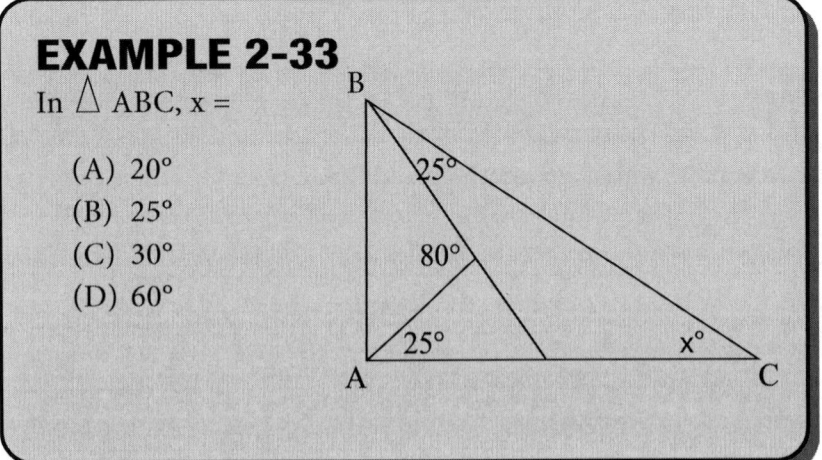

All triangles have 180°; when you know two angles, you can find the third—just add together the two given angles and subtract from 180. The left-hand triangle's given angle is 80°, so the other two will total 100 degrees. The sum of all the angles that make up A and B equal 150 degrees (100 + 25 + 25). So, if A and B equal 150, then x must equal 30 degrees, or answer (C). Notice C and D are the double or nothing pattern.

WEIRD SHAPES

FUN TIP
All Geometry formulas are found on the real test.

The *SAT* may give you an unusual geometric shape. Look closer—it is probably two regular figures that have been put together. Separate the two figures and use their respective formulas to find the answer. Don't forget about the extra line(s) that put them together—don't add the line(s) twice.

When you are required to look for a certain length or area, subtract the other lengths or areas of the figure. **The whole is equal to the sum of its parts**. Look at Example in 2-34.

EXAMPLE 2-34

The area of square WXYZ is 64, and points A, B, C and D are the centers of their own circles. What is the area of the square ABCD?

(A) 4
(B) 8
(C) 16
(D) 32

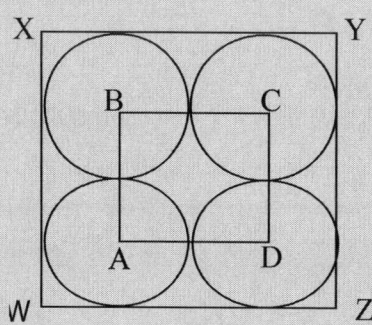

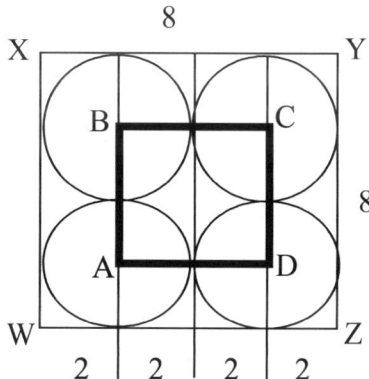

Always write in the information on the diagram.

The question is asking for the area *(l × h)* of the smaller square ABCD. Since points A, B, C and D are all center points of a circle, then the perimeter of square ABCD can be determined by adding the radii of the circles. The area of WXYZ is 64, so the length of one side equals 8. It also equals the combined diameter of two of the circles (or 4 radii), so each radius is equal to 2 (8 = 2 × 4). Draw lines to signify the measurements. One side of square ABCD is 2 radii or 4. To get the answer for the area, multiply length by height; 4 × 4, or **16, answer (C)**.

GEOMETRY FORMULAS TO REMEMBER

Lots of *SAT* geometry problems deal with the calculation of angles. You'll often find the answers with your knowledge of the properties of regular polygons like triangles, squares and quadrilaterals. There are also some very important rules about intersecting lines. Here are some fun angle and line rhymes to help you remember three important rules:

(1) Straighty equals 180

When there is a straight line, the sum of the angles equal 180. (Supplementary) X and Y are on a straight line, so their sum equals 180

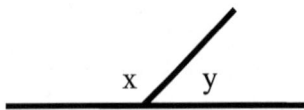

(2) Crossity equals opposity

When there are lines that cross, the opposite angles are equal to each other.

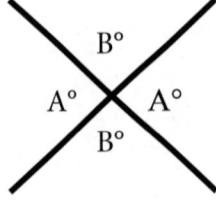

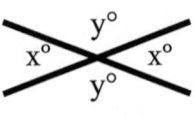

A is equal to A.
B is equal to B.

X is equal to X.
Y is equal to Y.

(3) Leany is in-betweeny

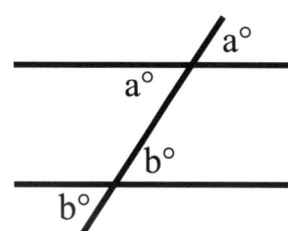 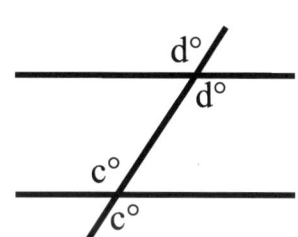

The leaning line is in-between a crossed line and a straight line.

a = b   c = d (opposites)
a = a   b = b   c = c   d = d (crossity lines)

When you put them together, you have a straighty so the leaning line is in-between the crossity line and the straighty line because both inside and outside angles are equal to each other.

b + c = 180°   a + d = 180°

In Example 2-35 since *x* is equal to its *crossity* line, it is also equal to the bottom *crossity* line. Bring the *x* down to the bottom. Now *x* and *y* are on the same straight line. *Straighty* equals 180, so *x* + *y* = 180: **answer (D).**

IMPORTANT TIP

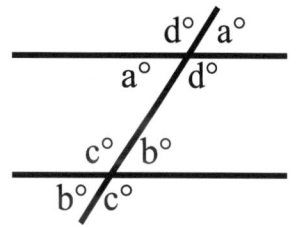

Notice how there are straighty and opposity angles.

EXAMPLE 2-35
In the figure below, RS ∥ TU, what is the value of x + y ?
(A) 45
(B) 90
(C) 120
(D) 180

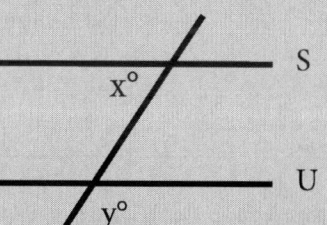

EXAMPLE 2-36

In the figure, line A is parallel to line B and both are intersected by lines P and Q. What is the measure of y?

(A) 45
(B) 60
(C) 105
(D) 150

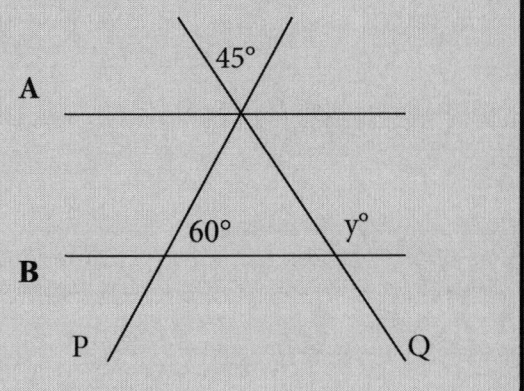

Notice in Example 2-36, line P intersects lines A and B to form one angle. Notice that line Q intersects lines B and A at another angle. Because lines A and B are parallel, these intersections give us cross lines (*crossity* equals *opposity*). Therefore, the angle opposite that of 45 degrees will also be 45 degrees. With two angles of our middle triangle (60, 45), you find the third angle. The sum of all angles equals 180 (180 – 60 – 45 = 75). Once you write the 75 degrees in the right-hand triangle, you can find y. Notice the 75-degree angle and the y lie on a straight line (*straighty* equals 180). So, subtract 75 from 180 which equals 105, or answer (C).

TRIANGLE RULES

EXAMPLE 2-37

In the triangle ABC, the length of BC is twice as much as AB. Which CANNOT be the length of AC?

(A) 8
(B) 10
(C) 12
(D) 15

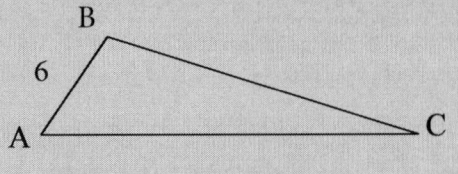

Figure Not Drawn To Scale

There is an important property of triangles you can employ here: The length of one side of a triangle can NEVER be greater or even equal to the total of the lengths of the other two sides. In Example 2-37, if side AB is 6, then BC is 12, 6 + 12 = 18. Therefore, AC is not equal to (D), as it breaks the rule, so **(D)** is correct. Also, don't be fooled by the diagram because it is NOT drawn to scale.

3–4–5 TRIANGLES

A Pythagorean Triple is a set of whole numbers derived using the Pythagorean Theorem. They are ratios of whole numbers that predictably repeat in right triangles. Look for this formula, often disguised in maths problems. Here it is hidden within the three sides of the following triangles: 3–4–5, 5–12–13, 7–24–25, 12–16–20, 9–12–15, 15–20–25. If the lengths of two sides of a right triangle are consistent with one of these ratios, the third side will fit the ratio. [See Example 2-38].

EXAMPLE 2-38

A policeman drives east on his two-wheeled vehicle 40 feet, then turns north and goes 30 feet. How many feet is he from his starting point?

(A) 25

(B) 35

(C) 50

(D) 60

Note: figure not drawn to scale

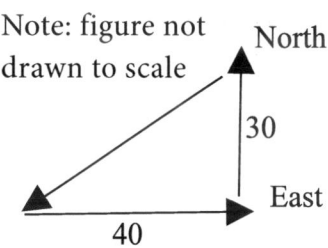

When you draw a diagram, it is easy to recognize this problem is based on the Pythagorean Theorem (a2 + b2 = c2) and the solution is represented in a 3–4–5 triangle. This question becomes easy to answer: travel from east to north is at 90 degrees, so the answer is obviously **(C) 50**.

TRIANGLES WITH CONGRUENT ANGLES

EXAMPLE 2-39

In the figure on the right, what is the perimeter of rectangle ABCD?

(A) 22
(B) 25
(C) 28
(D) 30

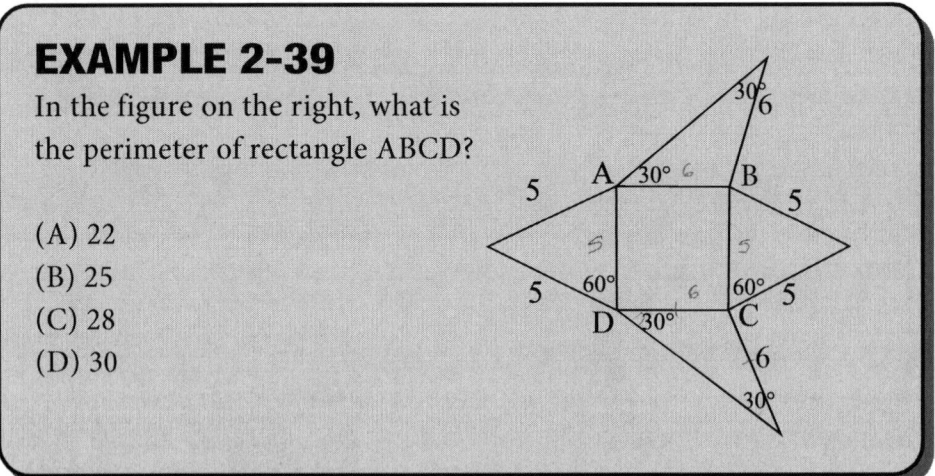

When a triangle contains two equal angles or two equal sides, it is called an isosceles triangle. If a triangle has two congruent angles, then the sides opposite the angles will also be congruent. The reverse is true: If a triangle has two congruent sides, the angles opposite the sides will also be congruent. If a triangle has two angles of 60 degrees, the third angle must also be 60 degrees, and it is an equilateral triangle. All sides and angles of an equilateral triangle are equal to one another.

In Example 2-39, use the rules of triangles with congruent angles. The triangles with the sides AD and BC are isosceles triangles because they have two equal sides. The angles opposite the congruent sides are also equal. If the opposite angle equals 60 degrees, then the two angles each equal 60 degrees, as must the third angle: Both triangles are equilateral triangles. The length of AD is 5, and the length of BC is 5. The triangles with lengths AB and DC have congruent angles, so they too are isosceles triangles and the sides opposite the congruent angles will be equal. Therefore, AB is equal to 6, and DC is equal to 6. The perimeter of the rectangle ABCD is the sum of all the sides (5 + 5 + 6 + 6). The **answer is 22 (A)**.

FUN TIP

The definition of an isosceles triangle is "a triangle with two equal sides." Therefore every equilateral triangle is also an isosceles triangle. However, NOT every isosceles triangle is an equilateral triangle.

TRIANGLES

Triangles always have 3 sides & 3 angles. The triangle's 3 angles ALWAYS add up to 180°.

In a right triangle, the Pythagorean Theorem: $a^2+b^2=c^2$ (where c stands for the hypotenuse), can be used to find the lengths of the triangle's sides.

In a right triangle, the sine of 1 acute angle ALWAYS equals the cosine of the other acute angle.

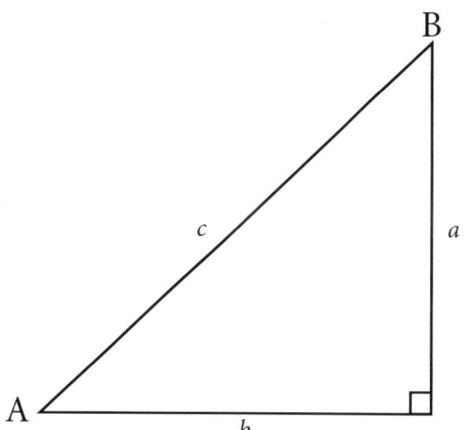

ISOSCELES TRIANGLES

Isosceles triangles have equal base angles & equal legs.

The exterior angle of a triangle equals the sum of the 2 opposite angles of the triangle $\angle E = \angle A + \angle B$

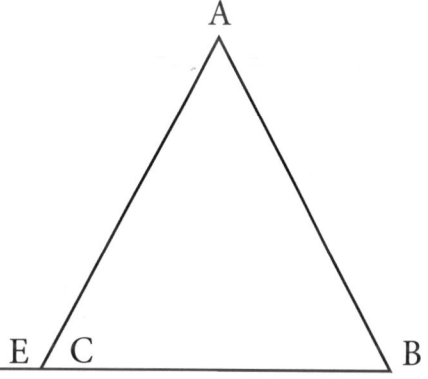

When parallel lines cut through a triangle, similar triangles are formed. This means all the corresponding angles are equal and the corresponding sides are proportional: AC:CE = BD:DF, and AC:AE = BD:BF.

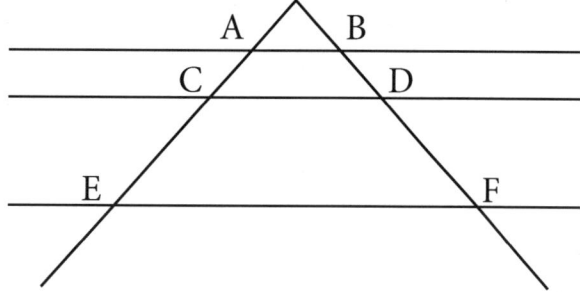

POLYGONS (3 OR MORE SIDES)

If the word 'regular' is used to describe a polygon, then all the sides of that shape are equal, and all its angles are equal.

Parallelograms (rectangle, rhombus, square):

The opposite sides are parallel and equal length. The opposite angles are equal.

Squares: all sides are equal; all angles are 90°.

To find the angles in a polygon: From a single vertex, draw lines to each of the non-adjacent vertices. This should form adjacent triangles. Every triangle has 180°. Count the number of triangles & multiply by 180°.

SQUARES

All sides are equal; all angles are 90˚.

To find the degrees in a polygon: From 1 vertex, draw lines to each of the non-adjacent vertices. This should form adjacent triangles. Every triangle has 180˚. Count the number of triangles & multiply by 180˚.

To find the area of a polygon: From the center point, draw lines to each vertex. Divide 360 by the number of triangles to get the measurement of the triangle's top angle. Take one of the resulting triangles and bisect it. Take that half triangle (which is now a right triangle) and find its area. Double that then multiply it by the number of triangles.

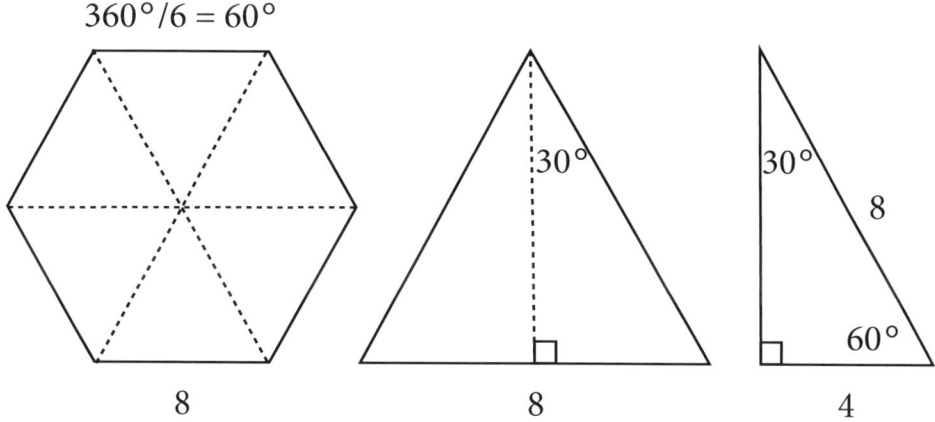

Area of right triangle = 1/2(4)(4 √ 3) = 8 √ 3
Area of equilateral triangle = 2(8 √ 3) = 16 √ 3
Area of polygon = 6(16 √ 3)=96 √ 3

XY-PLANE RULES

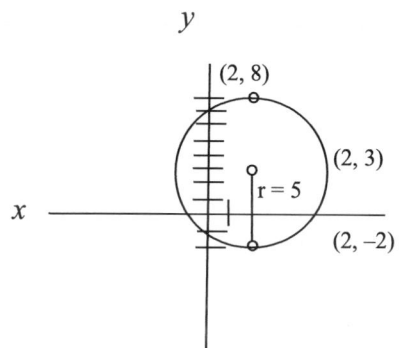

It's very important to be familiar with problems that require you to plot out questions on an *xy*-plane. "X" represents the horizontal line, and "Y" represents the vertical line. Always plot coordinates in order (x,y); x first along the horizontal, then y, on the vertical. Although not required in this problem, to find the slope of a line on a plane, find the rise (y) divided by the run (x)—the distance of y divided by the distance of x. In most cases it is a good idea to draw a diagram to help you solve problems like these. [See Example 2-40].

When you draw a circle to solve this problem the center is at (2, 3) and the endpoint is at (2, –2) and the radius is 5. You may be tempted to select the answer

EXAMPLE 2-40

In the xy-plane, the center of a circle has the coordinates (2, 3). If one endpoint of a diameter of the circle is (2, –2), what are the coordinates of the other endpoint of this diameter?

   (A) (3, 2)
   (B) (–2, 8)
   (C) (2, 5)
   (D) (2, 8)

choice (2, 5) because it includes the radius length. However, you need to chart out five spaces vertically from the center point (2, 3) by adding 5 to the *y* coordinate. Therefore, the correct point is **E, (2, 8)**.

Sometimes, simple logic can help you find the correct answer to an *xy*-plane problem. Try Example 2-41.

y = 4x - 8
y = 0
0 = 4x -8
8 = 4x
2 = x

EXAMPLE 2-41

In the xy-plane, the line with equation y = 4x – 8 crosses the x-axis at the point with coordinates (a, b). What is the value of a?

   (A) –8
   (B) –2
   (C) 0
   (D) 2

When a slope reaches the *x*-axis, the value of *y* is zero. In the equation above, only when *x* equals 2 will *y* equal zero. Since *a* equals the value of *x* in the coordinates, *a* equals 2. The correct answer is **(D) 2**.

As you move the x left or right, the y moves up or down. The slope is determined by the x moving right on the graph.

A positive slope is plotted when y moves up as x moves right, and down as x moves to the left. A negative slope is when y moves down as x moves right and up as x moves to the left.

CIRCLES

Here are several statements that will help you answer problems involving circles.

Every point on a circle is equidistant from the center point.

Every circle has 360° or 2π radians. A semicircle or half circle is 180° or π radians. The degrees in an arc are 360°.

The diameter (d) is a line from one side of the circle to the other that passes through the center point.

> **IMPORTANT TIP**
>
> The formula for the center-radius of the circle equation is:
>
> $(x - h)^2 + (y - k)^2 = r^2$, with the center being at the point (h, k) and the radius being "r".

The radius (r) is a line from the center of the circle to any point on the circle.

It is half of the diameter's length.

The distance around a circle is called the circumference: $C = 2\pi r$ or $d\pi$.

A central angle is an angle with the center point as its vertex. Its measurement is ALWAYS equal to the measurement of the arc it intersects.

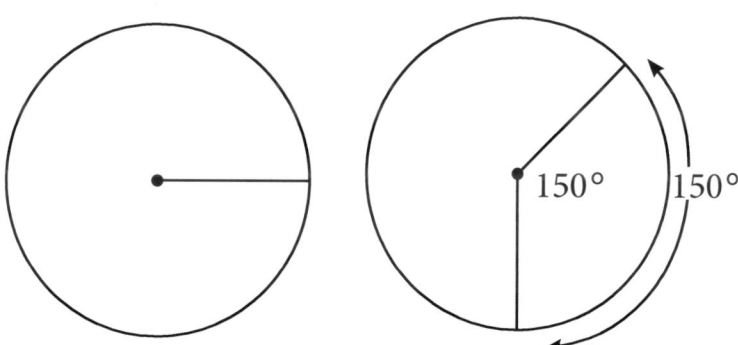

A tangent is an outside line that touches the circle at only one point. The tangent will ALWAYS form a right angle with the radius. If there are 2 tangent lines, each drawn from one point on each side of a circle, the tangents and radii form a quadrilateral which will ALWAYS form 2 congruent triangles when a line is drawn from the point to the circle's center.

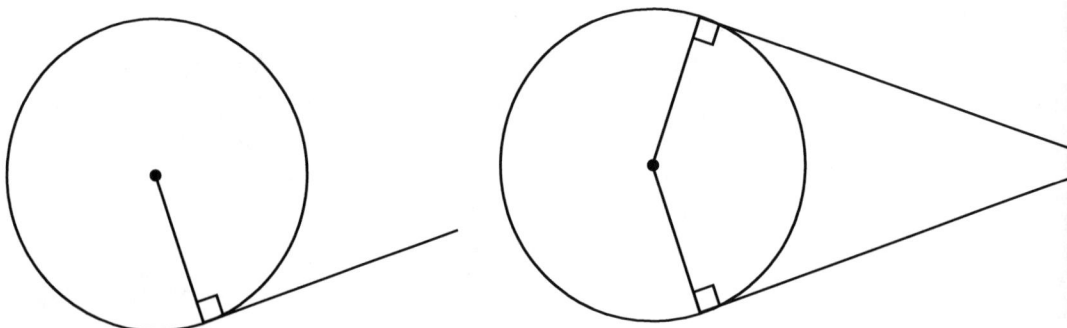

If there is a circle with an ordered pair on the curve, use that ordered pair to label the legs of a right triangle.

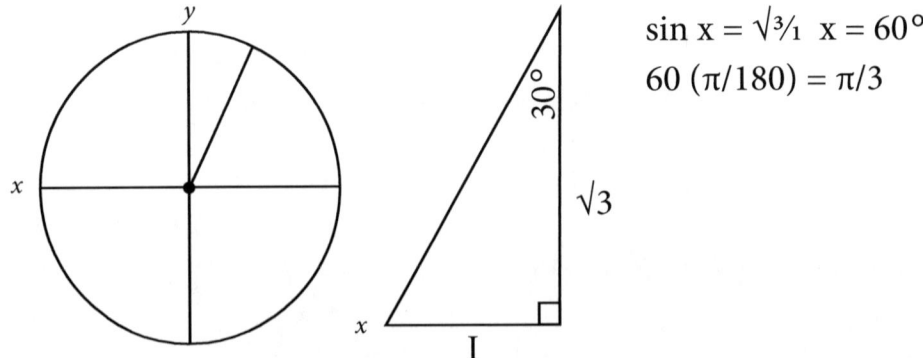

$\sin x = \sqrt{3}/_1 \ \ x = 60°$

$60 \ (\pi/180) = \pi/3$

SLIPPERY SLOPES

To find out if a line is a positive slope or a negative slope: start at the left side of the line and trace it to its right side. If the line goes up, it is positive or increasing. If it goes down, it's negative or decreasing.

A) Vertical Spaces   B) Horizontal Spaces   C) Slope = 2/5

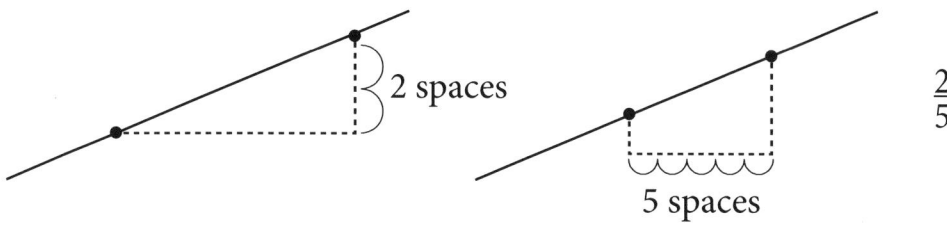

To find the slope of a line from a picture: first pick 2 points on the line. Count how many vertical spaces there are from the 1st point to the 2nd. Then count how many horizontal spaces there are from the 1st point to the 2nd. Lastly, divide the number of the vertical spaces by the number of the horizontal spaces.

$$(-6,1) \text{ and } (4,5) \qquad m = \frac{y_2 - y_1}{x_2 - x_1} \qquad \frac{5-1}{1-(-6)} = \frac{4}{7}$$
$$x, y, \qquad x_2\, y_2$$

To find the slope if there are just 2 points from a line: subtract the 1st y-value from the 2nd y-value; then subtract the 1st x-value from the 2nd x-value. Finally, divide the y-answer by the x-answer. That will be the slope of the line.

Parallel lines ALWAYS have the SAME slopes. Perpendicular lines have slopes that are negative reciprocals of each other.

If there are parallel lines cut by a transversal, all the big angles are equal amounts, and all the small angles are equal amounts.

In a linear equation that is solved for y: y= -5x +2.

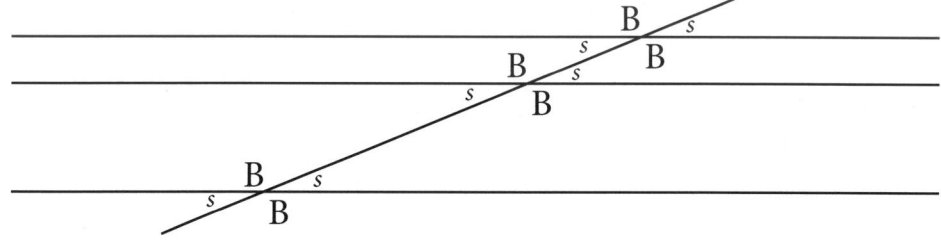

The coefficient of the x is the slope: -5.

STORY PROBLEMS

Story question-types are generally based on a fictitious life scenario or some theoretical / abstract concept. You need to find and extract the hidden math from the story and then set the problem up correctly. Here are the steps to solving this type of equation:

1. Circle all the key elements in the story and write them down next to the story.
2. Transform any math terms into correct math symbols and create an equation that illustrates the problem. (Knowing math terminology is a MUST.)
3. Now solve it like a normal math equation.

Here is a story problem that exemplifies a fictitious life scenario in Example 2-42:

EXAMPLE 2-42

The new hybrid car holds 30 gallons of gas. To fill the car when it is empty, the gas pump delivers g gallons every s seconds. In terms of g and s, how many seconds will it take the pump to fill up the tank?

(A) $\frac{30s}{g}$ (B) $\frac{30g}{s}$ (C) $30gs$ (D) $\frac{g}{30s}$

To solve this problem, start by circling the key elements and writing them down (30, s, g).

In this example 30 (full tank) = g/s (or gallons per second) which can be expressed as 30 = g/s. Multiply that out and you get 30s/g. Equally you can say: the gas tank capacity divided by the pump rate is 30/ (g/s) = 30s/g. The **answer is (A)**.

This is merely a *Rate multiplied by Time equals Distance* problem.

FUN TIP

Did you notice that (A) and (D) were "Opposites" so the answer was probably one of them. Also, the answer could not have 30 next to a "g" since they both represent gallons. This eliminated (B) and (C).

Here is a story problem that exemplifies an abstract concept:

In Example 2-43 to solve this problem: circle key elements (mean, nine, different, consecutive, median) and create a diagram (1, 2, 3, 4, 5, 6, 7, 8, 9). Transform math terms (mean = average, median = middle) and add them to the diagram. Here are two methods. You could work the problem by adding up all the numbers (45) and to get the mean and divide it by 9—the answer is 5, which is also the median (C). However, this question is designed to mislead you. In this instance, to add the 9 numbers just takes longer and is a waste of precious time. Knowing the mean of any set of 9 consecutive numbers is unnecessary. You can guess the average of an odd number of consecutive numbers will give you a mean of the middle number. But to find the answer here, you only need to know that the median is the middle number. If you know what median is, and you know there are 9 numbers and the middle number is n, then you don't even have to do any calculations.

> ## EXAMPLE 2-43
> If n is the mean of nine different consecutive numbers, what will be the median of those same nine numbers?
> (A) One number higher than the mean
> (B) One number lower than the mean
> (C) The same number
> (D) The mode of the numbers

> ## EXAMPLE 2-44
> Mike's unicycle wheel has a radius of 2 feet. How far has he traveled on a straight path if that wheel has made 6 complete turns?
> (A) 4π
> (B) 12π
> (C) 18π
> (D) 24π

Sometimes story problems require you to draw a diagram or picture in order to accurately see how to answer it. Example 2-44 can easily be solved with the equations to find circumference. **C=πd where d=2r.** If you cannot see the easy way then make a diagram to help things along.

When a question asks about tires, wheels or doughnuts—these are round, so you'll obviously think about circles. Draw a picture to help you out. Since the circumference formula is 2€r, then 2€(2) or 4€.

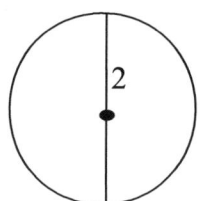

To answer the question, multiply 6 × 4€, so **(D) 24π** is correct.

REPEATING PATTERNS

EXAMPLE 2-45

Josie put one candy cane in a series of eight Christmas stockings. The first piece went into stocking one, the second into stocking two and so on. She does this pattern until 93 candy canes have been dispensed. In which stocking will the 93rd candy cane be placed?
- (A) Stocking number three
- (B) Stocking number five
- (C) Stocking number six
- (D) Stocking number seven

EXAMPLE 2-46

Cari's watch runs 5 minutes fast every hour. If her watch is reset at 8 am, what will be the real time when her watch chimes 1 pm on the same day?
- (A) 11:00
- (B) 11:10
- (C) 12:35
- (D) 1:05

Sometimes a hypothetical scenario will include a repeating pattern of numbers. This can be really simple as long as you look at the question logically. Look at Example 2-45.

Think critically to find the repeating pattern and answer this question quickly. Since there are eight stockings, you can write out a figure like (1, 2, 3, 4, 5, 6, 7, 8). If you divide 93 by 8 you will get 11 5/8. This means that after 11 rotations of filling stockings, stocking number 5 is the last one to receive a candy cane. So, the correct answer is **(B)**.

This hypothetical scenario in Example 2-26 exemplifies a repeating pattern. The best way to solve this problem is by creating a chart to illustrate the scenario. Keep in mind that when a timepiece "runs fast," it is ahead of time; if it "runs slow," it is behind time. Don't just look at the question or try and work it in your head—start writing down information. In this case, record the correct time (minus 5 minutes) from the watch that is fast.

Right Time	Cari's Watch
8:00	8:00
8:55	9:00
9:50	10:00
10:45	11:00
11:40	12:00
12:35	1:00

(C)12:35 is the correct answer.

ELIMINATE DON'T SEPARATE RULE

Example 2-47 follows the Eliminate, Don't Separate Rule. This math principle can be summed up in two steps: (1) Eliminate any answers that don't contain ALL the key elements. (2) Don't separate the action/function needed.

To solve this: circle the key elements in the story problem (x, y, 3). Now you will eliminate the answer choices that do not contain ALL three of these. Mark off (A) and (B). Now you need an answer that doesn't separate the action needed to work out the problem.

> ## EXAMPLE 2-47
> This Saturday, The Birthday Boom Company has x children divided among y parties. The company wants to purchase T-shirts for each child and have 3 back-up shirts for each party. How many T-shirts will The Birthday Boom Company buy?
>
> **(A)** $x + 3$ **(B)** $y + 9x$ **(C)** $(x \cdot y) + 3$
> **(D)** $x + 3y$

Party = y, and they need 3 extra T-shirts for each party. So, you will need $3 \times y$ or $3y$ in the answer. Any answer that separates the two elements can be marked off. Mark off (C). The **correct answer is (D)**. Notice how you don't need to solve for how many children are in each party, just how many T-shirts are needed.

MEAN, MODE AND MEDIAN

Terms like mean, mode and median can be very confusing. It is essential for students to learn and understand the definition of these items. They occur frequently on story problems and can be useful to know in your everyday life as well. Here are some *CPG Acronyms* to help you remember what they mean.

> ## EXAMPLE 2-48
> What is the mean of the following five numbers: 10, 14, 22, 30, & 49?
> To find the mean, we simply add all the numbers together and divide by the total amount of numbers.
> $$10 + 14 + 22 + 30 + 49 = 125$$
> $$125/5 = 25 \quad \text{The mean is 25.}$$

M ath
E quation's
A verage
N umber

EXAMPLE 2-49

What is the mode of the following set of numbers? {2, 7, 9, 2, 4, 1, 2, 8, 2, 6, 2, 7}

Mode is simply the number that shows up most often. In the case of this problem, that number is 2.

M ost
O often
D igit
E xposed

EXAMPLE 2-50

The median is a number that lies exactly in the middle of a set of numbers. When a set has an odd amount of numbers, simply choose the number in the middle.

Set A {980, 1023, 1112, 1476, 1599, 1643, 1755}

For Set A, the median is 1476 because it's in the exact middle by value. Even if the order of numbers were switched around, 1476 would still be the median.

If a set of numbers has an even amount of number, you must average the two numbers in the middle.

Set B {10, 14, 16, 20}

To find the median for Set B, we must take the two middle numbers and divide them by two.

(14 +16)/2 = 15   The median for Set B is 15.

M iddle
E xact
D igit
I n-between
A ll
N umbers

Never again forget the meaning of Mean, Mode and Median! These terms are so important to distinguish from one another. Make learning these a priority.

ROMAN NUMERAL PROBLEMS

Although the Roman numeral question is usually found in the *Math* section, occasionally it shows up in the *Reading* section also. Look at the math problem in Example 2-51.

This type of question has two parts: Segment 1 is on top and there are three Roman numeral numbers; Segment 2 on bottom is set apart by four answer choices, which contain one or more combinations of Roman numerals.

To solve this problem, start by ignoring Segment 2. Then work on the

> ### EXAMPLE 2-51
> If A is an integer greater than 1 and if $B = A - \frac{1}{A}$, which of the following must be true?
>
> **Segment 1: Set apart with Roman numerals** $\left\{\begin{array}{l} \text{I. } A > B \\ \text{II. B is a whole number} \\ \text{III. } AB \neq B^2 \end{array}\right.$
>
> **Segment 2: Answer choices** $\left\{\begin{array}{l} \text{(A) I only} \\ \text{(B) I and II only} \\ \text{(C) III only} \\ \text{(D) I and III only} \end{array}\right.$

problem as usual. When you find the right answer, put a check next to the corresponding number on Segment 1. Then match up Segment 1 (the top) with Segment 2 (the bottom), to determine the correct answer.

More than one answer from Segment 1 can be correct. Look to see if the question gives exact or vague details. If vague, work on the question from every possible angle.

To answer the above question, let's plug in a number for A (3 will work). So, B = 3 – 1/3 = 2 2/3 ,and B is 2 2/3.

A is more than B, so mark a check by Roman numeral I in Segment 1.
B is a fraction so put an "X" by Roman numeral II in Segment 1.
AB = 3/1 × 8/3 = 24/3 or 8
B^2 = 8/3 × 8/3 = 64/9 or 7 1/7
AB ≠ B^2 is true, so mark a check on Roman numeral III in Segment 1.

Now match up the top with the bottom—Roman numerals I and III is answer **(D)**. Option (C) could have been eliminated knowing Roman I is true; and (B) could be eliminated when Roman II was found to be untrue.

In the problem, notice the term "Must be true." It is very important to isolate the terms used in the problems and solve accordingly. [See Example 2-52]

EXAMPLE 2-52

At Fossil Lake High School's five-year reunion, students discovered that 16 couples that were high school sweethearts got married in the same year. In this group of 16 couples, which of the following statements must be true?

I. At least two of the sweetheart couples had a wedding in the same month.

II. At least two of the sweethearts married on the same day of the week.

III. At least two of the couples had a Friday wedding.

(A) I only   (B) III only   (C) II and III only
(D) I and II only

"Must be true" is a clue for you to eliminate wrong answers. Since there is no way to determine what day they married by this information, you can eliminate Roman numeral III. Consequently, any answer that contains Roman numeral III can be immediately marked off (B and C). Work this from every possible angle and check out each Roman numeral.

Since there are 12 months in a year and 16 couples, there are obviously duplicates, so put a check by Roman numeral I. Since there are 7 days a week and 16 couples, again, there must be duplicates, so put a check by Roman numeral II. Now, match up the top segment with the bottom segment. The correct answer, I and II, is answer **(D)**.

R emember to IGNORE Segment 2
O perate the question from every possible angle
M ark ALL correct answers on Segment 1
A nalyze answers marked
N ow match Segment 1 answers with Segment 2

STRANGE PROBLEMS

The *SAT* likes to add strange-looking problems to throw you off the track. These are not equations that the teacher taught in your Algebra class the day you were sick—instead, they are simply made up by the *SAT* test writers. They can be figured out through simple logic. By substituting the given numbers into the strange formula, you can find the right answer. Try Example 2-53.

Draw an arrow from each number to the appropriate letter in the problem to help you substitute accurately. To work the above problem, substitute the 3 for the S and the 4 for the T. $3 \times 4 + 4 = \mathbf{16}$.

EXAMPLE 2-53

Let $S \triangle T = ST + T$ What is the value of $3 \triangle 4$?

These types of problems can come in all sorts of shapes and sizes. The *College Board* is not limited to a certain type of strange problem. Nonetheless, every one of them can be solved through substitution and simple critical thinking. Try Example 2-54.

Substitute each symbol for numbers. When a number is odd (7), use $n + 5$ or $7 + 5 = 12$. When a number is even (4), use $n - 2$ or $4 - 2 = 2$. Therefore, $12 + 2 = \mathbf{14}$ **(D)**.

EXAMPLE 2-54

For all integers n, let $\boxed{n} = n + 5$ when n is odd, and $\boxed{n} = n - 2$ when n is even. What is the value of $\boxed{7} + \boxed{4}$?

   (A) 4
   (B) 6
   (C) 11
   (D) 14

Sometimes these questions don't even give you a formula to work. You will have to use your reasoning skills to come up with the correct answer.

EXAMPLE 2-55

In the following addition problem, the digit C could be equal to which of the following?

$$
\begin{array}{r}
2A6 \\
B5 \\
\underline{C4} \\
435
\end{array}
$$

I.   3
II.   6
III.   8

(A) II only
(B) III only
(C) I and III only
(D) II and III only

Example 2-55 is a strange problem with no straightforward equation to figure it out. A, B and C are mysterious letters, but they represent whole numbers between 0 and 9. The far-right column (6, 5, 4) add up to 15. This means you would carry the one to the middle column. This means that A + B + C + 1 will end in a 3.

A 2 has been carried over in the last column because 2 + 2 = 4. Now in the middle column, if you used 9 + 9 (the most they could be) for A and B, then there would need at least the number 4 to make 23. You can rule out I. Since this is a Roman numeral type question, once Roman numeral I is marked off, you can mark off all answers that contain I—which is (C). You know it can't be the number 3, because at least a 4 is needed to make 23. It doesn't matter what the number is—it could be 4, 5, 6, 7, 8 or 9. The question said "could" but not "must." There is no need to go on, because the correct answer is **(D)**.

NUMBER LINE PROBLEMS

A Number Line has infinite length with the center of 0 and can contain positive and negative numbers. The numbers are separated by evenly spaced tick marks.

The distance between two numbers is the same as the length of the same two numbers, and the distance can be found by subtracting the number on the left from

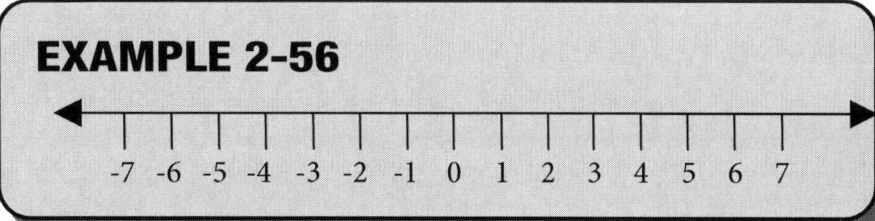

EXAMPLE 2-56

the one to its right. Example: 2 – 1 = 1. But it is NOT the same distance between two numbers when asked about the number of "positions" between the two numbers. The difference between 2 and 1 is 1, but in this case, count the tick marks, and the positions between will always be ONE less—so, there are 0 number of positions between 2 and 1. [See Example 2-56]

Sometimes number lines can be found in story problems. In this case, the fictitious scenario is about building a fence. When dealing with questions that mention "fence posts," remember there are two ends that need to be counted. [See Example 2-57]. This is why you would draw a diagram.

Be careful that you don't fall for the wrong answer. Most students would divide 60 by 6 and come up with the answer (D), 10. This is incorrect. Mark out the posts with a drawing.

EXAMPLE 2-57

Jack and Jared replaced their wooden fence posts by spacing them 6 feet apart. How many posts do they need to build a fence 60 feet long?
(A) 7
(B) 8
(C) 10
(D) 11

1	2	3	4	5	6	7	8	9	10	11

As you can see, there are two ends that must be counted, so the correct answer is **(D) 11**. *When dealing with number line problems, always draw a diagram to help you find the correct answer.*

GRAPHS

Number of Movies Rented in a Month by Seniors at Magnus University

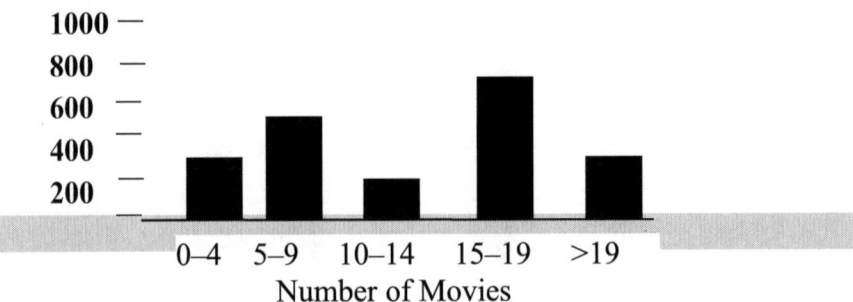

EXAMPLE 2-58

In the graph above, what percentage of seniors at Magnus University rent at least 15 movies a month?

  (A) 50%
  (B) 40%
  (C) 30%
  (D) 15%

The question in Example 2-58 wants to know the percentage of seniors who rented "at least" 15 movies. (This means you count 15 and every number above it.) The last two bars fall into that category.

Draw a line with your pencil to the left from the top of each column to see what number they each represent. Write the appropriate number above each column. (i.e. 300, 500, 200, 700, 300). Add the last two columns: 700 + 300 = 1000. Since there are a total of 2000 seniors (found by adding all the bars together), then 1000 would be 50%. So, **(A)** is correct.

Quick Reminder:

NEVER work problems in your head. By using your pencil to work it out, you minimize mistakes and clear up your thoughts for the next question.

AVERAGES AND RATIOS

There is a very simple formula for finding the average of a number. It's called the TAN formula; the total of all the numbers divided by the amount of numbers equals the average.

$$\frac{\mathbf{T}otal}{\mathbf{N}umbers} = \mathbf{A}verage$$

Use the TAN formula: $\frac{\mathbf{T}}{\mathbf{N}} = \frac{a + b + c}{3} =$ **A**verage or $\frac{39 + b + c}{3} = 42$

> ### EXAMPLE 2-59
> The average of three numbers is 42. If one of the numbers is 39, what is the sum of the other two numbers?
> (A) 3
> (B) 87
> (C) 129
> (D) 168

In Example 2-59, first, multiply each side by 3. Now you need the sum of b + c, so subtract 39 from both sides: 39 + b + c = 126. If 39 is subtracted from both sides, you get the sum of the other two numbers: Answer (**B**). As usual, wrong answer choices are there to throw you off. (A) is reached by subtracting 39 from 42; (C) is the wrong one if you didn't finish all the steps; (D) is a wrong choice if you multiplied 4 × 42.

Ratios are solved in a similar manner. A ratio is a share or portion of the total. A ratio of 4:3 means that one part has four shares for every three shares of the other part. See Example 2-60.

A quadrilateral is a four-sided polygon with four angles which always add up to 360. A line drawn from one angle to the angle opposite confirms this fact, as it will create two triangles (180 × 2).

> ### EXAMPLE 2-60
> A quadrilateral has four angles that are measured in the ratio 4:3:3:2. What is the measurement of the largest angle?
> (A) 45
> (B) 60
> (C) 100
> (D) 120

Add up all the shares (4 + 3 + 3 + 2) = 12. Take the whole (360) and divide by 12 to determine that every share is 30 degrees. The smallest angle has 2 shares (2 × 30), the two middle angles have 3 shares (3 × 30), and the largest angle has 4 shares (4 × 30). Multiply the largest angle: 4 × 30, to get **120 (D)**.

EXPONENTS AND SQUARE ROOTS

EXAMPLE 2-61

Which of the following is equivalent to $4^3 \times 4^2$?
(A) 4^5 (B) 4^6 (C) 8^5 (D) 16^6

When multiplying two exponents with the same base, keep the base the same and ADD the exponents. [See Example 2-61].

The correct answer is **(A)** 4^5 (3 + 2 = 5). Remember, if the bases are NOT the same, then you figure out each number individually and then multiply.

For example, $3^2 \times 4^3$ (3 × 3 = 9) and (4 × 4 × 4 = 64), so 9 × 64 = 576.

EXAMPLE 2-62

If x = 36, then $x^2 - \sqrt{x}$
(A) 72 (B) 212 (C) 806 (D) 1290

Here's a fun tip that can save you time when it comes to raising five or six to any power. No matter what power you raise a six to, the answer will ALWAYS end in six (and the same for five). [See Example 2-62].

When you square 36, the result is 1296. The question asks you to subtract 6, so the answer will end in a zero. Notice there is only one answer that ends in zero; **(D)**, 1290.

EXAMPLE 2-63

If $a^2 = 81$ and $b^2 = 36$, then what is the difference between the greatest possible value of (a − b) and the least possible value of (a + b)?
(A) 0 (B) 6 (C) 9 (D) 30

Don't forget that square roots can be either positive or negative, and you must assume all possibilities unless the question states otherwise.

In Example 2-63 this question is really asking how far apart is it if you to take the largest value of (a − b) and the least value of (a + b). In terms of square roots, *a* can equal 9 or −9, and *b* can equal 6 or −6. The largest possible value of (a − b), is 9 − (−6) which is 15. To get the smallest possible value, (a + b) then (−9) + (−6) is −15. Subtract these two values, 15 − (−15), to get answer **(D)**, 30.

New Concept Revealed

$i = \sqrt{-1}$

This means that the square of i is equal to -1.

I.e. $i^2 = \sqrt{-1}$

"i" is not a "real" number.

TOP HEAVY vs. BOTTOM HEAVY RULE

If a fraction has a numerator (top) larger than the denominator (bottom), the fraction will be larger than one. When fractions are bigger at the denominator (bottom), the fraction will be smaller than one. By recognizing this pattern, you can answer a question faster than using your calculator. [See Example 2-64]

EXAMPLE 2-64

What is approximately the answer for the following equation?

$$\frac{5^2}{4^2} + \frac{5^2}{4^2}$$

(A) –5/4   (B) $\frac{4^3}{5^3}$ (C) 16/25   (D) 3.125

Since the fractions are top heavy, the combined sum will be bigger than one. Only one answer is bigger than one. **(D)** is the correct answer. No calculator needed!

MUST RULE

It's very important to isolate the word "MUST" in *SAT* problems. In "MUST" equations, students need to find the only scenario that works the same every time. Try Example 2-65.

This question is about numbers but expressed in letters, and it's a bit confusing. Students could start plugging in numbers, however this can be a time waster. The answers (A) through (D) COULD be true because x "could" be positive or negative, but that is not what the question is

EXAMPLE 2-65

If x and y are integers and $x \neq 0$ and $-x = y$, then which of the following statements MUST be true?

(A) $x > y$

(B) $y > x$

(C) $xy < 0$

(D) $x - y = 0$

asking. If x and y have opposite signs, then a negative integer times a positive integer is negative—so, only **(C)** is absolutely true.

Example (2-65) illustrates this idea. Questions that involve the word MUST should be operated from every angle. Once a student finds an example that contradicts the MUST statement, that answer choice is wrong. Mark it off. This question allows for x to be either positive or negative, so students should try both. Plug in a number into the equation (-x = y or in other words y = -x) and see the results. For example if a student were to work out answer (A), it would look something like this:

(A) x = 6, y = -6, then 6>-6 which is a true statement. However if x = -6 and y = 6 then -6>6 is not true. A is wrong.

The "ALLSOME NONE" Rule/ ALL—SOME—NONE

When facing story problems that contain the words All, Some and None, it's important to know this rule: *ALL has SOME; SOME doesn't have ALL; and ALL and SOME don't have NONE.*

EXAMPLE 2-66

Some numbers in set A are odd.
If the above expression is true, which of the following is true?
  (A) If a number is odd, it is in set A.
  (B) If a number is even, it is in set A.
  (C) All numbers in set A are odd.
  (D) Not all numbers in set A are even.

By knowing the above definitions, you can answer Example 2-66 logically.

(A) This refers to "ALL" odd numbers. (Some doesn't have ALL.) — INCORRECT

(B) This refers to "ALL" even numbers. (Some doesn't have ALL.) — INCORRECT

(C) *The first word, "ALL" gives it away.* (Some doesn't have ALL) — INCORRECT

(D) Not ALL also means "SOME"— this is CORRECT.

THE ROAD LESS TRAVELED RULE (TRLTR)

There are always multiple problems on the *SAT* that deal with rate and distance. [See Example 2-67]

This is a problem of Rate times Time equals Distance (R × T = D). Manipulate the formula and then plug in the figures as the last step. If R x T = D, then T = D/R. T = 600/y which is answer D. Notice C and D are opposites.

There is a quick shortcut for story problems dealing with rate and distance. Every one of these questions can be answered easily with The Road Less Traveled Rule.

When questions ask about traveling, there is a long way and a short way to answer them.

EXAMPLE 2-67

John drove his new SUV to the border at a constant speed of y miles per hour. How many hours did it take him to travel 600 miles?

(A) 600 – y (B) 600y (C) $\frac{y}{600}$ (D) $\frac{600}{y}$

EXAMPLE 2-68

The Stevens family traveled 300 miles from home to the beach at 50 miles per hour. They came back home at 60 miles per hour. What was the average speed for their roundtrip to the beach?

(A) 54   (B) 54.5   (C) 55   (D) 55.5

THE LONG WAY:

In Example 2-68, you could make a tally chart and add in all the information: Rate, Time and Distance. Then divide the distance (300 miles) by each rate (50 mph and 60 mph), and you will get the time (6 hours there and 5 hours back). Next, divide the total distance (600 miles) by the total time (11 hours), and you will get the answer **(B) 54.5**.

Many students fall for answer (C) because they only average the speeds the Stevens family went, and not the amount of time they spent at the certain speeds of the trip.

THE SHORT WAY:

The Right answer is always a **L**ittle less **T**han the **R**ate's total average: **TRLTR.**

All you had to do is add the rates (50 + 60 = 110), divide in half to get the average (55) and the answer is a little less than 55. The answer is **(B) 54.5.** Since this is the multiple-choice section of the test, you don't have to work out the whole problem, just select the right answer. This rule will help you save time and always get it correct.

FUN TIP

The answer will never be the average since you have to factor in time.

 # STUDENT RESPONSE

THESE TYPES OF MATH problems do not have any answer choices. You are required to come up with the correct answers yourself and mark them using a grid-in box. There are no points counted against the overall score for wrong answers.

PICTURE OF ANSWER GRID

There are several rules for properly filling in the grid-in answer sheet. Pay attention to these tips. If you have the correct answer but bubble the answer sheet incorrectly, it will be counted wrong.

> **FUN TIP**
>
> Transfer each grid-in answer one at a time to minimize mistakes.

1. Start by writing the correct answer at the top of the box. This will help make sure you grid the numbers in the right spaces.
2. You can start on the left or right side. As long as the number is correct, it doesn't matter where it appears on the grid. However, if a zero is the first number, it has to go in the second box.
3. Mixed numbers (3½) will be read as 31/2 and will be wrong. Convert mixed numbers to improper fractions before gridding in (so, 3½ turns into 7/2).
4. Repeating decimals should fill up all the spaces (.555555 … MUST be bubbled in as .555 and **not** .55).

5. Long decimals should fill the entire grid as well. A number like .719857 should be bubbled in as .719 and **not** .71 Do not round the last number. Round up only if it is a repeating decimal: as in .666 to .67

6. Variables will not be counted as correct.

7. There is no need to reduce fractions if they fit in the four spaces. This saves time!

8. There are no negative answers!

9. There may be more than one answer, so just pick one of them.

10. The grid does not include the dollar sign ($) or percent symbol (%). Convert 100% into 1, 50% into 1/2 or .5, and omit the dollar sign.

11. The answer cannot have a square root or pi symbol, so if your final answer includes either of these, it is wrong. Please convert these equations to decimals.

If your answer is negative, a variable or longer than 4 spaces and cannot be reduced (except decimals), your answer is wrong. Go back and work on the problem again. Make sure you bubble-in the answers darkly and neatly. The machine only grades the bubbled-in answer. Even if you write the correct answer at the top of the grid, if you do not bubble it in, it will be counted as wrong.

EXAMPLE 2-69

A baby's toy block is marked only with an A and a B on two adjacent sides like the above picture. If the baby throws the block on the floor and it lands with one letter on top, what is the probability that the bottom side does not have a letter on it?

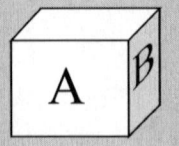

The student response section of the *SAT* can be intimating to some students. Unlike the multiple-choice section, there are no clues or hints to the answers. However, all the questions are made with the same patterns and you can reason them logically. Even though some of the questions may seem big and scary, keep in mind all the questions are designed to be figured out easily. Try Example 2-69.

The letters are side-by-side and NOT opposite of each other. There will never be a letter on top and on bottom. The answer is 100% or $\frac{100}{100}$

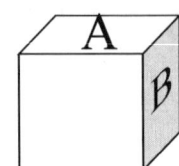

Since there is not a percentage mark on the grid-in box, and there are only four spaces, the answer MUST be written in as 1 or 1/1 or 6/6.

THINK SMALL LOGIC

Some questions try to trick you into writing out hundreds of numbers to solve them. Every question on the *SAT* is designed to be answered in less than a minute, so you automatically know that there is a faster way to answer it. Use logic and save time. Try Example 2-70.

Chart three spaces like this: 5 3 _ (5 in the hundreds place, 3 in the tens place and a blank for units). The *College Board* wants to know how many outcomes can be made using this scenario. There are only 10 digits (0–9) and each could be used, so the answer is **10**.

EXAMPLE 2-70
How many three-digit numbers have the hundreds digit equal 5 and the tens digit equal 3?

SCARY SCENARIO

The *SAT* likes to frighten you and will take a simple problem and make it seem scary. Read it carefully. Circle what the question is really asking. It's probably easier than you first thought. At first read, you could think you'll have to write out a long equation but that's unlikely.

Look at Example 2-71. The question is ONLY asking for the possible value of *t*. It is not asking for *r* or *s* so mark out these terms. You know that *t* is greater than 0, and you know that 1 squared equals 1. All you have to do is plug in a number greater than 1, and it will be correct. You can bubble in any number greater than one that will fit in the four spaces. So 2, or any number above 2 since there is more than one possible answer. Note the answer could not have been a fraction less than one, since a fraction less than one, multiplied by itself gets smaller.

EXAMPLE 2-71
If $t^3 > t^2$ and $t^2 > r^3$ and $r^2 < s$ and $t > 0$, what is one possible value for t?

SIMPLIFY AND TRY

Sometimes when you approach a complicated problem, the easiest thing to do is simplify the equation and test different numbers. A scary-looking problem can turn out to be quite simple. [See Example 2-72]

EXAMPLE 2-72

Each letter represents a digit that is less than or equal to 3. What three-digit number does ABC represent?

$$(A \times 4^3) + (B \times 4^2) + (C \times 4) = 108$$

Start simplifying the equation and work on the multiplication: $64A + 16B + 4C = 108$. Next, try out different numbers (less than 3, according to the question). Substitute 1 first: $64(1) + 16(1) + 4(1) = 84$ (this is 24 short of the desired answer, 108). A cannot be any larger than one, otherwise the grand total will be larger than 108, so you've found your first number. Now change the second and third number to 2: $64(1) + 16(2) + 4(2) = 104$. The answer is still 4 short. Change the last number to 3, to get the correct answer: $64(1) + 16(2) + 4(3) = 108$ (CORRECT).

You would bubble-in **123** as your answer.

THE PARC RULE

Pay Attention — Read Carefully

EXAMPLE 2-73

If the mean of three <u>different</u> positive numbers is 90, what is the greatest possible value for one of the numbers?

Don't be thrown off your game. Read the question carefully and circle all the key words.

Look at Example 2-73. The average of 3 numbers is 90, therefore the total of the three must be 270. You could start with three figures such as 89, 90, and 91, but 91 is NOT the greatest possible value. To have a "greatest possible value," the other two numbers must be the two smallest values: 1 and 2. Subtract 1 and 2 from 270 to arrive at **267**, the answer choice you would bubble-in.

When you circle the key words, *different* and *positive*, you know the answer cannot be 269 (two smallest numbers 0 and 1) or 268 (two smallest numbers 1 and 1). Keep your wits about you and read the details of every question.

FUN TIP

Notice the word "different" was underlined. This can cause you to miss the word "positive" (Zero is not positive).

TABLE TALK

The *College Board* likes to employ tables within questions. Always fill in all important information from the question and redraw the diagram if it's confusing. In Example 2-74, the big hint is that the cost of gasoline was the same each day. There is usually no need to fill in every box—just enough to find the answer.

The total expenses for Sunday if your target. Add the total food costs to give you 108: (35 + 41 + 32).

EXAMPLE 2-74

The partial table below is John's weekend spending spree for his trip to the city. If his gasoline expenses were the same each day, what were his total expenses for Sunday?

	Food	Gas	
Fri	35		
Sat	41		
Sun	32		
Total			162

The answer will be total food (108) + 3 × gas = 162

$$108 + 3g = 162$$
$$\underline{-108 \qquad -108}$$
$$3g = 54$$

Three days of gas cost $54. 54 divided by 3 = 18 (gasoline each day). You're being asked for Sunday's expenditure. So, to complete Sunday's column: 18 + 32 = **50**. Bubble-in 50 in the grid-in answer sheet. Remember, there are no dollar signs on the grid, so don't worry about notating the currency.

WORK BACKWARDS

EXAMPLE 2-75

On Sunday, Katie had a certain amount of money she had saved to spend on her vacation. On each subsequent morning, she had 1/2 the amount of the previous morning. On Friday, five days later, she had $1 left. How much savings money did she begin with?

When your efforts to work on a question head-on appear fruitless, sometimes tackling a problem backward will help you find the correct answer.

In Example 2-75 you are told Katie started with x money on Sunday, and on Friday she had $1. Each day she had half as much as the day before. Here's how to work this problem backward:

Make a simple tally chart with the given information.

Sun	Mon	Tues	Wed	Thur	Fri
					1

Fill a '1' in the last box to represent $1. You know from the information to double each amount. Fill in Thurs with a 2, Wed 4, Tues 8, Mon 16, and Sun 32. The correct answer is **32**. Bubble-in this number into your grid sheet. Do not bubble in-a $ sign.

Try Example 2-76. This question is perfect for the "think backwards" approach. Write down the information and subtract from the charge by working backwards. Stephanie paid a total of $21.00.

> Subtract $3.00 (first ½ mile)
> Subtract $6.00 (4 miles times $1.50)
> That leaves $12.00

Since each additional/partial mile is $1.00, then the taxi must have driven another 12 miles. But that is not the answer. You are asked for total mileage, so, add up all the miles. (1/2 + 4 + 12) = 16½, or answer (**D**).

EXAMPLE 2-76

The Red Robin Taxi Company charged Stephanie $3 for the first half-mile, $1.50 for each of the next 4 miles, and $1.00 for each partial or full mile after that. If the total charge for her trip was $21.00, which of the following could have been the total of the mileage that the taxi drove?

(A) 10   (B) 12   (C) 14¾   (D) 16½

THE P.A.W. LAW

Parts multiplied by the **A**verage equals the **W**hole. Conversely, the whole divided by its parts equals the average. Question types that contain parts and wholes can be figures out by using this P.A.W. law.

Try Example 2-77. First, circle and add all the **P**arts together: 8 + 10 + 6 = 24. Take the **W**hole (72) and divide it by the **P**arts (24) to get the **A**verage. The **A**verage = 3 ounces for each part.

EXAMPLE 2-77

The 72 oz. wedding punch was blended to put in a fountain. To fill the punch bowl, the caterers added 8 parts strawberry sherbet, 10 parts carbonated water and 6 parts sugar syrup. How many ounces of carbonated water are in the punch?

All that's left is to calculate the ounces of the carbonated water. Multiply the **Parts** (10) by the **A**verage (3) = **W**hole (30). The correct answer is **30**. Put this number in your bubble grid.

C. C. C.'s PIZZA RULE

Imagine questions involve probability, counting and placement in a pizza company. If you were to order a pizza, there would be three specialty problems available any way you slice it. The key to answering these correctly is the ability to differentiate the types of problems and knowing which formulas to use on each different problem.

There are three main course problems on our menu: *Chance, Counting* and *Combo*. To figure out which type of problem you are dealing with, you have to ask *IPM* questions. You start by circling the key elements of the formula. Then you connect the *IPM* question to the type of problem you're dealing with. To solve the question, chart out the correct spaces according to the formula.

Main Course (Three types)   IPM (Question to ask yourself)

Chance . . . . Is Probability Mentioned ?
Counting . . . . Important Positions Matter ?
Combo . . . . Irrelevant Placement of Members ?

Side Dish

Circle Key Elements 1st
Connect the Right IPM Question 2nd
Chart Spaces with Correct Formula 3rd

Here's the breakdown of each type of question, the correct formulas and some examples.

Chance Pizza

IPM: Is Probability Mentioned (in the question)?

Probability is always a fraction between 0 and 1.

FORMULA: The probability of an event will be:

$$\frac{\text{Number of desired outcomes (DO)}}{\text{Total number of ALL possible outcomes (TOP)}}$$

For Example 2-78

$$\frac{\text{Desired Outcome}}{\substack{\text{Total Outcomes} \\ \text{Possible}}} = \frac{\text{DO}}{\text{TOP}} = \frac{2}{8} = \frac{1}{4}$$

> ## EXAMPLE 2-78
> If a medium 8-slice pizza has only 2 slices with pepperoni on it, what is the probability that someone will pick a pepperoni piece at random?

1. Circle Key Elements: 8, 2
2. Connect Right IPM Question (Is Probability Mentioned?) YES
3. Chart Spaces with Right Formula

MORE CHANCE EXAMPLES:

1. If you toss a penny, what's the probability it will be a head?
    A penny has one head and one tail. The probability is 1/2.

2. What's the probability of rolling a 6 on a die?
    There are six numbers on a die, and only one is a 6. The probability is 1/6.

3. What's the probability of rolling an even number?
    There are six numbers on a die, and three of those (2, 4, 6) are even. The probability is 3/6 = 1/2.

Independent Probability vs. Dependent Probability

EXAMPLE 2-79

What's the probability of rolling a 3 on a die and getting tails from your tossed penny?

When doing chance problems, it's important to note the difference between independent and dependent probability. Independent probability deals with combining events that have no effect on each other. [See Example 2-79]

FUN TIP

On a probability question, the word "and" means to multiply and the word "or" means addition.

In this example, the number you roll on the die will have no effect on the outcome of the coin toss. They are independent of one another. Rolling it 3 times will not make it any more or less likely to flip the penny to tails. In fact, coin tosses are independent of one another. To solve it, multiply both probabilities together.

$$1/6 \times 1/2 = 1/12$$

EXAMPLE 2-80

What's the probability of tossing a dime three times and having it turn up heads each time?

In Example 2-80, each coin toss is still independent of one another, and the probability remains ½. In this case you have to multiply all the independent coin tosses together in order to find the probability of flipping the coin heads three times in a row.

$$1/2 \times 1/2 \times 1/2 = 1/8$$

EXAMPLE 2-81

The last three times the dime was tossed, it turned up heads. Assuming it is a fair coin, what's the probability that it will turn up heads on this toss?

The result of heads or tails from previous rounds of a coin toss has no relevance to the likelihood of a heads or tails outcome on subsequent tosses. Every coin toss is independent and has a probability of ½. If however, you're trying to find the likelihood of flipping a coin a certain way, you must multiply the independent variables.

In Example 2-81 this toss is INDEPENDENT of the other tosses, so it is 1/2.

For dependent probability, the number of outcomes is affected by previous actions. Try Example 2-82

EXAMPLE 2-82
There are 9 black, 12 purple and 8 orange marbles in a bag. If you draw out an orange marble and don't put it back, what's the probability of drawing out a black marble on your second draw?

There is a total of 30 marbles and 8 of those are orange: 8/30 = 4/15. Once you take a marble out, only 29 marbles remain. The number of outcomes is affected by a previous part of the problem (hence, this is a dependent probability question). Out of 29 total marbles, 10 of those are black. The probability is 9/29.

COUNTING PIZZA

IPM: Important Positions Matter?

In this type of question, order matters.

EXAMPLE 2-83
The Triple C Pizza Parlor Menu has 4 soups, 15 pizzas and 5 desserts. How many different meals can be made?

FORMULA: If a choice can be made in A ways, and after that, if a second choice can be made in B ways, the number of total possibilities is A × B.

For Example 2-83
(1) Circle Key Elements: 4, 15, 5

(2) Connect Right IPM Question: Important Positions Matter? YES! Soup cannot be substituted for pizza or dessert or vice-versa, so order DOES matter!

(3) Chart Spaces with Right Formula

__ × __ × __ =

4 × 15 × 5 = **300**

COUNTING PIZZA EXAMPLES

EXAMPLE 2-84

How many 3-letter "combinations" can be made from the letters in the word ANCHOVY if no repetition is permitted? If repetition is permitted?

For Example 2-84. Important Positions Matter! Chart your spaces: __ __ __ there are 7 letter choices, so in the first space put a 7__ __. You are not permitted to repeat a letter which leaves 6 choices for the second space, and 5 choices for the last one (7 6 5). Multiply them: 7 × 6 × 5 = 210. If repetition is allowed, then there are 7 choices for the first space, and 7 choices for both the second and third spaces: 7 × 7 × 7 = 343. *(There will never be a question on the test that asks for more than one answer.)*

EXAMPLE 2-85

There are 5 cards, each a different color. How many different ways can they be placed in a row if red can't be on the end?

For Example 2-85. Important Positions Matter! Because there are restrictions, you need to deal with them first. There are five different color cards and five spaces. There are two ends and neither end can hold a red card. Place your numbers thus: 4 _ _ _ 3. You've used 2 cards, which leaves you with 3 card choices for the second space (4 3 _ _ 3); you have 2 cards for the third space (4 3 2 _ 3); and lastly, 1 card for the fourth space: 4 × 3 × 2 × 1 × 3 = 72.

EXAMPLE 2-86

How many three-digit passwords can you make using the numbers 0 to 9 without using repetitions? Allowing repetitions?

For Example 2-86. Important Positions Matter! You need three digits. 0 to 9 equals 10 different digits, so you'll have 10 choices for the first space, 9 for the second space and 8 for the third space: 10 × 9 × 8 = 720. If numbers can be repeated, you'll have 10 choices for each of the three spaces—10 for the first, second and third spaces: 10 × 10 × 10 = 1000.

For Example 2-87. Important Positions Matter! The road trip will use 4 roads: one road from Grapevine to Somerville; one road from Somerville to Beach Cove; one road from Beach Cove back through Somerville; and lastly, one road from Somerville back to Grapevine. Don has the choice of 3 roads to go to Somerville, and 4 roads to go to Beach Cove (3 4 _ _). On the way back to Somerville, he cannot use the same road, so 3 choices (from 4) remain (3 4 3 _), and on the way back to Grapevine, 2 unused roads (from 3) can be chosen (3 4 3 2). So, $3 \times 4 \times 3 \times 2 = 72$.

EXAMPLE 2-87

There are 3 roads from Grapevine to Somerville, and 4 roads from Somerville to Beach Cove. If Don rides his motorcycle from Grapevine to Beach Cove and back, and passes through Somerville both times and does not go on any road twice, how many different routes for his journey are possible?

FUN TIP

If the question said that the roads could be repeated, then chart out the spaces with 3 4 4 3 because Don has the same amount of roads both ways.

COMBO PIZZA

IPM: Irrelevant Placement of Members?

In this question type, order DOES NOT matter.

FORMULA: Since order doesn't matter, you will eliminate the number of possibilities where order does matter. Use the counting method to find the total number of possible arrangements and then divide that by the factorial of the number you are looking for. **A factorial is the product of all integers up to and including a given integer.**

FACTORIAL EXAMPLE:
$5! = 5 \times 4 \times 3 \times 2 \times 1 = 120$.

EXAMPLE 2-88

In how many ways can 4 pizza delivery drivers be chosen from a group of 8 employees?

For Example 2-88

(1) Circle the Key Elements: 4, 8
(2) Connect Right IPM Question: Irrelevant Placement of Members? The order in which employees are picked does NOT matter. They are in the same group regardless of what order they are chosen in.
(3) Chart Spaces with the Right Formula

<u>8 7 6 5</u>   Counting formula
4 3 2 1   divided by the factorial (4!)

$(8 \times 7 \times 6 \times 5) / (4 \times 3 \times 2 \times 1) = \mathbf{70}$

COMBO PIZZA EXAMPLES

EXAMPLE 2-89

In a deck of 52 cards, how many different 4-card hands can a dealer make?

For Example 2-89 irrelevant Placement of Members! The order in which the cards are dealt does not matter. You have the same cards, no matter what order you receive them in.

<u>52 51 50 49</u>   Counting formula
 4 3 2 1   divided by the factorial (4!)

$52 \times 51 \times 50 \times 49 / 4 \times 3 \times 2 \times 1 = \mathbf{270{,}725}$

EXAMPLE 2-90

For a taste test at the mall, 4 people will be chosen at random from a group of 10 people. How many ways can this be done?

For Example 2-90 irrelevant Placement of Members! It doesn't matter if a person is chosen first or last—either way, they're still in the group—so, order needs to be eliminated. Four people will be chosen (__ __ __ __) from the group of 10. There will be 10 choices for the first person, 9 for the second, 8 for the third, and 7 for the fourth ($10 \times 9 \times 8 \times 7 = 5040$). Since it is a Combo problem, and order doesn't matter, eliminate the 5040 (Counting) by dividing by the factorial of the number of people that are being picked (4!). Or, $4 \times 3 \times 2 \times 1 = 24$.

10 9 8 7 Counting formula
 4 3 2 1   divided by the factorial (4!)

$10 \times 9 \times 8 \times 7 = 5040 / 4 \times 3 \times 2 \times 1 = 24$
$5040 / 24 = \mathbf{210}$

PULL THE MATH OUT

Often, you can simply pull the math out of the equation by finding the key elements and converting them into math terms found in the answer choices. Always consider the question and answers as one entity first, as often the answer is evident.

In example 2-91, circle "length" and put an l to denote length, above it.

EXAMPLE 2-91

In meters, the length of a box is 3 meters less than twice its width. Which of the following gives the length of the box in meters, in terms of the width of the box in meters?

(A) I = 1/2w + 3
(B) I = w - 3
(C) I = 2w + 3
(D) I = 2w – 3

Circle "is" and put an = above it.
Circle "3" and put a 3 above it.
Circle "less" and put a minus sign above it.
Circle "twice its width" and put a "2w" above it.
Find the Correct answer that contains all the key elements: **D** is correct.
No calculations! See the math; don't do the math.

FUNCTION JUNCTIONS

There are usually several function questions on the test. There are three parts to the function question: input, relationship and output. Think substitution when working out the problem.

EXAMPLE 2-92

Let the function f be defined by $f(x) = 3x2 + 2x + 1$

What is the value of $f(3)$?

In example 2-92, there are two values: x and f(x).

Note: x is what goes in; f (x) is what comes out.

FUN TIP

The functions are even if they have an even exponents:

$$f(x) = f(-x)$$

This is not applicable for odd exponents.

Everywhere there is an x you are going to replace it with a 3:

$f(3) = 3 (3)2 + 2(3) + 1$

Simplify and solve the equation:

$f(3) = 27 + 6 + 1$

$f(3) = 34$

"CHIEF" SOHCAHTOA

FUN TIP

There are only 2-3 trig. questions so if you skipped/missed them, you can still get an amazing score.

There are elements of trigonometry on the redesigned *SAT* so students need to learn the *CPG Acronym*, SOHCATOA. It stands for:

Sine = Opposite / Hypotenuse

Cosine = Adjacent / Hypotenuse

Tangent = Opposite / Adjacent

SOHCATOA a:

$\sin a = O/H = X/Z$

$\cos a = A/H = Y/Z$

$\tan a = O/A = X/Y$

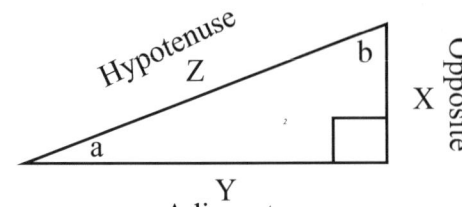

SOHCATOA b:

$\sin b = A/H = Y/Z$

$\cos b = O/H = X/Z$

$\tan b = O/H = Y/X$

SOHCATOA =

$\sin a = X/Z = \cos b$

$\cos a = Y/Z = \sin b$

$\tan a = X/Y = 1/\tan Y$

SOHCAHTOA 90: $a = 90 - b$

$b = 90 - a$

Trigonometry values use percentages.
1. Adjacent means "next to."
2. Opposite-opposite to.
3. Hypotenuse means "long side."

The calculation is simply one side of a right-angled triangle divided by another side. "SOHCAHTOA" helps you know which sides to compute.

Sine and cosine are complementary angles. Given cos π/7, sine of the complementary angle will be the same value.

$\pi/2 - \pi/7 = 7\pi/14 - 2\pi/14 = 5\pi/14$. Therefore $\sin 5\pi/14 = \cos \pi/7$

EXAMPLE 2-93
Which of the following is equal to cos (π/7) ?
A. $-\sin(\pi/7)$ B. $-\cos(\pi/7)$
C. $\sin(5\pi/14)$ D. $\cos(5\pi/14)$

FUN TIP

Pi' is a measure of radians. If you are going to calculate this using a calculator, you MUST change your calculator from 'degrees' to 'radians'. "pi" and degrees will give WRONG answers. Using radians on the calculator, cos(pi/7) and sin(5pi/14) each equal 0.9009688

Here are the justifications for the answer (C).

A.) The opposite cosine cannot be negative.
B.) The negative of a number can't equal that number (unless the number is zero).
C.) **CORRECT.**
D.) You cannot multiply top by 2 and bottom by 2 to get this answer.

THE SCATTER PLOT THICKENS

On a scatter plot question, the diagonal line that goes through the points is called the "line of best fit."

A line of best fit depicts the estimated location through the 'middle' of the points and in the same overall direction as the points. The line may or may not pass through any points. It shows the relationship between the 2 sets of data more clearly than the points by themselves. Its slope is the estimated slope for the scatter plot.

There will be 4 types of questions on a scatter plot diagram.

1. Interpretation of the correlation of data

    a. strong positive (from left to right, the scatter plot is a fat line that slopes up)
    b. strong negative (from left to right, the scatter plot is a fat line that slopes down)
    c. weak positive (from left to right, the scatter plot is in an ovoid shape that slopes up)
    d. weak negative (from left to right, the scatter plot is in an ovoid shape that slopes down)
    e. little or no correlation (the data is in a circle-like shape or square of points with no discernible up or down direction)

2. Use of a horizontal value and the line of best fit to predict a vertical value.

3. Identification of data that greatly varies from the line of best fit.

4. The ratio of increase or decrease between the horizontal data and the vertical data (or the slope of the best fit line).

First, decipher one point on the scatter plot: carefully examine the horizontal and vertical information where the point intersects.

Next, circle key information in the question and on the graph.

Then, circle key information in answer choices and eliminate ones that don't match up. Finally, match up the exact cross-reference from the graph and the correct answer.

In example, 2-94, locate the axis of time (the horizontal axis). Go straight up from the 5 until you reach the line of best fit (the diagonal line). Next, go straight left until you reach the horizontal number: **95** is correct.

EXAMPLE 2-94

Based on the line of best fit, predict the test score for someone who studied 5 hours.

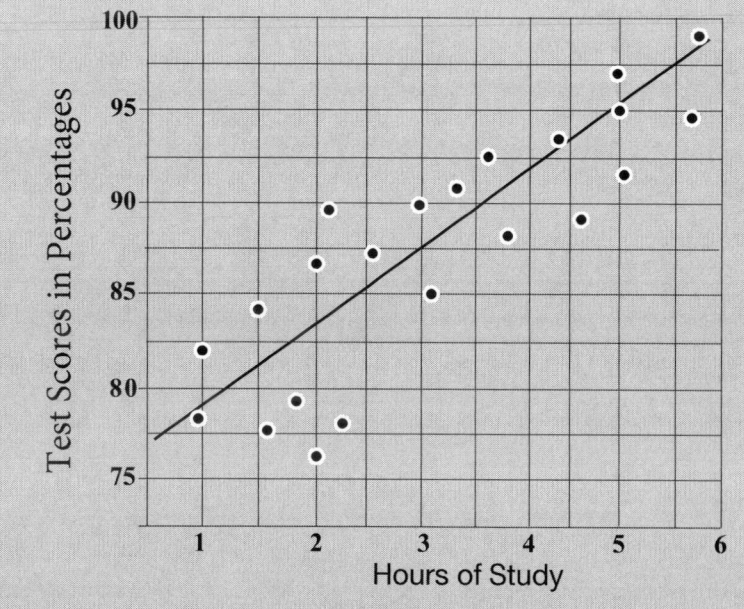

Use this picture with examples 2-94 and 2-95.

In example 2-95, the points from left to right go up (positive), the points are close to the "line of best fit" and exhibit a (strong) correlation. Answer **(A)** is correct.

EXAMPLE 2-95

What is the best interpretation of the correlation of this data?

(A) Strong positive
(B) Strong negative
(C) Weak positive
(D) Weak negative

$100 DOLLAR STORE

EXAMPLE 2-96

The price of a car was increased last week by 10 percent, but during a blowout sale next weekend, this price will be decreased by 25 percent. The price of the car at the blowout sale will be what percent of the original price?

(A) 78%
(B) 75%
(C) 80%
(D) 82.5%

When a question asks you for a percentage, always work from a base value where the item in question is 100 regardless of the other numerical information; i.e., here you will make the initial value of the item $100.

Thus, in example 2-96, the initial cost of the car is $100. The price increases by 10 percent so you multiply 100 x 110% (or 1.1) = $110. For the blowout sale, you deduct 25 percent from $110. You now multiply $110 by 75% or .75 to arrive at $82.5. You can instantly see the relative value lies at 82.5% of the original price! The answer is (D).

Math Completion Process

1. **Easy** is the math. The questions you'll be asked are mostly about logic. Read all questions very carefully and use logic to solve them.

2. **Asking** what? Circle all the key elements and determine what the question is asking of you.

3. **Set** up the math problem with the elements you circled.

4. **You** should write the rule (if there is one) next to the question.

5. **Make** a new diagram.
   Draw it correctly or you could get the wrong answer.

6. **Add** in ALL the information to the diagram.
   The *SAT* test often leaves out information on the given diagram. Assume it is incomplete and retrieve the missing information from the question.

7. **Test** the answers from answer (C).
   Start at (C); then you'll know whether to go higher or lower since the answers are presented in order.

8. **Hidden** Patterns now exposed (Clone answers, Double or nothing, Opposites)

   E asy math, logical answer
   A lways circle what question is asking
   S et up the math problem
   Y ou write the rule

   M ake new diagrams
   A dd in given information
   T est answer from answer (C)
   H idden patterns exposed

Learn the acronym back to front and then write **EASY MATH** at the top of your test page for the strategies to trigger you to work effectively.

FUN TIP

The test is not testing how smart you are in math, but rather your critical thinking skills on a math problem. Learn to SEE the math and not do the math!

IMPORTANT TIP

EASY MATH steps are not always in this order and all steps may not apply to all questions. E.g. You may not have to set the question up or a Clone Invasion pattern may be noticed right away.

PART IV:
WRITING AND LANGUAGE

WRITING AND LANGUAGE

Know and understand the basics of grammar to do well in this section.

THE *WRITING AND LANGUAGE* section contains four passages, forty-four questions, and thirty-five minutes to complete it. The questions will correspond to underline portions of the passage. The Writing section is separate on the test, but the score is combined with the *Reading* section.

Since the score is integrated with *Reading*, it is equally as important to do well in this section for the total possible score of 800. It is worth noting the *Writing* section is now deemed to be of greater importance by colleges.

This chapter will lay out many strategies to conquering this part of the test. To allow you to confidently approach it, you'll need to:

1. Learn the strategy ACRONYMS.
2. Know the fundamental grammar rules.
3. Read and understand the rules for this section before taking the real test.
4. Practice taking the *Writing and Language* section in actual *College Board* tests.

Let's get started.

UNDERLINED PASSAGES

This section contains passages with questions that correlate to an underlined portion of the text. Read it first. If there is an error, you will need to correct it from one of the answer choices.

If there is no error, then pick answer *A - NO CHANGE* **when offered.** *There is no set number of answers that will be without an error.*

If there is an error, you will be looking for an answer that generally <u>revises or restates</u> the <u>underlined section</u>. Since the underlined portions are now in a passage, it is **not necessary** to read the entire text. Although sometimes you will need to read the sentences immediately <u>before or after</u>, especially when asked to revise information.

Noteworthy points:

- Even if you believe there is a better way to write the sentence, don't dwell on it. Your job is to see if there is an error in the underlined portion.
- Your goal is to find any error in the underlined portion and the correct answer that correlates with that question number.
- By simply understanding some <u>basic grammar rules</u> and <u>identifying common patterns</u>, you can do very well in the *Writing* section.
- Remember the subject is **NEVER** found in the prepositional phrase so draw a line through it to find the subject and verb.
- There is no room to improve a sentence by changing it to an active voice.
- Your *only* objective is to <u>find the error</u> if there is one. Otherwise mark answer <u>A – NO CHANGE</u>.
- Occasionally you will need to read the <u>first and last lines of the paragraphs</u> just as in the *Reading* section, in order to grasp the context. The <u>title</u> is often a clue to answers.
- The **C.O.A.T**. acronym (later in this chapter) can still apply to make sure answers are **justified** by the passage.

STRATEGY 1

When you recognize and learn the recurring patterns, you can find the correct answer in the shortest amount of time. Be aware that the test-makers often add stuff to the correct sentence to **create problems with structure or wording**, so pay attention to concise answers to verbose ones.

Look for answers that contain the 3 <u>Shorts</u> of being right:

A.) **Shortest Answer in Length** Very often the correct answer is simply the <u>shortest</u> answer in linear length. This pattern is very common and may occur up to 75% of the time!

B.) **Shortest Number of Suffixes** Look for answers with the **shortest** number of words with suffixes such as *-ed, -est, and -ing*. Be leery of answers with "having" and "being" as these words often create a problem within the sentence.

C.) **Shortest Number of Succinct Words** To be concise, the correct answer usually has the **shortest** number of small concise words such as: *he, she, it, as, but, and…*

STRATEGY 2

The *Reverse Clone Invasion* pattern often occurs in this section as in *Math* where you find answers by looking for similarities in the answer choices.

For example:

Joseph left the party and then he went to his house.

A.) NO CHANGE
B.) And Joseph left the party and went to his **house.**
C.) **Joseph** left his house and went to the party.
D.) **Joseph** left the party and went to his **house. Correct**

Three answers start with the subject, "Joseph" and three answers end with the noun "house". This is a clue that the correct answer is *probably* a clone and starts with "Joseph" and ends with "house".

STRATEGY 3

Always eliminate the wrong answers first. Then insert the remaining answer choices into the sentence to find the correct answer. Read it back. The right answer will be **concise, grammatically correct** and **make the most sense.**

STRATEGY 4

If there is a chart or graph…just as in the *Reading* section, simply find the answer that has the correct information found on the diagram and that will be the correct answer.

Read the title, description and the horizontal information. Decipher data on one entire row, bar, column or slice to understand the diagram.

Beware of extra info. Always read all information around the chart or graph, including the title, italicized parts, chart description and subtitles. Circle key points in the question, in the answers and match them up on the chart.

STRATEGY 5

Always whisper to yourself (loud enough for just you—and nobody else—to hear) the complete sentence to yourself. This is an easy way to hear something that sounds weird or off or wording that contains poor grammar. Your ears can often pick up an error even when your eyes can't see it. This is because grammar is processed in the left inferior frontal gyrus (IFG) in the cerebrum of the brain which is strongly connected to our hearing.

STRATEGY 6

If the problem does not have a prompt-question, and the answers are very similar, then it generally tests grammar. *Grammar is the set of rules on how a sentence is constructed.*

E.g.   A.) NO CHANGE
         B.) spends
         C.) spending
         D.) has spent

Or

A.) NO CHANGE

B.) running, near the river,

C.) running near the river,

D.) running near the river

Your goal would be to find the answer that best restates the underlined portion.

In the second example, instead of reading the answers in a linear fashion, read them up and down or vertically. Notice the main differences are grammatical. There is a comma in B after "running" but not one in C and D. There is a comma after "river" in B and C but not after D. Knowing test-makers like to use clones a lot, the answer that has the most elements of the others is usually correct. Answer (C) has the most in common and it is correct.

STRATEGY 7

If the problem does not have a prompt-question and the answers are more <u>varied</u>, then it generally tests style. ***(Style is pertaining to a sentence sounding clear and effective. Read and listen carefully to how the sentence sounds and what may seem awkward.)***

E.g.   A.) NO CHANGE

B.) First and foremost, I didn't hesitate.

C.) It makes sense, that, I absolutely would not hesitate.

D.) I did not hesitate, as repercussions thereof.

Answer B sounds the best and is correct.

Or

A.) NO CHANGE

B.) money-smart

C.) being good with money

D.) economical

Answer D is the best sounding answer and is correct.

Your goal is to find the answer that best <u>restates</u> the underlined portion. These are style questions.

STRATEGY 8

If the problem has a prompt-question and the answers are more varied, then it generally tests reading analysis. ***Read the sentences before and after the underlined portion to find the answer that fits the surrounding context.***

E.g. Which choice most effectively sets up the information that follows?

    A.) Californians are known for being adventurous.
    B.) Surfers usually hit the beach in the morning.
    C.) There are three types of mountains on the west coast.
    D.) Many northerners move to California because of the tempered weather.

Your goal would be to find the answer that best revises the underlined portion. Read above and below the underlined portion in the passage to find the context.

Here are some examples of the three types of shorts:

1.   SHORTEST IN LENGTH

Some author's talents go beyond words written on a page.
<u>Don Miller is of the same brilliant writer and equally poetic storyteller.</u>
His book, *Blue Like Jazz,* was a runaway best-seller.

    A.) NO CHANGE
    B.) Don Miller is equally a brilliant writer and poetic storyteller.
    C.) Don Miller is a brilliant writer and poetic storyteller.
    D.) A poetic storyteller and of the same brilliant writing, is Don Miller

Draw a line at the end of the answer choices to note the shortest one and start there. It makes logical sense that if the shortest answer is grammatically correct, then it will be the right answer. Notice that the correct answer—**C**—

is concise and the shortest answer in length and it also makes the most sense. This pattern often occurs **up to 75%** of the time on the actual test.

2.   SHORTEST NUMBER OF SUFFIXES

Whether an athlete chooses to do several sets with reps or subscribes to the slow burn ideology, lifting weights can be very beneficial. There are also risks that need to be taken into consideration. **Overworking their muscles, weightlifting is an exercise that many people do wrongly.** Often a professional trainer can give clear direction.

> A.) NO CHANGE
> B.) Weightlifting is wrongly performed because people are overworking their muscles.
> C.) Many people having overworked their muscles in exercising in weightlifting do it wrongly.
> D.) Many people overwork their muscles in weightlifting by exercising wrongly.

Draw a line at the end of the answer choices to note the shortest one.

Notice that the wrong answers have taken a perfectly correct sentence which is **D** and added a lot of unnecessary and awkward suffixes like "-ing, -ly, -ed." Circle these suffixes to bring attention to them. There is "having" in there as well which usually indicates a wrong answer and should be a **red flag** to you. The correct answer (**D**) has the shortest number of suffixes as well as it is the shortest linear answer.

3.   SHORTEST NUMBER OF SUCCINCT WORDS

Throughout the last century, Encyclopedias reigned supreme as the resource of choice to gain information about our world. The creation of the internet, known as the information super highway, it has transformed people in their personal lives by and revolutionized our world globally. At the touch of a finger, we now have access to countless millions of topics almost immediately.

A.) NO CHANGE

B.) it has transformed people; but as in their personal lives by and it revolutionized

C.) it has not transformed people in their personal lives but also revolutionized

D.) has transformed people's personal lives and revolutionized

Notice that the correct answer—**D**—has the **shortest number of succinct** words such as "it, has, as…" and it ended up being the shortest linear answer. Always circle these extra little words to draw your attention to them.

INSIDE ANSWERS

A standardized test, by its very nature means that each test follows the same patterns, concepts and ideas every time. In the *Writing and Language* section, the test-makers repeatedly use the same grammar problems.

You can do very well in this section when you use the *College Prep Genius* **INSIDE ANSWERS** acronym.

I—"ing" Words

Words that end in -ing are usually wrong, especially "having" and "being". This should be a red flag. **Circle these words!**

Many constituents complain about the mud-slinging commercials made by candidates being arisen during political campaigns in a voting year.

A.) NO CHANGE

B.) that arise

C.) being that they arise

D.) having arisen

B is correct.

N—Notwithstanding Words Defined

There is a significant number of words at the beginning of a sentence that require the use of a comma. These transition words **keep repeating** *on the test so* <u>be sure of their definitions</u> *and logical relationship to the sentence:*

AN ADDITION:
furthermore, similarly, likewise, moreover, in addition

A CONSEQUENCE:
accordingly, consequently, therefore

A SEQUENCE:
finally, after all, thereafter

IN CONTRAST:
notwithstanding, however, nevertheless

Due to the objectivity of the test, if you find two or more answers with a word similar to those above, all those answers are wrong.

Example:

   A.) Nevertheless, we should set the oven at 350 degrees.
   B.) Notwithstanding, we should set the oven at 350 degrees.

Answers A and B both start with words that mean the same thing (in contrast) which means both are wrong. This sentence calls for a sequence word.

S—Substitute Words

Often an underlined word in this section will not be the best word for the sentence so you will need to substitute another word that rephrases the meaning better.

E.g. Bonnie was <u>pretty pumped</u> when she found out her present was a pony.

    A.) NO CHANGE
    B.) Ecstatic
    C.) Really very happy
    D.) Over the Moon

B is Correct

I—Idiom Problems

E.g. The bug ate <u>at</u> the plant.

The bug ate <u>up</u> the plant.	**Correct**
Honey serves <u>to be</u> a good alternative to sugar.	
Honey serves <u>as</u> a good alternative to sugar.	**Correct**

Make sure the correct preposition is represented.

Prior to the internet, phone books were used to serve as a means <u>through</u> distributing contact information for families.

Prior to the internet, phone books were used to serve as a means <u>of</u> distributing contact information for families.   **Correct**

D—Dash and Comma Rules

<u>Dash</u>—is used to bring attention to the next word(s)
I got a new car—a corvette!

<u>Comma</u>—is used for a pause, a series of words or to set apart and an appositive. (The Oxford comma is used before the word "and" in a series.)
I like hot dogs, hamburgers, pizza, and sushi.
My brother, Bill, is a doctor.

Semi-colon—longer pause that separates two full sentences of equal weight and can replace a period. Since a semi-colon can replace a period and vice versa, then if there are two answer choices, one with a semi-colon and one with a period, both are wrong.

My mother is studying nursing; college has been her life-long dream.

My mother is studying nursing. College has been her life-long dream.

Colon—is used to expand or define (as in a word or list) If the word "namely" can replace the colon, it is used correctly.

There are four types of dogs: docile, hyper and alert.

There are four types of dog namely docile, hyper and alert.

E—Exchanged Words

Sometimes the correct words are replaced with similar sounding possessive words with the wrong meaning, such as "whose" and "who's".

E.g.

He remembered that the projector has **it's** own remote control.

He remembered that the projector has **its** own remote control.

The first class section was like the **president's** airplane.

CAUTION: This is a possessive adjective and is describing the airplane, not the actual president and his aircraft, therefore using the word "he" afterwards would not be correct in this scenario.

A—Among/Between/Into

Among   used when items are not distinct

He moved among the crowd.

Between—used when items are distinct

Between Sydney and Lexi, they have forty dollars.

Into—movement inside a place. Together "in" and "to" form an adverb. When they are not connected they form a preposition.

She moved into the stairwell for safety.

N—Not only/but also; Neither/nor—Either/Or

"Not only" must be followed by "but also"
Not only is she smart, but she is also pretty.

"Neither has a "nor" and "either" has an "or"
She neither has a job nor does she have any prospects.
I will either go home or go to the store.

S—Subject/Verb agreement

Watch out for unbalanced subject/verb agreement—singular vs plural. To make sure they agree, draw a line through the prepositional phrase then circle the subject and underline the verb. Remember, the subject is never found in the prepositional phrase.

My friend with two of the most beautiful horses have won numerous races.

Rule out prepositional phrase and find the subject (friend) and verb (have) do not agree.

W—Who Rules

Students often don't know when to use "who" or "whom"
Who is doing what to whom?

- **Who**—gives action (replace who with he/she) E.g. Which is correct? "**Who/whom** went to the store?" **Whom** went to the store-doesn't make sense. **He** went to the store. If the word "he" or "she" makes sense when substituted, then the word *who* is the correct choice.
- **Whom**—receives action (replace whom with him/her) E.g. Which is correct? Who/Whom can we turn to in a time of crisis? If the statement or question makes sense when you substitute "him" or "her" then use *whom*. Can we turn to **she,** doesn't make any sense. Can we turn to **her**? makes sense so you would use "whom."

- **Who** goes with people, **where** with places, **which/that** with things.
- People **who** believe…The house **where**…The car **which**…

E—Effect/Affect; Access/Excess

These types of words are commonly used incorrectly so be on the alert.

- <u>Effect</u>—(result)
  The effect of too much sun was third-degree burns.
- <u>Affect</u>—(influence)
  Drinking coffee after six will affect my ability to sleep.
  "a" as in affect is the first letter so it comes first,
  "e" as in effect comes later so it is the result.

- <u>Access</u>—admittance
  He received access to the backstage of the concert.
- <u>Excess</u>—overabundance

She brought an excess of food to the picnic.
"a" as in access is first letter so it comes first,
"e" as in excess comes later so it is the result.
You will find more diction mistakes on page 209.

R—Redundancy

These words are <u>**saying the same thing**</u> and **one** of them should be <u>**eliminated.**</u>

<u>**Here are some examples**</u>: reason why; add an additional; end result; repeat again; usual custom; unintended mistake; years' time; false pretense; added bonus…

He is rich and has a lot of money.
She is always late and never shows up on time.
The employee was lazy and unwilling to work.
The plane was airborne as it flew high in the sky.

S—Structurally Parallel

Read the sentence to make sure words/phrases are parallel, especially if they are being compared.

E.g.

He went fishing, hiking and to go swim. **INCORRECT**
He went fishing, hiking and swimming. **CORRECT**

E.g.

Her painting-with-a-purpose company teaches ordinary people how to expand their hidden talent by showing them step-by-step how to transform a blank canvas into a field of majestic flowers, with daisies toweri**ng** in the background, fireflies connect**ing** the skyline with luminous lights, and 5 <u>delicately placed</u> <u>animals such as rabbits nesting in the tall green grass.</u>

    A.) NO CHANGE
    B.) delicate animals nest**ing** in the tall grass. **CORRECT-"ing" is consistent**
    C.) delicately placed rabbits who are nesting in the tall grass.
    D.) delicate rabbits that nest in the tall grass.

To make the sentence logically parallel, compare "daisies towering" and "fireflies connecting" so answer (B) has "animals nesting" which is correct.

INSIDE ANSWERS Acronym

I—"-ing" words
N—Notwithstanding Words Defined
S—Substitute words
I—Idiom problems
D—Dash and comma rules
E—Exchanged words

A—Among/Between/Into
N—Not only/but also; Neither/nor-Either/Or
S—Subject/Verb agreement
W—Who Rules
E—Effect/Affect; Access/Excess
R—Redundancy
S—Structurally Parallel

BEST RESTATEMENT STEPS

1. Write the acronym **RESTATE** to remind you what to do.
2. Write the acronym **INSIDE ANSWERS** to remind you of the most common grammar errors.
3. Start by drawing a straight line/vertical line at the end of all the answer choices from top to bottom. This perpendicular line will automatically **highlight the shortest** answer, which **tends to be correct** up to 75% of the time.
4. Since the <u>shortest answer</u> could be in the underlined portion, use your pencil to <u>measure it</u> against the other answers.
5. Always try the shortest/linear answer first in the sentences to save you time! If it fits, move on. <u>Whisper the sentence out loud to make sure.</u>
6. If it is not the correct answer, recall the INSIDE ANSWERS rule to identify which of the common grammar and punctuation errors has been applied.
7. **Insert answer and read back** to make sure you have chosen well. Listen carefully!
8. Correct answer is **obviously exposed**.
9. **To remember the steps to success, here's an acronym**

RESTATE

R—Review answers. Draw a straight line.
E—Examine underlined part with pencil length.
S—Shortest answer/suffixes/short words usually right.
T—Try answer in sentence (if not).
A—Apply INSIDE ANSWER rules.
T—Totally restates best.
E—Exposed answer!

READING ANALYSIS

When the problem has a prompt-question and the answers are varied, your reading analysis skills and comprehension are being tested. **Often** a revision of the underlined portion is advised to determine if it sounds effective and logical!

Reading **the entire passage is unnecessary!**
These answer types are found in context, around it, or 1st & last lines **of each paragraph.**
Revision questions have more varied answer choices.

· **Remember-they are NOT seeking your opinion!**

Objective: Answers are found in the text and always objective!

Deductive Reasoning: Eliminate obvious wrong answers first!
Correct answers will rephrase information from the passage. Incorrect answers can contain irrelevant, obscure, contradictory or additional information. Use the *CPG* **C.O.A.T. acronym**.

Strategy 1 Read right before and right after the underlined portion to understand the most logical answer to the question.

Strategy 2 Read the first and last lines of the paragraph as well as the title to get the main idea to answer questions about the overall passage.

Strategy 3 Always eliminate <u>obvious</u> wrong answers <u>first</u>, and those unsubstantiated by the passage.

*Strategy 4 If a question asks you to delete a sentence in the passage, only do so if it suggests any <u>*new* information</u> that can't be reinforced from information already in the passage.

*Strategy 5 If a question asks you to add a sentence in the passage, only do so if the information can be confirmed by other information already found in the surrounding part of the underlined text.

*For these 2 types of questions, there will be two "No" and two "Yes" answers so first determine "which" it should be and then determine "why".

This information is usually found in the sentences right before and after. Correct answers MUST be justified by the passage!

E.g

12. At this point, the author is considering deleting the sentence. Should the writer make this change here?

    A.) Yes, because the Arabic and Spanish languages should be given equal importance.

    B.) Yes, because it doesn't provide a logical flow to the next sentence.

    C.) No, because it provides a transition between popular languages and college courses.

    D.) No, because it continues to maintain a clear chronological order of events.

Read the lines before and after the underlined portion for question 12 and if necessary. Read the title and the first and last lines of the paragraph to find the correct answer. First determine if whether it should be deleted (yes or no) and lastly determine why.

Here's our acronym for REVISE:

R—Read only what is necessary, before/after/first and last lines, and the title.
E—Eliminate unsubstantiated answers (C.O.A.T.).
V—Version must be the best.
I—Insert info if justified by passage. Delete if not.
S—Specific questions need specific support.
E—Effective and accurate is the answer.

The writing question may ask about a specific numbered-sentence. The bracket number will be at the beginning of the sentence no matter where it falls. E.g. [1] The numbers for the questions will still be encased in a black square and will correlate with the actual questions.

BASIC GRAMMAR RULES

To do well in this section, it is very important to know and understand the basics of grammar. Memorize all the grammar rules found in this book as a starting point to prepare or refresh yourself.

BASIC SENTENCE STRUCTURE

EXAMPLE 3-1
Sue sang.

It is important to go over the basic structure of a sentence. A proper one will have one subject and one verb. [See Example 3-1]

Although simple, this sentence is grammatically correct because it contains the two necessary elements. This is also considered an independent clause, because it can stand alone and is proper without adding anything.

EXAMPLE 3-2
Although she had a sore throat.
And she read the prayer.

A dependent clause is a phrase that modifies the independent clause. These phrases tht begin with either a coordinating conjunction (for, and, nor, but, or, yet, so i.e. use the acronym

FANBOYS) or a subordinating conjunction (although, because, if, since, that, which, until, while, etc.). Please note coordinating conjunctions are used for clauses with equal emphasis. The independent clause and subordinating conjunctions are used for phrases that have unequal emphasis to the main clause. [See Example 3-2]

IMPORTANT TIP

If two conjunctions are next to each other, the answer is wrong. E.g. and yet, but so, or so...

Notice, these dependent clauses cannot stand alone and must connect to an independent clause such as that in Example 3-1. Sometimes the *SAT* will include sentences that are merely dependent clauses; these are called fragments. They demonstrate improper sentence constructions. Both these dependent clauses make complete sentences when added to the independent clause. [See Example 3-3]

EXAMPLE 3-3

Sue sang although she had a sore throat.
Sue sang and she read the prayer.

These are both proper sentences because they still only contain one independent clause. Please note; *however*, *therefore*, *besides*, *hence*, *also*, *consequently*, *nevertheless*, *thus*, *moreover* and *furthermore* are not proper conjunctions. These cannot join two independent clauses without a proper conjunction added to them. If a sentence has two independent clauses, it is considered a run-on, and is incorrect.

EXAMPLE 3-4

Sue sang, it was the county fair.

Example 3-4 has what is called a comma splice, because it links two independent clauses with only a comma. There are several ways to fix run-on sentences. Replace the punctuation: Because they are both independent clauses, they can both stand alone, so you could separate them with a period. You can also join two independent clauses with a semicolon. [See Example 3-5]

EXAMPLE 3-5

Sue sang. It was the county fair.
Sue sang; it was the county fair.

Now the sentences are grammatically correct. You could also join the two clauses by making one of them a dependent clause with the use of a conjunction. [See Example 3-6]

EXAMPLE 3-6

It was the county fair, and Sue sang.
Sue sang because it was the county fair.

Both the sentences above properly turn one of the independent clauses into a dependent clause. The *College Board* very often uses fragments and run-ons in the *Writing* section to confuse students. Knowledge of proper sentence is essential to help you find the errors.

Some underlined sentences include prepositional phases to confuse the subject, but the subject is NEVER found in the prepositional phrase. (Hint: Memorize all the prepositions from the list on the page 207.) Start by drawing a line through all the prepositional phrases. When you find the subject, circle it and underline its verb to make sure they agree. If they agree, put a check above them to remind you they're correct. Say each sentence to yourself quietly. Very often, you can pick up errors simply by listening to the sound of the sentence.

SUBJECT—VERB AGREEMENT

EXAMPLE 3-7

Sub. V. Prep. Phrase
The dog ran <u>under the tree</u> to get away.

Agreement is the first thing to look for. Circle the subject and underline the verb, then make sure they agree.

- ✔ singular subject = singular verb   plural subject = plural verb
- ✔ subjects joined by *and* = plural verb
- ✔ subjects joined by *or, either, neither, nor, not only, but also* = the verb will agree with nearer subject
- ✔ subjects joined by *along with, as well as, besides, in addition to, together with* = the verb will agree with first subject
- ✔ amounts as subject = singular verb (e.g., "One-hundred dollars is…")
- ✔ indefinite pronouns relating to individuals = singular verb (e.g.,

anybody, each, everyone, no one, something, amount, anyone, anything, everybody, everything, someone, somebody, either, neither, none, nobody, nothing, one)

- ✔ indefinite words relating to groups = plural verb (e.g., both, few, many, several)
- ✔ some indefinite words require singular or plural verb depending on the noun they modify (e.g., all, any, enough, most, you, who, which, what, that)
- ✔ groups of people require singular verbs (e.g., team, jury, crowd, class, committee)
- ✔ words that look plural but have a singular verb (e.g., physics, news, measles, mathematics)

PREPOSITIONAL PHRASE RULE-OUT

To make sure you have found the correct subject, rule-out the prepositional phrase by lightly drawing a line through it (even if it's an underlined portion). The subject is **NEVER** in the *prepositional phrase*. [See Example 3-7]

A *prepositional phrase* starts with a preposition and ends with a noun or pronoun. Study your prepositions. The most popular prepositions are listed below:

aboard, about, above, across, after, against, along, amid, among, around, at, before, behind, below, beneath, beside, between, beyond, but, by, down, during, except, for, from, in, into, like, near, of, off, on, over, past, since, through, throughout, to, toward, under, underneath, until, unto, up, upon, with, within, without

OBJECTIVE/SUBJECTIVE CASE PROBLEMS

Know what is *doing* the action and what is *receiving* the action.

EXAMPLE 3-8

Andy kicked <u>him</u>. CORRECT ("him" received the action)
He disagrees with <u>her</u> and <u>me</u>. CORRECT ("her/me" received the action)

<u>She</u> and <u>I</u> think alike. CORRECT ("She/I gives the action)
<u>Whom</u> did he kick? CORRECT ("whom" receives the action)

Subject: I, you, he, she, it, we, they, who (These pronouns GIVE action.)

Object: me, you, him, her, it, us, them, whom (*These pronouns RECEIVE action.*)

If any of the pronouns are in the wrong case, that answer choice is wrong. [See Ex. 3-8]

EXAMPLE 3-9

The constant fighting between my best friend and I started after he accused me of stealing his homework.

In sentences with multiple subjects/objects, to determine whether "I" or "me" is correct, simply remove the other person and insert "I" or "me" to see which one works.

By removing "my best friend" and inserting "between I" or "between me", it is clear that "me" is the correct answer. [See Example 3-9]

EXAMPLES 3-10

Define *as*, different *from*, frown *upon*, object *to*, use *as*, accuse *of*, arrive *at*, believe *in*, attribute *to*, abide *by*, according *to*, try *to*, preferable *to*, credit *with*, affinity *with*, argue *with*, catering *to*, intends *to*, superior *to*, ought *to*, partake *of*, different *from*, aim *at*, dispute *over*, agree *to*, agrees *with*

TENSE

Make sure there is no unnecessary shift in tense if the action stays the same. A shift in the tense should occur only to show actions at different times.

regular verb: add -ed for past
irregular verb: (you should study them for tense)

> **EXAMPLE 3-11**
> Margaret watched the kids play at the hill.

IDIOM

An idiomatic expression is a phrase containing the pairing of a specific verb with a specific preposition that is commonly accepted as correct. [See Example 3-10] There are no specific rules with regards to idioms. It's just how Americans form certain verb/ preposition constructions. Studying idiomatic use of prepositions is recommended but could take a long time (*English Prepositional Idioms* by Frederick T. Wood is a good reference). If you read the prompt sentence slowly, you can usually pick out problems with idioms. Here are a few examples of commonly accepted idioms: [See Example 3-10]

> **FUN TIP**
> If a sentence has a conditional structure (*If he had…then he would have…*), always use the tense = *had + verb…would have + verb.*

In Example 3-11 sentence, the idiom "at" is used incorrectly. The correct idiom is "up."

DICTION PROBLEM/WRONG WORD

One of the underlined portions of the sentence might contain a word used out of context. Here's a list of the most common ones:

it's (it is)	or	**its** (possessive)
they're (they are)	or	**their** (possessive)
you're (you are)	or	**your** (possessive)
who's (who is)	or	**whose** (possessive)
imminent (about to occur)	or	**eminent** (famous)
accept (to receive)	or	**except** (exclude)
ascent (upward)	or	**assent** (agree)
eminent (prominent)	or	**imminent** (impending)
a part (a portion)	or	**apart** (to pieces)
precede (go before)	or	**proceed** (onward)
illusion (deception)	or	**allusion** (reference)
lead (escort)	or	**led** (directed)

(*a is before e, so remember you must* first *receive before you can exclude*)

real (colloquial)	or	**really** (adverb, means "very")
good (colloquial)	or	**well** (adverb/adjective means "good health")

Most verbs take the word "well", but linking verbs (to be, and those of the five senses: sight, sound, smell, touch, taste) use the adjective "good."

bad is used after verbs relating to human feelings. ("I feel bad about your accident.")

badly is used after a verb
amount (used when something cannot be counted) or **number** (when it is countable)
fewer (used with a plural verb on things you can count—e.g., months, hours, people)
less (used with a singular verb and can't be counted—e.g., rain, time, love)

*NOTE: Adjectives are used to modify nouns. Adverbs are used to modify verbs or adjectives. Add "ly" to an adjective to make it an adverb. *She ran quickly*, **NOT** *she ran quick.*

These are common misspellings of correct words.

alot should be spelled **a lot** (2 words)

(*Remember, 2 words are a lot more than 1 word)*

irregardlessssess	should be spelled	**regardless**
would of	should be spelled	**would have**
could of	should be spelled	**could have**
kinda	should be spelled	**kind of**
sorta	should be spelled	**sort of**
altogether	(entirely/completely)	**all together** (everyone together)

WRONG/FAULTY COMPARISON

When comparing items, make sure they are structurally correct. [See Example 3-12]

When comparing two items, use the suffix **-er** [See Example 3-13]

When comparing three or more items, use the suffix **-est** [See Example 3-14]

(*Remember, er has* two *letters and est has* three *letters.)*

Beware of phrases that double emphasize the comparison like "*more bigger*". The phrase should be either "*more big*" or simply "*bigger*".

EXAMPLE 3-12
Her car was faster than her mother. (INCORRECT)
Her car was faster than her mother's car. (CORRECT)

EXAMPLE 3-13
Joe is strong**er** than Bill.

EXAMPLE 3-14
Between Joe, Bill and Steve, I believe Steve is the strong**est**.

DOUBLE NEGATIVE

EXAMPLE 3-15
Worrying <u>won't hardly</u> change the future.

There are words with built-in negatives (scarcely, hardly, never, neither). Watch out for added negative words that can create a double negative such as: no, not, can't, don't, isn't, doesn't. [See Example 3-15]

EXAMPLE 3-16
The vase is almost perfect. INCORRECT (It is either perfect or it is not.)

Already Complete Words—These are words that are complete and cannot be considered less or more (e.g., unique, perfect, naked). [See Example 3-16]

PRONOUN PROBLEMS

EXAMPLE 3-17
The average <u>student</u> will take 200 tests during <u>his</u> or <u>her</u> college life.

Pronoun/Antecedent Agreement

Singular antecedents require singular pronouns; plural antecedents require plural pronouns. Use feminine and masculine pronouns for words like "student." [See Example 3-17 and 3-18]

EXAMPLE 3-18

Pronouns	Antecedents
I, you, he, she, it, they.	James, Cathy, the bank, people.

James thinks <u>he</u> will be home on time.
Cathy will come later and <u>she</u> will bring the drinks.

Noun/Pronoun Agreement

In Example 3:18b, it is unclear what "it" is referring to since there is no noun to connect it to.

Change in Person

If the sentence starts in first person, it cannot properly switch to third or second person in mid-sentence. Watch out for an improper switch. [See Example 3-19]

This sentence contains a switch in persons. It starts in second person—"you"—and then switches to third person—"one". It should read: *If you eat lots of vegetables, you will be very healthy* **or** *If one eats lots of vegetables, one will be very healthy.*

MODIFIER (MISPLACED OR DANGLING)

A modifier is a phrase that modifies a noun. Modifiers work like adjectives. They can be created by prepositional phrases (preposition + noun), subordinating conjunctions (although, that, when, etc.), appositives (a noun phrase that renames) or participial phrases (verbs with an "ing" or "ed" ending not acting as adjectives).

A modifier directly modifies a specific noun in the sentence. Modifiers must be clear; they require an obvious antecedent and must be placed right next to it. Otherwise it will be confusing and wrong. [See Example 3-21]

Dangling Modifier—A group of words that modifies something we are unsure of.
[See Example 3-22]

EXAMPLE 3-18B

According to the newspaper poll, most people would want the chance to do it all over again.

EXAMPLE 3-19

If you eat lots of vegetables, one will be very healthy.

EXAMPLE 3-20

She <u>neither</u> wants a dog <u>nor</u> does she have time for one. <u>Either</u> you will stay <u>or</u> you will go.

EXAMPLE 3-21

My neighbor *in the house next door* loves me. (Prepositional Phrase)
My neighbor *although mean to other kids* loves me. (Sub. Conjunction)
My neighbor, *Mrs. Brown*, loves me. (Appositive)
My neighbor *sitting in the rocking chair* loves me. (Participial Phrase)

EXAMPLE 3-22

Worrying too much about failure, competitions can be a scary ordeal.

EXAMPLE 3-23

Burning, crackling and popping, the singer stood frozen at the microphone as the wires caught on fire.

Misplaced Modifier—Modifies the wrong word that it is next to. [See Example 3-23]

The above examples are incorrect because modifying phrases must be placed next to the word(s) they modify. It appears in the example sentences that competitions worry (though they are inanimate) and the singer was burning, crackling and popping.

Know the rules of punctuation and determine if the answer choices have broken any of the rules.

Capitalize what is appropriate:

First word of sentence or direct quote; proper nouns; names of ships, aircraft, trains, deities, geological periods, astronomical bodies, personifications, historical periods, associations and government offices; first and last word of a title; newspaper and magazine titles; radio and TV call letters; regions; specific military branches; political groups; nationalities; days; holidays; months; and trademarks.

Italicize** the bigger item—**Put the smaller item in quotations

Book (*Jane Eyre*)	Chapter of book ("My Day")
Movie (*Spider-Man*)	TV Show ("Jeopardy!")
Newspaper *(New York Times)*	Story ("My Summer")
Magazines (*Good Housekeeping*)	Poem ("Stopping by Woods on a Snowy Evening")

Quotation marks—periods and commas go inside quotation marks while question marks, exclamation points, colons and semicolons go inside only if they are part of the quoted material.

PART V:

ESSAY SECTION

THE ESSAY

THE *SAT* ESSAY IS optional and is administered after the test is finished. However, there are very compelling reasons why you should ALWAYS opt in and write it. An extra *SAT* essay score may earn you a better scholarship, it will never hurt your chances, and it makes a more complete college profile. At some colleges, writing a good essay can exempt you from required writing classes. And if a college admission's counselor is on the fence about an application, they often use the essay as the determining factor. If you opt out of the essay and later decide to go to a school that requires it, you will have to <u>take the entire *SAT* again</u>—not just the essay section. To check to see if your school absolutely requires the essay, go to: collegeprepgenius.com/requiredSATessay and for the ACT: collegeprepgenius.com/requiredACTessay

FUN TIP

Students who opt-in for the essay are usually exempt from the possible fifth, experimental section.

Does the thought of writing an *SAT* essay strike fear in your heart? It seems irrational but once you understand the formulaic nature of the essay challenge, you'll be able to prepare for it, just like you can for every other section. You are given 50 minutes to write an essay on a completely unknown topic. The paper will be based on a high-quality piece of writing. It follows a pattern, and if you can accurately imitate this pattern, you can do really well on this portion of the test. Practice copy work with the eCourse essay templates. Receiving a perfect essay score is not as hard as you may think.

When you sign up for the new *SAT*, you can opt then and there to add (or not add) the essay portion. You change your mind, and opt-in at the school at check-in time. Admission will be based on availability of rooms and material. *This is not an option at some testing centers.*

Score Choice and Super Score still apply to the new *SAT* essay portion! If you score badly, you can simply take it again on another test and get your scores higher!

The *College Board* judges are not looking for perfect papers, but they want to make sure that each paper includes a few key ingredients. There is no need to cram information in preparation for it, because you won't know your essay topic until the moment you open the test booklet. That's okay. The test-makers don't expect you to be an expert on the given subject matter, but they will want to see how well you understand an author's perspective on the piece. I.e. You are analyzing not summarizing the given work.

The essay measure your ability to evaluate the author's use of language and express how effectively the ideas are conveyed. Rather than specifically test your writing ability, it tests your ability to follow instructions and create a logical paper that shows how the author of the given work builds their argument. The essay reveals if you can make a coherent point and then support information from the given passage. Your essay should be insightful, analytical, and make logical sense and conform to the rules of Standard Written English—which means a clear understanding of syntax, diction, sentence construction and punctuation.

The following section presents an overall outline of how to write your essay for the *SAT*. It is a tried and tested formula. Don't be tempted to veer off this guideline and become creative—just stick with what works. Students who have learned to copy this proven guideline have received excellent essay scores.

Essays should contain the four C's of Composition.

INGREDIENTS OF A GOOD ESSAY

All good *SAT* essays should contain certain basic ingredients. At CPG we call these the four Cs of Composition. They should **C**learly state a thesis; add **C**ompetent given examples; and be **C**onsistent with the **C**oncepts of the main theme. *Essays* should also include the four Ss of syntax. Every sentence should contain **S**olid information (no fluff), **S**ound intelligent (word choice) and have a varied and complex **S**entence Structure.

The *Four Cs* of Composition
Clear
Competent
Consistent Concepts

The *Four Ss* of Syntax
Solid
Sound
Sentence Structures

GRADING THE ESSAY

There are more than 3600 judges across the United States. Each essay is graded by two judges who have the minimal qualifications of a college degree, several years of experience teaching writing, and they must understand the rules of *Standard Written English*.

Judges look for good organization, appropriate punctuation, supported examples, solid sentence structure, clear presentation, developed ideas and good vocabulary choices. By picking out the most important components, you demonstrate comprehension of the text and the author's argument; this creates a paper that focuses on analyzing only the relevant details. A few grammar and spelling errors are acceptable, but more than five tend to have a negative impact on the overall score. The judges realize that you only have 50 minutes to develop and write your composition. They're not looking for perfected papers. They just want to read work that is effective and SOUNDS SMART.

A good essay should express a wide range of experience and knowledge found in the given work.

"Standard Written English" is the form of language most widely accepted as being clear and proper. It includes word choice, word order, punctuation, and spelling. Standard English is especially helpful when writing because it maintains a fairly uniform standard of communication which can be understood by all speakers and users of English regardless of differences in dialect, pronunciation, and usage.

After the test, the essays are scanned into a computer and dispersed to the judges. For ten days, they are reviewed by two judges who grade them on three scales: writing, reading and analysis. Section-scores are between one and four marks. Both three-part scores combine to create the student's overall essay score. An 8/8/8 or total score of 24 is a perfect score.

In this new format, the lowest possible score from each individual judge is 1/1/1 and the highest is 4/4/4. After scores are combined, the final score ranges from 2/2/2 to 8/8/8 and can be any combination within these ranges. **E.g. 5/2/6, 4/3/2, 2/2/3.** This score will <u>NOT</u> be combined with the *Writing and Literature* section of the *SAT* or any other portion that comprises the regular *SAT* score out of 1600.

Judges award points for every major scoring element within the essay.

If there is more than a one-point difference between the scores of the two judges in all three sections, a third judge (*Master Judge*) will be brought in to make the final decision. The score of the master judge (1 – 4 in each section) will be the overriding score and will be doubled for the final score. The other two scores will be thrown out. A score of 0 can be given if the essay is illegible, written in ink or if the essay is off topic. If a student who has opted in for the essay leaves early, the essay will be given a zero.

The judges read your paper one time through fairly quickly and then grade it immediately for its first impression. However, they go back through it to make sure it has all the key elements for a great essay. Your score will then be adjusted accordingly. Generally, the judges award points every major scoring element within the essay. They are looking for attention to detail, relationship to central ideas and an insightful perspective on the author's claims.

They use the 3 Fs to grade the essay:

- Fast (read through quickly)
- First (one time through)
- Feeling (overall impression)

You are given four pages to write the essay so shoot for the fourth page; the longer the better! Judges do use an objective grading system on a subjective essay and paper length is a popular grade influencer with five complete paragraphs as the goal. Judges tend to skim the paper and only spend about thirty seconds to a minute grading each essay so in that short timeframe, length can be a major contributor to a better score.

COLLEGE BOARD RUBRICS:

"*Reading* **Rubric:** *Successful essays demonstrate thorough comprehension of the passage, including the interplay of central ideas and important details, and use textual evidence effectively.*"

In other words … do you comprehend the article enough to understand its main points and find the keywords? Can you articulate them through skillful use of paraphrasing and direct quotations? And can you express yourself succinctly and accurately to capture details of the central claim?

"**Analysis Rubric:** *Successful essays demonstrate skill in evaluating the author's use of evidence, reasoning, style, and other stylistic or persuasive techniques and support and develop claims with well-chosen evidence from the passage.*"

In other words … do you understand the arguments laid out in the excerpt? Can you explain how the words worked with the evidence cited and demonstrate a sophisticated understanding of the analytical task, and can you offer a possible reason for examples given and their overall effect on the audience?

"**Writing Rubric**: *Successful essays are focused, organized, and precise, with an appropriate style and tone that varies sentence structure and follows the conventions of standard written English.*"

In other words … does your essay flow well, does it incorporate decent grammar and proper style to demonstrate a cohesive and highly effective use and command of language; a consistent use of precise word choices and phrases; and does it exemplify advanced writing proficiency?

SCORING OVERVIEW

The optional *SAT Essay* is scored using a carefully designed rubric. Two different, official scorers will read each essay response and give the essay a score of 1-4 for each of the three rubrics. These two scores are added, and in the end, you'll receive three scores: one for each dimension of the essay:

reading, analysis, and writing.

- A score of 4—Advanced—demonstrates **thorough** comprehension of the source text, **insightful** analysis and a **well-considered** evaluation of the text. The essay is **cohesive** and uses **masterful** language and claims effectively.
- A score of 3—Proficient—shows effective comprehension of the text, and an understanding of the analytical task. It also includes a central claim or a controlling idea, surrounded by an effective introduction and conclusion.
- A score of 2—Partial—still shows an understanding of the text's main idea or ideas but leaves out important details. While it lacks cohesion and shows limited language skills, it holds reasoning and notes persuasive elements of the provided text.
- A score of 1—Inadequate—demonstrates little to no understanding of the source text, nor does it offer analysis or understanding of the task. The essay lacks a statement and supporting details.

TYPES OF ESSAY TOPICS

The essay prompt is a 600-750-word high-quality published piece of work such as an article, document or excerpt from a book and it cites numerous sources and data. The writers of the *SAT* consistently use the same type of prompts for every test. Therefore, you can prepare yourself by becoming familiar with general types of topics. They vary each time the test is given, but all the passages will:

- Address a broad audience.
- Convey an argument.
- Express nuanced views on complex subjects.
- Use logical reasoning and various forms of evidence to support substantive claims.
- Examine ideas, debates, trends, and the like in the arts, the sciences, and civic, cultural, and political life.
- The passages are carefully chosen to ensure they are appropriately and consistently complex.

The essay will never test on previous knowledge, so you cannot study for upcoming essay topics. The essay judges DO NOT want personal experiences, outside sources or other such materials in the essay. The judges DO NOT want you to agree or disagree with the author. DO NOT use personal pronouns such as "I" or "me". They want you to critically look at the work and then analyze how the author uses evidence to build an argument.

THE ESSAY STRUCTURE

Once you know your essay topic, the first thing you should do is skim the paper for important elements. There is no need to read the essay first but it is crucial that you read the prompt question in the box so you have instructions to follow. There is generally a question at the end of the essay with an overview of the article. Quickly do a vertical scan of the document and circle your thesis and three examples used from the author.

Make the structure of the essay like this:

- A good opening sentence with an attention-grabbing hook
- Five paragraphs
- Three supporting examples
- Closing sentence that sums up the thesis

You can create an outline that is applicable to any essay and give you a solid head start during the 50 minutes' test time. You can actually develop about 50-75% of the essay ahead of time before even reading the essay. Do not add in outside sources or personal experiences. The judges will be strictly looking for citations from within the prompt itself.

Don't panic about having to fill in an exceptionally long piece of prose in order to win over the judges. Length can be impressive but it's not essential. Several perfect scoring *SAT* essay samples had just five paragraphs (with the longest being 592 words). These essays filled up three plus pages. The judges measure the strength of the paper on how well a student portrays the author's use of B.I.C.E.P.S.

...the first thing you should do is skim the paper for important elements.

Builds Argument
Ideas Expressed
Connects Evidence
Elaborates Facts
Persuades Audience
Supports Claims

Write your essay using the **active voice** instead of the passive voice.

Remember, if you get off-topic, it can result in a score of zero, so it is very important to state your thesis very early to demonstrate your comprehension of the given document. This is reassuring to the judge and helps to keep you on the right track. Use given examples and restate your thesis stance at the end of each body paragraph.

Write first and rewrite second. Write the body of the essay as fast as you can and then come back and edit it. Practice writing essays in forty minutes. Use the other ten minutes to correct any mistakes and to embellish the paper. The eCourse essay templates will help you formulate the paper.

THREE TO FOUR VOCABULARY WORDS

Appear smart by using three to four good vocabulary words in your paper.

Appear SMART by using three to four good vocabulary words in your paper as this can be a very good score-booster. Don't overdo it though. If your essay reads like a thesaurus and is inconsistent with your writing style, it could count against you. Spell correctly and use your vocab appropriately. An example of three words used on a recent essay with a perfect score on the redesigned *SAT*, were words morose, guttural and amass.

You don't have to learn thousands of words to sound knowledgeable, just a handful that you can recycle and reuse on each paper you write. See how many ways you can make the same words fit into different practice essays. The judges repeatedly read the same topic for 10 days (from 7 am to 10 pm if they so choose). Your goal is to make your paper stand out above the rest. The judges will be amazed that you were able to add great words "off the top of your head."

Best use of time is to write the paper first, then go back over it. If you have time, erase two to three lazy words and add in some good vocabulary replacements if not included already.

Here are a few examples of vocabulary substitutions:

Wrongdoing → **malfeasance**

Pain → **throes**

Lucky → **providential**

Fun → **jollity**

Quiet → **tranquil**

Wonderful → **prodigious**

Joy → **ecstasy**

Success → **triumph**

Hard → **painstaking**

Enemy → **antagonist**

Excited → **innervated**

Scare → **affright**

Loud → **tawdry**

Funny → **risible**

Fast → **posthaste**

Leniency → **laxity**

Make sure to use transition words (bridges) in between paragraphs to help connect your essay together and give it a cohesive flow. Some good bridges are *"Another example,"* *"Next,"* *"Finally,"* *"In addition,"* *"however,"* *"despite this,"* *"as a result,"* *"therefore,"* etc. Practice adding or changing out these words or similar ones when you copy the essay templates on the eCourse.

STAGGER SENTENCE LENGTH

Varying sentence length keeps your reader's attention and prevents somnolent monotony.

Vary sentence length to keep your reader's attention and prevent somnolent monotony. In keeping with the previous rule about vocab use, I have used good substitutes for *boring* and *monotonous*! Now, as you write your paper, stagger sentence length. Follow a couple of longer sentences with one that is short and punchy, even with just three words. You need to break up the rhythm so it's not (unconsciously) predictable. This will help your essay seem polished and educated. Practice writing a few of them and then try to reuse them repeatedly. Adjust them to fit the given topic. Here are a few examples:

> She's batting 400.
> Children trust her.
> Life is short.
> God is love.
> Lying ruins friendships.
> Parents know better.
> Tennis owns him.

Use smart sounding phrases that mimic information from the given essay by restating key parts of the paper. Here are a few topics and examples:

SUCCESS—Great gain is often preceded by some loss.
IGNORANCE—He who knows nothing, doubts nothing.
EAVESDROPPING—The night has ears.
WISDOM—Those who rise early will gather wisdom.
SICKNESS—Without health, no one can be rich.
RUMORS—One who scatters thorns should not go barefoot.
LIFE—Where there is fire and water, anyone can live.
LEADERSHIP—If you want to really know someone, give them authority.
GROWTH—To be better, one must first be worse.
WORDS—The body can be ruined by the mouth.
LIES—A lie will multiply seven times.
PEACE—Revolution causes violence; revelation brings peace.
JUDGEMENT—If you live in a glass house, you should not throw stones.
PERFECTION—A person not yet dead is not yet clear of defects.

FREE—The best things in life are usually free.

OBESITY—Eating a lot will lead to eating a little.

RICHES—Money is flat, therefore meant to be piled up.

CHARACTER—Suffering a hardship can build character.

IMPRESSION—One never gets a second chance to make a good first impression.

GIFTS—We are truly happier when we are giving gifts rather than getting them.

JUSTIFICATION—Sometimes the end justifies the means.

POWER—Power is greater than money.

STUBBORNESS—You can't teach old dogs new tricks.

PERFORMANCE—Practice makes perfect only if it is perfect practice.

FRIENDS—Cheerful company can shorten the journey.

LONGEVITY—Those who live the longest, see the most.

STEPS TO ESSAY SUCCESS

DON'T READ THE PROMPT-ESSAY

It is too long and a time-waster to read it.

1. Read the directions in the box (info at the top) and the prompt-question at the end of the essay.

2. Go through the essay and circle the main theme, i.e. the author and the article's name and first couple of lines. Skim and circle 3 examples from the essay. Look for numbers, (dates) surveys, personal anecdotes, quotes, statistics…

3. Now, use the acronym HOT POWERFUL PAPER to fill in your essay. Remember the formula from the essay templates on the eCourse.

FUN TIP

Think of other topics and notate a smart sounding phrase to go with them and use them when presented with that topic on the given essay.

THE HOOK

Grab the judges attention quickly with a hook. It can easily be taken from the article's name, the author and the first couple of lines. The question at the end of the essay is a big clue to the article's content. Skim through and circle key parts to create your opening hook. Here's an example:

Adapted from Davis Brandon, "Roofs for Everyone" © by The Star Gazette. Originally published September 21, 2003.

> Write an essay in which you explain how Davis Brandon builds an argument to persuade his audience that homelessness in America can be easily eradicated. In your essay, analyze how Brandon uses one or more of the elements in the prompt question (or one of your own) to strengthen the logic and persuasiveness of his argument. Be sure your analysis focuses on the most relevant feature of the passage.

Hook Examples:

In response to our nation's growing homeless problem, writer Davis Brandon argues that this epidemic can be easily eradicated in his article, "Roofs for Everyone".

Davis Brandon, a sophisticated and passionate writer, gives a persuasive argument about destroying homelessness in America in his article, "Roofs for Everyone".

The compelling article about homeless Americans, "Roofs for Everyone" was written by a compassionate humanitarian—Davis Brandon.

The first and last sentences of the essay are extremely important as the judges will read the paper one time through quickly and immediately write down their first impression. Make them count!

THREE SUPPORTING EXAMPLES

Find three detailed examples from the document to support your thesis statement. The given paper usually has several examples that can be used for your essay. Without reading the given paper, skim through and pull out three that seem the most important. Circle them to make it easy to find, categorize and then write about them. Look for dates, survey, statistics and personal stories. In each of the following samples, three elements are alluded to, not their specific details.

> *He effectively builds his argument by using a personal anecdote, a national statistic and a historical fact to show how he came to this conclusion.*
>
> *Three occurrences from a historical fact, a personal story and The Census Bureau will demonstrate why he believes this to be true.*
>
> *Three strong reasons he believes the way he does are found in his personal life, a national statistic and a historical fact.*
>
> *He gives compelling evidence to support this decision by using the U.S. Census, a well-known fact and a rhetorical question.*

Be consistent with your thesis stance in every paragraph and restate it differently with each example. Restate key words as well. E.g. trusses, ceiling, rafter, canopy…could be used for "roof". This means you've probably restated it four to five times before the end of your essay." Make sure each example is clear and accurate from the prompt-document.

Find three detailed examples from the document to support your thesis statement.

FUN TIP

Here are some template ideas you can use to practice writing analytical essays, regardless of topics presented.

To get a higher score, elaborate on the author's examples.

To get a higher score, elaborate on the author's examples.

> **Bad Example**: His next example comes from the book, *My Sister's Secret*, where the main character hopes for a new life.

> **Good Example**: His next example comes from Arden Peyton's historical fiction, *My Sister's Secret*, which demonstrates the protagonist's unrelenting desire to hope for a new life.

TEMPLATE-HOW TO SOUND SMART

When you learn this template, the outline of your essay will be largely written before you walk in the door. Just fill in the missing info from the given passage!

1. EXPLOSIVE OPENING—START OFF WITH A GOOD HOOK THAT SETS UPS THE ESSAY!

TEMPLATE EXAMPLE:

John Doe, a respected and passionate writer offers a convincing argument…

In this very insightful article, John Doe…

From the very beginning, John Doe draws us into…

In response to the article, "Timeout for Parents," the writer eloquently…

2. SHORT PHILOSOPHICAL STATEMENT OR THESIS OVERVIEW

TEMPLATE EXAMPLES:

He vividly reminds us that a nation's most vulnerable citizens are lives worth fighting for, as he reminisces about the sacrifice once made for our country.

He shows us that we need to understand today's homeless society. It is the key to prevent the repeat of past failures and crucial to the growth of future generations.

His overall purpose is to guide readers through the painstaking reasons why a huge population of our citizens is facing such a dilemma.

3. USE THREE CONCRETE EXAMPLES FROM THE ESSAY: GIVE RELEVANT EXAMPLES FROM THE ESSAY TO SHOW HOW THE AUTHOR BUILDS THEIR CLAIM.

TEMPLATE EXAMPLE:

1. He effectively builds an argument by using a personal story, a statistic and a historical fact.
2. Key strategies John employs are from a personal anecdote, allusions to art and a rhetorical question.
3. She uses literature, a famous speech and a state law to deliver a powerful argument.
4. Three compelling reasons from an old quote, a personal journey and a little-known fact effectively demonstrate why he came to his conclusion.
5. John convincingly makes his point by using an award-winning movie, recorded data and a popular book.

IMPORTANT TIP

Make sure any quoted words or phrases are enclosed with quotation marks.

4. USE STRONG VOCABULARY WORDS AND TRANSITION/BRIDGES

Replace 3-4 lazy words with big/smart words and bridges. Try to draw from a pool of words you can reuse each time you write the essay.

TEMPLATE EXAMPLE:

VOCAB—morose, guttural, amass (words found in a perfect scoring essay) Have an arsenal of about 10-15 good words to rely on: SOUND SMART!

BRIDGES—next, my first example, finally, sometimes, in conclusion, as a result…

5. FIVE PARAGRAPHS—STAGGER PARAGRAPHS

Vary the length of paragraphs by using different number of sentences. Also use a varied length of sentences. Your first paragraph could have four sentences, one of which could be noticeably short. From there attempt to avoid uniformity among paragraphs and sentence length: don't repeat the same patterns. Stagger sentence length by using occasional short sentences of less than a handful of words.

SHOOT FOR THE FOURTH PAGE!

Length does matter and may be used in the objective grading system for a subjective essay.

6. DRAMATIC ENDING: END WITH A BANG AND A LASTING IMPRESSION!

A powerful way to sum up the way the author uses persuasion in their argument or claim.

TEMPLATE EXAMPLE:

1. He held my attention by making use of a personal anecdote, literary facts and a recent poll.
2. She persuasively builds this claim without apology using a legal document, a poem and an age-old question.
3. This writing was enthusiastically persuasive…
4. He builds a valid claim…
5. The foundation for her credible argument…
6. Her evidence is conclusive by…

There are thirty template paragraphs on the eCourse that you can mix and match. Use them as copy-work to learn how to write a high-scoring essay. As you memorize and write the paragraphs, make them your own. These can help you have as much as 75% of the essay written before the test.

AUTHOR'S BRAGSHEET:

Do not agree or disagree with the author but do elaborate on their expertise. It is important for you to maintain a neutral stance. Use statements in your essay that reiterate the author's sound knowledge about the subject matter. Here are some examples:

She has a sophisticated understanding of…

He makes a solid case against…

I appreciated his consistent use of the precise word choice…

She gave a well-considered evaluation of…

I was impressed by his strategically chosen support…

His claims consistently focused on…

The author uses vivid language to…

Her use of relevant details…

He deliberately uses a highly effective progression of ideas…

Her use of emotion thoroughly explains the impact on the reader…

The author is well-organized and a master of clarity…

She is a master at linguistics…

He bombarded us with overwhelming evidence…

You should be writing at least one essay a week for practice using the given techniques. You will learn to reuse hooks, bridges and vocabulary words for many different essays despite not knowing what the subject in advance. Besides practice topics—found online or in *College Board* books—useful short articles are in newspaper editorials, speeches, historical documents or any opinion-piece of writing.

You should be writing at least one essay a week for practice using the given techniques.

TIMING THE ESSAY

You are only given 50 minutes to complete the essay section. Use it all up!

Take a watch with you and keep track of exactly how much time has passed on your own timepiece. During the real test, the proctor should give you a five-minute warning prior to the end of the allowed time, but if he or she doesn't, you will rely on your own watch.

Use a chronometer watch or analog watch with the long hand that indicates minutes, set to point at 12:00. You will track time around to the 9 on the dial to indicate five minutes remain, and 10 for the end of the allotted time for the essay. This makes it easier to keep track because you need only glance at the watch without the need to calculate.

Write the acronym in this section on your essay pages. It's a guideline to help you remember how to format each paragraph. Write it on the outside of the grid lines. The goal is to make the 3 body paragraphs fill up at least 3/4 of a page each. Even though there are four pages to write the essay, a winning essay is usually at least three pages long but the longer the better.

You are only given 50 minutes to complete the essay section. Use it all up!

PARAGRAPH 1: OPENING

- Restate the author's topic sentence/main argument, using the same key words.
- State overall purpose of the article, including who the author is trying to appeal to.
- Cite three strategies the author uses in their article to **BUILD THE ARGUMENT** (such as polls, data, articles, reports, etc.).

PARAGRAPH 2: FIRST CITATION

Repeat first + second paragraph's key words and argument. What does the author say?

- Explain what kind of writing patterns the author uses, such as comparing, contrasting, using a personal anecdote, analyzing data, etc.
- Explain how the writing patterns give the writer credibility for the **IDEAS EXPRESSED!**

PARAGRAPH 3: SECOND CITATION

- Select another paragraph from the article and **identify** what references the author makes.
- What citation does the author use in that new paragraph? Identify it and **expand** on why the author would want to use that citation to make it effective.
- Is the author **CONNECTING EVIDENCE?** Is the author using more than one source? **Harp** on this, and analyze how those arguments work together.

PARAGRAPH 4: THIRD CITATION

Cite one more paragraph, preferably one that **ties** in the previous two paragraphs you cited.

- What is the author pushing toward? Are they appealing to the emotional side of persuasion, logical side, or something completely different?
- **ELABORATE FACTS** and give a final explanation on how the author makes a strong argument.

PARAGRAPH 5: STRONG ENDING

- Finish with a **repeat** of the main argument and tie it back to your first paragraph.
- Put a **summary** of how the author **PERSUADED THE AUDIENCE.**
- End the essay with a **razzle-dazzle,** such as a surprising or powerful fact or opinion presented of how the author **SUPPORTED THE CLAIM.**

SUMMARY OF PARAGRAPH 1:

Hook—Grab their attention. Cite an amazing claim or fact from the introduction paragraph and include the title and author's name.

Overview—Give a thesis that firmly explains what you will discuss from the essay; including who the author intended to have read the essay.

Three citations—Impress the judges by focusing on three ways the author BUILDS their argument, such as citing a study, a survey and a quote from the essay.

PARAGRAPH 2:

Pull the first argument and cite IDEAS expressed.
Observation—Show what the author uses to back up that claim.
Word choice—Use a good vocabulary word.
Expound—Add details to why the citation works.
Result—Explain how it relates to being persuasive.

PARAGRAPH 3:

Fresh example—Use a new citation from the paper.
Useful outcome—Explain how the citation relates to the PULL example and how it fits with the main argument and CONNECTS evidence.
Language choice—Use another good vocabulary word here.

PARAGRAPH 4:

Press the argument—Tie the two previous examples together with one more the author cites.
Analyze—ELABORATE facts on ow the argument appeals to the pathos, ethos or logic of a person to make their point.
Polish—Make it sound good with a new vocabulary word.

PARAGRAPH 5:

Elaborate Thesis—Sum up how the author PERSUADES the audience.
Razzle-dazzle—Leave a final impression of how the paper effectively SUPPORTS claims with either an emotion from the essay or a strong piece of evidence from it, summarizing the (3) types of evidence used.

H   P
O   A
T   P

P   E
O   R
W
E
R

Write the above acronym on the outside of the lines for each paragraph with a goal of finishing on the fourth page. *When the essay is finished, remember to erase the lines you've drawn and the acronym.*

FUN TIP

Use 2-3 dashes for emphasis and at least one semicolon or colon and a couple of commas in your essay to make your paper LOOK SMART.

PART VI:

SCHOLARSHIP SEARCH

THE SCHOLARSHIP SEARCH

NOW THAT YOU'VE TAKEN the SAT, practiced hard and received your ideal score, it's time to start looking for scholarships. College scholarship money is usually awarded to a student based on merit or winning a contest. Most colleges and universities offer scholarship opportunities based on your *SAT* score combined with your high school GPA. Below is a chart that represents how your score can affect institutional financial aid.

SAT	REPRESENTS	POSSIBLE OUTCOME
800–950	high school equivalency	Junior College Entrance
960–1000	college ready	Moderate College Entrance
1100–1250	excellent preparation	Possible one-third to two-thirds scholarship to certain colleges
1260–1450	remarkable preparation	Possible "full ride" to mid-range colleges
1460–1600	extraordinary student	Possible "full ride" to high-end colleges

Many colleges give "full ride" scholarships to students with scores upwards from around 1400. If you receive scholarship money directly from the school, here are some tips to help get **more** scholarship money after they've decided your financial award.

1. Appeal for more money to the financial aid department. Do this after you have received an award letter. Ask for any extra scholarship money awarded to students who decided not to attend the school. Ask to be considered for award redistribution after the semester starts.

FUN TIP

A Bachelor's Degree can yield 182% more money per week.

2. Many schools will award more money if you raise your *SAT* score higher after you are already enrolled in school.

Keep on friendly terms with the financial aid advisor during this process. Be sure to send a personal thank-you note for working on your bbehalf.

FINDING OUTSIDE SCHOLARSHIPS

There are many scholarship opportunities outside of institutional aid.

There are many scholarship opportunities outside of institutional aid. Your goal should be to apply for as many of these as possible. Start your search by checking out the web sites provided in this book. Keep that list current and check off the sites you visit, record essays you complete and responses you receive. Check with local high schools, organizations and community groups (e.g., religious institutions, private foundations, athletic clubs, Lions Club, parent's employer, veterans, etc.) for other scholarship contests. Many scholarships have specific prerequisites so apply only for those scholarships for which you qualify.

The applications or essays generally require you to describe yourself or particular aspects of your life to convey who you are, where you are going and what you have to offer the college (or those awarding the scholarship). Many contest judges base their determinations solely on this piece, since they will probably never meet you.

EXAMPLE
Just call me Superwoman Extraordinaire. Not only have I been president of the Spanish Club, Captain of the Drill Team and Secretary of Student Government, but I've also maintained a 4.0 GPA, won volunteer of the year in my city and won four local art contests, all while working part-time as a cashier in a grocery store.

Your application or essay should immediately make an impression on the judges. Give this crucial element of your application some significant thought. You want a good "hook" at the beginning that will make them want to read on. Your "hook" should sum up who you are in just the first few sentences.

This will be your time to shine and to **SELL** yourself to the judges. Be specific about your accomplishments and talk about yourself every chance you get. It is highly likely the judges will be reading many other submissions and yours needs to stand out.

Stay away from expressions of negativity. Your personal strengths should be conveyed but not compared to someone else's weaknesses. Do not write about misfortunes and hard times. Rather, express how you have triumphed over adversity and immense challenge.

Communicate how—if given the opportunity—you can benefit the college or society by being a successful future leader.

A scholarship application is generally not the forum to announce that you have won other scholarships. The judges usually want to give the scholarship money to applicants who **have not** already won a big contest. Only divulge other scholarships if this is a specific condition of the application.

Include ALL volunteer work, leadership opportunities, awards won, extracurricular activities, works you have initiated, etc. The more of everything you enclose, the more impressive. Letters of recommendation—written on appropriate letterhead—from teachers, employers, church leaders, and other influencers in your life are worth including. Always sign the bottom of the essay and include a recent photograph of yourself. You will want to put a face to your name so the judges will remember you in their consideration. Read essays that have won in the past to seed your inspiration. They are an excellent place to start because they demonstrate what the scholarship judges are looking for. Look on the Internet for creative or non-traditional winning essays.

Don't leave any form-blanks empty. If a question does not apply to you, insert *N/A* (for "not applicable"). Use only black ink when filling out your application or essay.

More detailed scholarship information can be found at www.CollegePrepGenius.com in the book *High School Prep Genius*.

> **Stay away from negative topics. Your personal strengths should be conveyed but not compared to someone else's weaknesses.**

FUN TIP

You may consider typing your essay to really make it stand out. An actual typewriter can be found at most libraries if using the school's form.

LOANS AND GRANTS

If you're having a hard time finding good scholarships, don't worry. Scholarships usually make up less than 10 % of financial aid for most students. Generally, about 40% comes from financial grants, and loans usually make up the remainder.

College loans are usually obtained by parents, with low interest, from the college, a bank or The *College Board*.

College loans are low-interest loans, usually obtained by parents from the college, a bank or the *College Board*. They must be paid back over time. Grant money is given to students based on need* and is distributed on a first-come basis. Here is a list of grants that most students qualify for:

1. *Federal Pell Grant*: This is based on Federal (*FAFSA*) guidelines and **MUST** be applied for early. *If your first student has received a full scholarship, very often his or her Pell Grant can be applied and awarded to a second student—along with their own Pell Grant.*
2. *Federal Supplemental Education Opportunity Grant*: Is an instrument usually destined for the most needy. It can be applied for at the financial aid office.
3. State grants: Many states have free money, based on need, and they may also target studies in certain fields.
4. Institutional grants: These are from the schools and sometimes take the place of a loan to encourage a student to come.

The earliest date to apply to *FAFSA* is October 1 of the senior year. This is first come—so apply early! For more information call (800) 433-3243 or go to the website www.fafsa.ed.gov.

*Keep limited funds in your banking/savings account as it can be counted against monies given or awarded to you. Keep your resources detached from your parents' assets.

SCHOLARSHIP WEBSITES

THERE ARE MULTIPLE SCHOLARSHIPS and college resources available on the web. For ease, I have divided them into three major categories: organizations that offer scholarships college resources and scholarship search sites. The list of online scholarship resources in this book is by no means a comprehensive representation, but it is an excellent place to start your search for information. A more exhaustive scholarship list is in *High School Prep Genius* (paid product).

Important: Set up a separate email account for college and scholarship information. You'll have one place to check.

ORGANIZATIONS WITH SCHOLARSHIPS

There are thousands of organizations, funds and companies that offer scholarships to college students. I have included a small number of them.

The following is a representative sample of the kinds of places you can investigate: careers, religious groups, mature students, and those who maybe re-entering the workforce, single parents, cultural groups, women's societies, philanthropic centers, minority groups, groups of universities, college-specific, state-specific, federal instruments, music, arts, and so on…(just off the top of my head)!

Check the links below to see which of their scholarships may apply to you. Please note some of the websites may require you to search for "Scholarship" in the index.

> USDA: Animal and Plant Health Inspection Service
> Scholarships for study in veterinary medicine and biomedical science
> www.aphis.usda.gov

There are multiple scholarships and college resources available on the web.

American Political Science Association
Scholarships and grants for research and study
www.apsanet.org

Ayn Rand Institute
Essay contest
www.aynrand.org/contest

Common Knowledge Scholarship Foundation
Scholarship contest based on quiz scores
www.cksf.org

Elks National Foundation
Scholarships for leadership and Elks legacy
www.elks.org/enf

Kohl's Corporation
Scholarships for volunteer service
www.kohlscorporation.com

Microsoft Careers
Scholarships for computer science and related technical disciplines
https://careers.microsoft.com/careers/en/us/collegescholarship.aspx

Hispanic Scholarship Fund
Scholarships for many types of degrees
www.hsf.net

National Collegiate Athletic Association
Scholarship and internships for athletes
www.ncaa.org

The Roothbert Fund, Inc.
Scholarships for students with spiritual values
www.roothbertfund.org

Siemens Foundation

Scholarship competition for math, science and technology
www.siemens-foundation.org

Thurgood Marshall College Fund
Scholarships for the 47 TMCF Colleges and Universities
www.thurgoodmarshallfund.net

COLLEGE RESOURCES

Upromise
Earn scholarship money by making everyday restaurant or grocery purchases
www.upromise.com

Wall Street Journal: Education
Latest news about university education and financial resources
www.collegejournal.com

College Savings Plan Network
Information about developing a 529 Plan
www.collegesavings.org

GrantsNet
Database of searchable grants
www.grantsnet.org

Foundation Grants to Individuals Online
Resource for finding grants
www.gtionline.fdncenter.org

National Association of Student Financial Aid Administrators
Information regarding laws and regulations of financial aid
www.nasfaa.org

Sallie Mae
Information about student loans
www.salliemae.com

City of College Dreams
Resource for all types of college information
www.cityofcollegedreams.org

College for All Texans
Resource guide for universities in Texas
www.Collegeforalltexans.com

Federal Student Aid
Information about programs and resources from the U.S. Department of Education
www.federalstudentaid.ed.gov

Guaranteed Scholarships
An alphabetical listing of scholarship offers from colleges across the nation
www.guaranteed-scholarships.com

SCHOLARSHIP & UNIVERSITY DATABASES

There is a multitude of websites available that allow students to research scholarships and universities. Below is a list of some of the most popular ones. Each is put into a grid to help you utilize these resources to the best of your ability. As you find scholarships, use this table to note the scholarship name, the deadline, whether an essay is required and the date you mail the application. This will help you keep track of your work.

Scholarship Web Sites	Password	Contest Name	Deadline	App.	Essay	Mailed
www.aie.org		1._____	_____	_____	_____	_____
		2._____	_____	_____	_____	_____
		3._____	_____	_____	_____	_____
		4._____	_____	_____	_____	_____
		5._____	_____	_____	_____	_____
www.BrokeScholar.com		1._____	_____	_____	_____	_____
		2._____	_____	_____	_____	_____
		3._____	_____	_____	_____	_____
		4._____	_____	_____	_____	_____
		5._____	_____	_____	_____	_____
www.careertools.org/ scholarship		1._____	_____	_____	_____	_____
		2._____	_____	_____	_____	_____
		3._____	_____	_____	_____	_____
		4._____	_____	_____	_____	_____
		5._____	_____	_____	_____	_____

Scholarship Web Sites	Password	Contest Name	Deadline	App.	Essay	Mailed
www.collegeispossible.org		1._____ 2._____ 3._____ 4._____ 5._____	_____ _____ _____ _____ _____	_____ _____ _____ _____ _____	_____ _____ _____ _____ _____	_____ _____ _____ _____ _____
www.collegenet.com		1._____ 2._____ 3._____ 4._____ 5._____	_____ _____ _____ _____ _____	_____ _____ _____ _____ _____	_____ _____ _____ _____ _____	_____ _____ _____ _____ _____
www.collegexpress.com		1._____ 2._____ 3._____ 4._____ 5._____	_____ _____ _____ _____ _____	_____ _____ _____ _____ _____	_____ _____ _____ _____ _____	_____ _____ _____ _____ _____

Scholarship Web Sites	Password	Contest Name	Deadline	App.	Essay	Mailed
www.Fastweb.com		1._____	_____	_____	_____	_____
		2._____	_____	_____	_____	_____
		3._____	_____	_____	_____	_____
		4._____	_____	_____	_____	_____
		5._____	_____	_____	_____	_____
www.gocollege.com		1._____	_____	_____	_____	_____
		2._____	_____	_____	_____	_____
		3._____	_____	_____	_____	_____
		4._____	_____	_____	_____	_____
		5._____	_____	_____	_____	_____
http://aid.military.com/ scholarship/search-for-scholarships.do		1._____	_____	_____	_____	_____
		2._____	_____	_____	_____	_____
		3._____	_____	_____	_____	_____
		4._____	_____	_____	_____	_____
		5._____	_____	_____	_____	_____

Scholarship Web Sites	Password	Contest Name	Deadline	App.	Essay	Mailed
www.petersons.com		1._____	_____	_____	_____	_____
		2._____	_____	_____	_____	_____
		3._____	_____	_____	_____	_____
		4._____	_____	_____	_____	_____
		5._____	_____	_____	_____	_____
www.scholarship-page.com		1._____	_____	_____	_____	_____
		2._____	_____	_____	_____	_____
		3._____	_____	_____	_____	_____
		4._____	_____	_____	_____	_____
		5._____	_____	_____	_____	_____
www.Scholarships.com		1._____	_____	_____	_____	_____
		2._____	_____	_____	_____	_____
		3._____	_____	_____	_____	_____
		4._____	_____	_____	_____	_____
		5._____	_____	_____	_____	_____

Scholarship Web Sites	Password	Contest Name	Deadline	App.	Essay	Mailed
www.supercollege.com		1._____	_____	_____	_____	_____
		2._____	_____	_____	_____	_____
		3._____	_____	_____	_____	_____
		4._____	_____	_____	_____	_____
		5._____	_____	_____	_____	_____
www.collegeanswer.com		1._____	_____	_____	_____	_____
		2._____	_____	_____	_____	_____
		3._____	_____	_____	_____	_____
		4._____	_____	_____	_____	_____
		5._____	_____	_____	_____	_____
www.Financialaidofficer.com		1._____	_____	_____	_____	_____
		2._____	_____	_____	_____	_____
		3._____	_____	_____	_____	_____
		4._____	_____	_____	_____	_____
		5._____	_____	_____	_____	_____

Scholarship Web Sites	Password	Contest Name	Deadline	App.	Essay	Mailed
www.finaid.org		1._____	_____	_____	_____	_____
		2._____	_____	_____	_____	_____
		3._____	_____	_____	_____	_____
		4._____	_____	_____	_____	_____
		5._____	_____	_____	_____	_____
www.studentaid.com		1._____	_____	_____	_____	_____
		2._____	_____	_____	_____	_____
		3._____	_____	_____	_____	_____
		4._____	_____	_____	_____	_____
		5._____	_____	_____	_____	_____

SCHOLARSHIPS FOR STUDY ABROAD AND INTERNATIONAL PROGRAMS

Scholarship Web Sites	Password	Contest Name	Deadline	App.	Essay	Mailed
www.iefa.org		1._____	_____	_____	_____	_____
		2._____	_____	_____	_____	_____
		3._____	_____	_____	_____	_____
		4._____	_____	_____	_____	_____
		5._____	_____	_____	_____	_____
www.iesabroad.org		1._____	_____	_____	_____	_____
		2._____	_____	_____	_____	_____
		3._____	_____	_____	_____	_____
		4._____	_____	_____	_____	_____
		5._____	_____	_____	_____	_____
www.internationalscholarships.com		1._____	_____	_____	_____	_____
		2._____	_____	_____	_____	_____
		3._____	_____	_____	_____	_____
		4._____	_____	_____	_____	_____
		5._____	_____	_____	_____	_____

Scholarship Web Sites	Password	Contest Name	Deadline	App.	Essay	Mailed
www.internationalstudent. com/		1._____	_____	_____	_____	_____
		2._____	_____	_____	_____	_____
		3._____	_____	_____	_____	_____
		4._____	_____	_____	_____	_____
		5._____	_____	_____	_____	_____

This compilation is in no way an endorsement of any particular website. The inclusion or omission of any particular website does not reflect the beliefs or opinions of *College Prep Genius* or *Maven of Memory Publishing*. This website list was reproduced for your benefit and serves as a launchpad for your own investigations. This listing is for informational purposes only and is no way a guarantee of scholarship awards.

PART VII:

JOURNAL FOR
TEST-SUCCESS

WHY KEEP A JOURNAL?

B Y NOW YOU MUST know the *SAT* and PSAT/NMQT are standardized tests that have recurring patterns. The key to doing well is to learn how to recognize the hidden patterns, use strategies to find the correct answers...and practise, practise, practise. The *Journal for Test-Success* is a way for you to keep records of your progress. As you take practice-exams, fill out the journal pages with the questions that you missed.

If your outcome is to improve your test-scores (and I'm guessing that's why you're reading this book), then when you miss a question, your goal should factor in how to master that particular pattern. The next time you retake that practice test or when that pattern arises again, you will know how to conquer it.

These are tests of logic, reasoning and critical thinking. With practice you will train your mind to look for the correct answer by exposing the patterns and observing the relationships between the question and its answer.

The *Journal for Test-Success* is a way for you to keep records of your progress.

Here is how to use these journal pages

The first step to set up your journal is to make copies of the journal pages and put or compile them in a notebook. In it you will keep a record of test dates and scores on the *Test Record* page.

1. Copy down all missed questions and include all its answers in the corresponding section.
2. Reference the type of question. Was it...?
      Reading (Use, Citation, Command, Chart, Passage)
      Math (TRLTR, Top Heavy vs. Bottom Heavy)
      Writing (Grammar, Style, *Reading*)
3. Make a note of which wrong answer you selected.

4. Rework it correctly.

5. Think…did.

6. Think…did you miss the answer or work it the long way? How can you shortcut the process?

7. Review of missed questions is one key to your success. Periodic revision ensures you can still answer them correctly and quickly.

> Once a month (for minimal recall)
>
> Once a week (for a good refresher)
>
> Nightly (for optimal review)

8. Compare your improvements the next time you take the same test.

9. Practise writing at least one essay a week using published articles in newspapers or online.

> Reuse and recycle the same key points learned in the essay templates.
>
> Make sure it contains all the elements in the acronym.

10. Form a study group with others who will be practicing for the tests.

> Conduct friendly competitions (weekly, bi-weekly).
>
> Divide into groups (boys vs. girls, etc.).
>
> Reward the individual and the group with the best improvement.

TEST RECORD

Date	Prep Book/Official Test	Test #	Reading/ Writing Score	Math Score	Essay Score	Total Score

READING

(Passage-Based Reading)

Test #	Problem	Answer Choices	Answer Details	Question Type	Error
Date	5	(A)	C	C	A
		(B)			
Page #		(C)			
Quest. #		(D)			
Date		(A)			
		(B)			
Page #		(C)			
Question #		(D)			
Date		(A)			
		(B)			
Page #		(C)			
Quest. #		(D)			
Date		(A)			
		(B)			
Page #		(C)			
Quest. #		(D)			

MATH

(Multiple-Choice)

Test #	Problem	Answer Choices	Answer Details	Question Type	Error
Date		(A)			
		(B)			
Page #		(C)			
Quest. #		(D)			
Date		(A)			
		(B)			
Page #		(C)			
Quest. #		(D)			
Date		(A)			
		(B)			
Page #		(C)			
Quest. #		(D)			
Date		(A)			
		(B)			
Page #		(C)			
Quest. #		(D)			

MATH

(Student Response)

Test #	Problem	Grid-in Box	Answer Details
Date			
Page #			
Quest. #			
Date			
Page #			
Quest. #			
Date			
Page #			
Quest. #			
Date			
Page #			
Quest. #			

WRITING

Test #	Problem	Answer Choices	Answer Details	Question Type	Error
Date		(A)			
		(B)			
Page #		(C)			
Quest. #		(D)			
Date		(A)			
		(B)			
Page #		(C)			
Quest. #		(D)			
Date		(A)			
		(B)			
Page #		(C)			
Quest. #		(D)			
Date		(A)			
		(B)			
Page #		(C)			
Quest. #		(D)			

PRACTICE ESSAY - Topic

H

O

T

P

O

W

E

R

F

U

L

P

A

P

E

R

Prefixes, Root Words and Suffixes

Pos Prefix	Definitions	Examples
am	friend	amicable—friendly
amphi	two	amphora—a jar with two handles
ben	good	benefit—promoting well-being
bene	well	beneficent—producing good
con	together	congregation—a gathering of persons
cred	belief	credulous—ready to believe
dyn	power	dyne—a unit of force
dynamo	power	dynamic—having explosive force
em	into	empower—give power to
en	make into	enchant—make magical
eu	pleasant	eulogy—words or praise
hyper	over	hypertension—high blood pressure
intra	within	intragroup—within a group
macro	large	macrotous—having large ears
magni	large	magnificent—great in deed
neo	new	neophyte—beginner
omni	all	omniscient—all knowing
para	beside	parallel—laying side by side
pro	forward	procedure—method of going towards a goal
super	above	superior—of higher rank, pompous, arrogant
supr	great	supreme—of the highest quality
sur	over	surcoat—overcoat
syl	together	syllable—one or more letters which form one sound
sym	along with	symbolize—to present a symbol
syn	along with	synthesis—a combination of parts to make a whole
sys	with	system—a method
ultra	beyond	ultrasonic—beyond sound
vita	long life	vitality—vigor in living
viv	life	vivacious—lively character

Neg Prefix	Definitions	Examples
a	in	abed—in the bed
a	without	amorphous—without shape
ab	not	abnormal—not being normal
an	absence of	anemia—not enough red blood cells
ante	against	antebellum—before the war
anti	opposite	anti-Semitic—against the Jews
apo	away from	apocope—a cutting off
beli	warlike	bellicose—inclined to start wars

Neg Prefix	Definitions	Examples
cata	down	catagenesis—evolution going backwards
contra	opposite	contraception—against conceiving
contro	against	controversy—opposite views
counter	opposite	counterclockwise—going in a direction opposite of clockwise
de	down from	denounce—putting down
di	two	dichotomy—a separation into two parts
dis	not	dislike—to not like
dys	poor	dysfunctional—functioning poorly
e	out	eject—to throw out
ec	out	eclipse—to hide
ef	out	effete—worn out
ex	out of	expect—to look out for
hypo	too little	hypotension—low blood pressure
hyper	too much	hypertension—high blood pressure
il	not	illegal—not legal
im	not	immature—not mature
in	not	innocent—not guilty
ir	not	irresponsible—not responsible
mal	evil	malicious—having evil intentions
mal	bad	maladjusted—ill-adjusted
mis	wrong	mispronounce—pronounce incorrectly
miso	hate	misogyny—hating women
mor	die	mortuary—place for dead
non	not	nonabrasive—not abrasive
ob	against	obviate—prevent a situation
of	against	offense—go against the law
pseudo	false	pseudodox—a false opinion
se	apart	secret—something hidden
un	not	uninformed—not informed

Neutral Prefix	Definition	Examples
ad	to	addict—towards a habit
amb	about	ambidexter—one who uses both hands with skill
ambi	around	amble—to walk leisurely about
ana	up	anabasis—a journey upward
be	intensive	bedeck—to cover up
bi	two	biceps—large muscle fastened in two places
bin	two	binocular—an instrument with two eyes
bis	twice	bisection—something divided into two equal parts

Neutral Prefix	Definition	Examples
circ	around	circumspect—to look around
circum	around	circumfluous—flowing around
demi	half	demisuit—half armor
dia	through	dialysis—the separation into elements
em	in	embalm—to insert preservatives
en	into	encamp—set up camp
epi	upon	epidemic—a spreading among people
hemi	half	hemisphere—half of a globe
inter	among	interaction—action for mutual advantage
intro	into	introduce—lead into
mon	one	monad—a unit
mono	one	monodrama—a play with one actor
per	through	perceive—to understand
peri	around	pericardium—around the heart
post	after	postfix—to add to end of syllable or word
pre	before	preamble—an introduction
re	back	rebuild—build again
semi	half	semicircle—a half circle
sesqui	one and a half	sesquicentennial—relating to a century and a half
sub	under	subaltern—under another
trans	across	transatlantic—across the Atlantic

Root Word	Definition	Examples
acer	bitter	acerate—shaped like a needle
acid	sour	acidic—acid building
acri	sharp	acrid—stingingly bitter
ag	do	demagogue—one who stirs people up for profit
agi	move	agenda—the program of work to be done
ago	go	agitate—keep moving
ali	other	alias—an assumed name
allo	other	allograph—forgery
alter	other	alternative—another choice
anni	year	anniversary—the annual return of an event or a day
annu	year	annual—relating to a year
anthrop	man	misanthropy—hatred of mankind
arch	ruler	genarch—the head of the family
aster	star	asterisk—a tiny star
astro	star	astrophile—one interested in star lore
aud	hear	audible—can be heard

Root Word	Definition	Examples
aus	listen	auscultation—the act of listening to sounds within the body
aut	self	automat—a self-service cafeteria
auto	self	autocrat—an absolute monarch
bene	well	benefit—an advantage
bio	life	biology—the study of living organisms
bon	good	bonny—sweet and attractive
calor	heat	caloric—like heat
cap	take	capias—a writ for arrest
capit	head	capital—amount of accumulated goods
capt	chief	captain—the head
cause	cause	accuser—one who charges another with a crime
cede	go	cede—to yield
ceed	yield	abscess—a localized collection of pus due to infection
cep	receive	exception—something left out of general use
cept	take	interception—to gain possession
cess	surrender	recession—act of going back
chrom	color	chromophilic—easy to stain
chron	time	chronic—continuing for a long time
cide	kill	fratricide—the killing of one's brother
cise	cut	incise—cut into
civ	citizen	civil—trained
claim	declare	clamor—a shouting
clam	call out	exclaim—cry out
clud	shut	recluse—one who shuts himself
clus	shut	include—to take in
congnosc	know	cognition—the act of knowing
coni	dust	otoconia—ear dust
cor	heart	core—the heart
cord	heart	cordial—cheerful
corp	body	corpse—a dead body
corpor	body	corporal—relating to the body
cour	heart	courage—to have heart; bravery
crea	create	creant—having the urge to create
cred	believe	credo—set of opinions
cub	lean back	accubation—posture of lying down
cumb	lie down	encumber—to place a burden upon
cus	motive	excuse—the reason for an action
cuse	motive	causal—relating to motive

Root Word	Definition	Examples
cycl	wheel	cyclical—moving in a circle of cycle
cyclo	circle	cyclitis—inflammation of the tissue behind the eyeball
dem	people	demophile—a friend of the people
demo	people	democrat—one who believe in democracy
dent	tooth	dental—relating to teeth
dic	say	dictacte—command
dict	declare	diction—language
dont	tooth	orthodontia—straightening of irregular teeth
dorm	sleep	dormancy—state of being static
drome	running	prodrome—an early warning of disease
dromos	running	hippodromist—a circus rider
duc	lead	abduct—to take away
duce	lead	induce—to persuade
duct	lead	educate—to develop
end	within	endoral—within the mouth
endo	within	endotrophic—nourished from within
enni	year	sexennial—occuring once every six years
fac	make	factive—making
fact	make	facsimile—a copy that is exact in every detail
feal	faith	fealties—intense fidelity
fect	make	proficient—able to do things well
feder	trust	federal—united
fer	bring	deference—respect for
fic	make	affect—make an impression upon
fid	faith	infidel—one who has no faith
fide	faith	fealty—loyalty
fila	thread	filate—slender
fili	thread	filet—lace made of fine threads
fin	end	final—relating to the end
finis	end	confine—to keep shut in
fix	fix	fixate—to become fixed
flect	bend	flection—the act of bending
flex	bend	flexible—able to bend
flu	flowing	fluid—a liquid
fluc	flowing	flue—a passageway for a flow of air
fluv	flowing	fluvial—in relation to a moving stream
flux	flowing	fluxion—the act of changing
forc	strong	fort—a stronghold for protection

Root Word	Definition	Examples
fort	fortune	fortress—a fortified place
fortuna	chance	fortuitous—happening by chance
fum	smoke	fumy—smoke-like; a funny smell
ge	earth	geobios—life of earth
gen	race	general—relating to all kinds
geo	soil	geophilous—growing or living on or under ground
germ	vital part	germin—to bud
gest	carry	gestant—pregnant
gnosi	know	agnosy—state of not knowing
grad	step	gradient—increase or decrease in a slope or property (such as temperature or concentration)
graph	write	graphite—soft, black carbon used for pencils
grat	pleasing	gratify—to please
grav	heavy	grave—serious
gravi	weighty	gravid—pregnant
gravito	heavy	graviton—a hypothetical particle with zero charge
gred	degree	gradual—processing by small steps
greg	herd	aggregate—to collect
gress	walk	ingress—the act of entering
hab	have	habitat—the natural abode of a plant or animal
habit	live	habile—able
helio	sun	heliod—like the sun
hema	blood	hemoid—like blood
hemo	blood	hemoptoe—hemorrhage of the lungs
hum	earth	humus—earth
human	ground	humble—lowly
hydr	water	hydrotherapy—the therapeutic use of water
hydra	water	hydrophobia—morbid fear of water
hydro	water	hydraulic—acting by water power
hypn	sleep	hypnobate—a sleepwalker
hypno	sleep	hypnotic—soporific
intellect	power to know	intellectualisms—devotion to the exercise of intellect
intellig	power to know and think	intelligent—having the power to think and know
jac	throw	dejected—low in spirits
jec	lie	eject—to throw out
ject	throw	projection—the act of thrusting forward
join	join	conjoin—unite
jud	judge	judicial—relating to administration judicial power

Root Word	Definition	Examples
judi	lawyer	abjudicate—reject the case
judic	judge	injudicious—not having sound judgment
junct	join	junction—act of joining; place of meeting
jur	law	conjure—to swear together
jus	law	adjustive—tending to put into proper order
koni	dust	koniscope—an instrument for estimating the dust in the atmosphere
lav	wash	lavish—flowing like water
leg	law	legal—lawful
letter	letters	letterpress—the process of printing from an inked raised surface
liber	free	liberal—relating to freedom
lic	permit	license—freedom to act
licit	permit	illicit—illegal
lit	letters	literal—according with the letter of the scriptures
liter	letters	literacy—the state of being educated
litera	letters	litany—a prayer consisting of invocations and responses
liver	free	delivery—freedom; liberation
loc	speak	soliloquy—a long speech to oneself
loco	place	dislocate—to move away from its place
log	word	logogriph—a word puzzle
logo	word	logical—reasonable
loqui	speak	soliloquy—solo speech
lot	wash	immunoblot—radioactively labeled antibody is used as the molecular probe
luc	light	lucid—clear
lum	light	luminary—a heavenly body
lun	light	lunacies—intermittent insanity believed to be related to the moon
lus	light	luster—a glow of light from within
lut	wash	launder—to wash and iron clothes
magna	great	magnify—to intensify
magni	great	magnum—great; in size, a large bottle of wine
man	by hand	manifest—seen at hand
manu	by hand	manual—relating to the hand
mar.	sea	marine—a sailor
mari	pool	mere—a lake
matri	mother	matrix—the womb
matric	mother	matricide—the murder of one's mother
matro	mother	matronymic—mother of one's ancestor
medi	half	mediate—come between
mega	large	megadont—having large teeth

Root Word	Definition	Examples
megalo	large	megascopic—enlarged
mem	remember	memory—the ability to recall
mer	sea	merman—mythical male sea creature
meter	measure	mete—to measure
micro	small	microbe—a minute organism or germ
migra	wander	migrate—to wander
mis	wrong	misadventure—an accident
miso	bad	misalliance—an improper union
miss	bad	missile—something which can be sent through the air
mitt	send	remit—pay back
mob	move	mobile—capable of moving
monstr	show	monstrous-extreme
monstri	show	demonstrate—to display
mors	death	remorse—torture of conscience
mort/mori	death	mortuous—deathlike
mot	move	motive—cause
mov	move	removable—able to be taken or carried away
multi	much	multifold—folded many times
multus	many	multiple—consisting of more than one
must	show	muster—to put on display
nasc	to be born	renascent—to be reborn
nat	to spring forth	natal—relating to birth
neo	new	neolatry—the worship of the new
neur	nerve	neurism—nerve force
nounc	warn	denounce—accuse
November	new	novalia—new-plowed fields
number	number	numerant—used in counting
numer	number	numerous—of great number
nunci	declare	enunciate—to pronounce carefully
omni	all	omnify—enlarge
oper	work	opera—a drama set to music
opus	work	opuscule—a small petty work
oss	bone	ossify—to make into bone
osteo	bone	osteal—relating to bone; osteoporosis
pac	please	pacer—calm
pan	all	panacea—a cure for all ills
pater	father	patron—a wealthy person who supports a cause or a person; patriot
patr	father	paternal—relating to a father; paternity

Root Word	Definition	Examples
ped	foot	pedantry—display of learning
pel	drive	propel—drive forward
pen	hang	impending—hanging over one, as in doom
pend	hang	pendant—hanging
phil	love	philliter—a love potion
phila	love	philanthropist—a lover of mankind
phile	love	philematology—the science of kissing
philo	love	philomuse—a lover of poetry and arts
photo	light	photon—a unit of light intensity
pict	paint	depict—to form a likeness
picto	paint	pictury—tending to look like a picture; pictograph
plais	please	implacable—cannot be soothed
plu	more	plural—more than one
plur	more	plurennial—a plant living many years
plus	think	nonplussed—perplexed
pneuma	breath	pneumonia—a disease of the lungs
pneumon	breath	pneumatic—pertaining to air
pod	foot	podium—a platform
poly	many	polyanthus—a type of plant
pon	set	to set forth to float; pontoon
pop	people	populace—the people
port	carry	portable—able to be carried
portion	part	portion—the one who divides
pos	place	posit—set firmly in place
posse	power	possessorship—complete ownership
poten	power	potent—powerful; potential
potes	power	possible—able to be
pound	power	impoundment—refusal of the presidents of the United States to spend money
prim	first	primal—original
prime	first	primacy—state of being first in rank
puls	push	expulsion—drive out
punct	point	punctuate—to place a point at the end of a sentence
put	think	compute—to calculate
ri	laughter	riantly—laughingly; hilarious
ridi	laughter	ridicule—laughter at the expense of another
risi	laughter	risible—to dispose to laughter
rog	beg	derogate—to lessen
roga	ask	arrogant—proud

Root Word	Definition	Examples
sangui	blood	sanguine—confident
sat	enough	satisfy—to give pleasure
satis	enough	saturate—to soak thoroughly
scope	watch	telescope—instrument for viewing distant objects
scrib	write	scribble—meaningless writings
scrip	write	conscript—to be drafted into military service
sign	sign	signate—sign or seal expressing authority
signi	mark	design—intention; signify
silic	flint	silica—silicon dioxide
simil	like	similize—to compare; similar
simul	resembling	simulate—pretend
sist	stand	persist—stand firmly
soph	wisdom	sophic—full of wisdom
spec	watch	specious—pleasing to the eye but deceptive
spect	see	spectacle—a show
spectro	observe	spectrohelioscope—instrument to view the sun
sphere	ball	atmosphere—the mass of air surrounding the earth
spond	answer	respond—to answer in kind
spons	pledge	sponsor—to assume responsibility
sta	stand	standard—established
stereo	solid	stereotype—anything reproduced without variation
stet	chest	stethogoniometer—apparatus for measuring curvature of the chest; stethoscope
stit	stand	persist—stand firmly
stru	build	construe—to explain
struct	build	construct—to build
sume	take	assume—to suppose
sump	use	consume—to use up
tact	touch	tactus—the sense of touch; tactile
tain	hold together	containment—prevention of hostile incurment
tang	touch	intangibility—quality of not being touched
techni	skill	technicality—a detail of skill and procedure
technic	art	pyrotechnics—a fireworks show
tempo	time	contemporary—those who lived at the same time
tempor	time	temporal—limited by time; temporary
ten	hold	tenant—occupant; tenacious
tend	stretch	extend—stretch forth
tens	strain	intensify—quality of strain
tent	hold together	maintain—to keep up

Root Word	Definition	Examples
tent	strain	detente—relaxation of strained relations
test	to bear witness	testate—leaving a valid will which has been witnessed; testament
the	God	thearchy—government under God
theo	God	theology—the study of elements of religions
tig	touch	contiguous—touching; in contact
ting	touch	contingency—possibility
tinu	hold	continually—without stopping
tract	draw	traction—the act of pulling
trah	pull	detract—to draw away from
trib	pay	contribute—to give money to a cause
tuit	teach	tutoriate—a body of tutors; tuition
tut	guard	tutor—one who teaches a pupil
ultima	last	ultimate—final
uni	one	unify—make into one
vac	empty	vacate—to make empty
vale	strength	valediction—a farewell
vali	worth	validate—establish legitimacy
valu	valor	valuation—estimation of worth
ven	come	adventure—a remarkable experience; ventral; ventriliquist
veni	come	event—a happening
vent	come	adventitious—not usual
ver	true	veracity—truth
veri	genuine	veridify—genuineness
vers	turn	versus—against as in legal actions
vert	turn	divert—turn attention away from
vest	clothe	vested—clothed in authority
vicis	substitute	vicarious—being substituted; vicissitude
vict	conquer	victor—winner
vid	see	video—visual part of television
vinc	conquer	vincible—being overtaken
vis	see	vision—something seen
vita	life	vitamin—of the essential constituents
viv	alive	vivacious—lively in temper
vivi	live	vivid—sharp/clear
volcan	fire	volcano—a mountain erupting molten lava
vulcan	fire	vulcanist—a metal worker

Suffixes	Definition	Examples
able	able	capable—able to do things well

Suffixes	Definition	Examples
ad	result of action	myriad—a collective number
ada	result of action	armada—a fleet of warships
ade	result of action	blockade—the act of isolating an enemy
age	act of	carriage—the act of carrying oneself
al	relating to	sensual—relating to the senses
an	native of	American—a native of America
ance	action	assistance—the act of giving help
ancy	process	militancy—a fighting spirit
ar	one who	burglar—one who commits burglary
ary	relating to	burglary—the act of breaking in
asis	condition	oasis—fertile condition
ata	result of action	enigmata—something hard to understand
ate	cause	dedicate—to set apart with a purpose
cian	having a certain skill	logician—an expert in the science of logic
cule	very small	reticule—a small net handbag
dom	quality	freedom—state of being free
ee	one who receives the action	employee—paid for action
en	made	silken—made of silk
ence	action	difference—state of being unlike
ency	state	efficiency—the ability to get things done
er	that which	reporter—one who reports
ery	quality	bakery—a place where food is baked
esis	process	genesis—act of coming into being
ful	full of	frightful—able to make one full of terror
fy	make	vitrify—to make into glass
ian	relating to	Orwellian—resembling the work of George Orwell
ible	can do	credible—can be believed
ic	nature of	endemic—native to a particular people or country
icle	very small	funicle—a small cord
ile	suited for	docile—easy to teach
ine	nature of	divine—godly
ion	act of	diction—choice of words
ish	origin	boorish—a lout
ism	doctrine	alcoholism—a condition of addiction to alcohol
ist	one who	alarmist—one who excites alarms needlessly
ite	quality of	appetite—craving
ity	state of	amenity—state of being pleasant
ive	causing	declarative—tending to make a statement

Suffixes	Definition	Examples
ize	make	acclimatize—to adapt to a new condition
less	without	careless—without care
ling	very small	duckling—a baby duck
ly	like	listlessly—like one who is without spirit
ment	act of	attainment—state of having reached a goal
ness	state of	baselessness—the state of being baseless
oid	like	asteroid—like a star
logy	study	biology—the study of living creatures
or	one who	exhibitor—one who shows things
ory	place where	factory—a place for manufacturing
osis	action	ketosis—the action of ketones
ous	full of	delicious—having a delightful taste
ship	office	hardship—suffering
sion	state of	confusion—state of being confused
tion	result of	reflection—an image thrown back
tude	condition of	similitude—the condition of likeness
ty	quality	plenty—quality of having much
ure	act	censure—to blame
y	inclined	faulty—inclined to be at fault

Appendix B:

Math Terms

MATH TERMS

T IN ORDER TO DO well on the *Math* portion of the *SAT* and *PSAT/NMSQT* it is essential know and memorize math terms and rules. I have created a handy table below to include the most important of these. I have left you two free columns. The best way to use the table is to write in an example in column three and then, when learned, check it off ✔ in the last column to confirm your comprehension. You can use words, draw diagrams or make equations to guarantee a thorough understanding.

Math Terminology	Definition/Properties	Make an Example	Know It ✔
1 to 1 Ratio	A ratio equivalent to one.		
30–60–90 Triangle	A right triangle with interior angles equal to 30°–60°– 90°. The length of each side will follow the ratio 1:2: √3.		
360 Degrees	The sum of the central angles in a circle.		
45–45–90 Triangle	When two of three interior angles equal 45°, then the third angle equals 90°. The hypotenuse will be the length of one side multiplied by the square root of 2.		
90-Degree Angle	The right angle formed by perpendicular lines, segments and rays.		
Absolute Value	The distance of a number from the origin (e.g., both –5 and 5 have an absolute value of 5).		
Abstract Fractional Equation	A fractional equation where all or most of the terms are different variables.		
Acute Angle	An angle that measures more than 0 degrees and less than 90 degrees.		
Additive Identity	Zero (since 0 + a = a).		
Additive Inverse	For any number a, a + (-a) = 0		
Adjacent Angles	Two angles that share the same side or vertex.		

Math Terminology	Definition/Properties	Make an Example	Know It ✓
Algebraic Expression	An expression which has at least one variable; they can be added, subtracted, multiplied and divided.		
Alternate Interior Angles	For two lines cut by a transversal, a pair of nonadjacent angles located between the two lines and on opposite sides of the transversal. (Alternate Exterior Angles are also congruent).		
Altitude	A line segment that extends from one vertex or a plane to the opposite side, forming a right angle.		
Angle Bisector	A ray, line or segment that passes through the vertex of an angle and divides the angle into two equal parts.		
Angle	Two rays joined by their endpoints.		
Arc	The arc of a circle is a portion of the circumference of a circle. A circle is 360° all the way around. Therefore, if you divide an arc's degree measure by 360°, you find the fraction of the circle's **circumference** that the arc makes up.		
Area	A two-dimensional space covered by a flat object.		
Area of a Circle $A = \pi r^2$	The product of 3.14 multiplied by the square of the radius of the circle.		
Area of a Square	The product of one of the sides of the square squared. ($A = S^2$)		
Area of a Rectangle	The product of the length and the width. ($A = L \times W$)		
Arithmetic Sequence	A sequence in which the difference between any two consecutive terms is the same.		
Arithmetic Series	The sum of the terms of an arithmetic sequence.		
Arrangement	An ordered grouping of elements.		
Associate Property	For any real numbers a, b, and c: $(a + b) + c = a + (b + c)$ and $(a \times b) \times c = a \times (b \times c)$		

Math Terminology	Definition/Properties	Make an Example	Know It ✓
Asymptotes	A line that a curve approaches but does not touch the line.		
Average	The sum of a set of values divided by the number of values—whereby all data points contribute equally to find the final average. **Weighted Average**—where some data points contribute more than others. **Combined Average**—where the average totals of a group of two or more are taken and added together, then divided by the total of members.		
Axiom	A statement assumed to be true without proof.		
Balance	An amount that remains.		
Base	The bottom-part measurement of a triangle used to calculate the area.		
Base Angle	An acute angle that's opposite the congruent sides.		
Bar Chart	A chart with rectangular bars with lengths proportional to the values they represent. They're used to compare two or more values taken over time or of different conditions, usually on small data sets.		
Binomial	A quantity which consists of the sum or difference of two monomials.		
Bisect	To divide into two congruent parts.		
c times	*as old as* Jim = $(c \times$ Jim's age$)$		
Capacity	The maximum amount a 3-dimensional object can hold.		
Center	The point in the interior of a circle from which all points are equidistant.		
Central Angle	An angle with its vertex at the center of a circle.		

Math Terminology	Definition/Properties	Make an Example	Know It ✓
Chord	A segment which has endpoints on a circle.		
Circle	A set of points on a plane that are equidistant from a single point (also called the center). $(x – h)2 + (y – k)2 = r2$		
Circumference	The distance around a circle; similar to the perimeter of a polygon. $C = \pi d$ or 2 pi R		
Clockwise	Moving in the direction of a clock.		
Coefficient	The numerical part of a term.		
Collinear	Lying on the same line.		
Confidence Interval	A range of values that signifies a 95% confidence level that the average of a population lies in between.		
Combinations	Different ways you can group elements in a set.		
Common Factors	Factors that two numbers have in common.		
Commutative Property of Multiplication	Property that states if x and y are two real numbers, then $x \times y = y \times x$.		
Complementary Angle	Adds up to a 90-degree angle.		
Complex Fractions	Fractions that contain more than one fraction line.		
Composite Functions	A combination of two functions, where you apply the first function and get an answer, and then fill *that answer* into the second function.		

Math Terminology	Definition/Properties	Make an Example	Know It ✓
Compound Interest $A = P(1 + r/n)^{nt}$:	Where: A = the future value of the of t years including interest P = the original principal investment r = the annual interest rate (decimal) n = the number of times that interest is compounded per year t = the number of years the money is invested or borrowed for		
Congruent	Identical in shape or measurement.		
Conjunction	A statement of two conditions, of which both must be true in order for the statement to be true.		
Conjugate	Binomials of the form $a + bc$ and $a - bc$.		
Consecutive Integers	Two integers whose difference is one.		
Constant	A quantity whose value is known and does not change.		
Conversion	When you write a given quantity and use two different units of measurements.		
Coordinate Plane	A plane with a coordinate system that can be used to designate the position of any point on the plane.		
Corresponding Angles	Angles formed by two lines crossed by a transversal.		
Cross-Multiply	To set the cross-products of a proportion equally. $\frac{a}{b} = \frac{c}{d} \rightarrow ad = cb$		
Cube	1) A regular solid with six congruent square faces. 2) To raise a number to the third power.		
Cube Root	The cube root of a number is a special value that, when used **three times** in a multiplication, gives that number.		
Cylinder	An object shaped like a tube; a shape with straight sides and circular ends of equal size.		
Decimal	A number written in decimal form.		

Math Terminology	Definition/Properties	Make an Example	Know It ✓
Decrease from x to y	$x - y$		
Degree of Polynomial	The degree of the term in the polynomial that has the highest degree (the sum of the exponents of all the variables in that term).		
Degree	The unit measurement for angles > 45 degrees ├ 90 degrees — 180 degrees		
Denominator	The bottom number of a fraction.		
Density	The amount of weight per the amount of space. I.e. mass compared to volume.		
Dependent Probability	Probability questions with more than one scenario.		
Dependent Variable	In a function, the variable whose value depends on the value assigned to another variable.		
Determinant	One real number associated with a square matrix.		
Diagonal	A segment that extends from one vertex of a polygon to a vertex that's non-adjacent.		
Diameter	The distance from one edge to another on a circle through the centerpoint; it can be broken into two opposite radii so the length is equal to twice the circle's radius.		
Difference	The result when one number or quantity is subtracted from another number or quantity.		
Digit	Any integer including and between 0 and 9.		
Dimension	The number of spatial directions needed to create a geometric figure.		
Direct Variation	A linear function described by $y = m - x$, where $m \neq 0$.		
Directly Proportional	When the increase of one quantity results in the increase of the other quantity (vary directly).		

Math Terminology	Definition/Properties	Make an Example	Know It ✔
Discriminate	The value of $b2 - 4ac$ from $ax2 + bx + c = 0$.		
Disjunction	A statement of two conditions in which only one condition must be true in order for the statement to be true.		
Distance	The length of the shortest path between two geometric objects.		
Distance Formula	For two points on a plane with coordinates (x, y) and $(x2, y2)$ is d = $\sqrt{(x^2 - x)^2 + (y^2 - y)^2}$		
Distinct	Not equal.		
Distribute (Properties)	Multiply term by the variable in front of the parentheses. $a(b + c) = a \times b + a \times c$		
Dividend	A number or quantity that is divided by another number or quantity.		
Divisible	Divided evenly by a certain number with zero left over.		
Division	An inverse operation of multiplication.		
Divisor	A quantity which divides into another quantity.		
Domain	A set of all first coordinates of the ordered pairs of a relation.		
Domain of a Function	The complete set of possible values of the independent variable in the function/ the set of all possible x values which will make the function "work" and will output real y-values.		
Elements	Objects or numbers within a set.		
Eliminate Method	To eliminate one variable by adding equations.		
Ellipse $(x - h)2$ $(y - k)2$ = 1 $a2$ + $b2$	A set of all points such that the sum of the distances from two given points (called *foci*) is constant. 2a (longer side) is the same for positions of an ellipse.		
Empty Set	A set that has no members, denoted by {}; also called a *null set* Ø.		
Endpoints	Points in between which all other points lie on the line segment.		

Math Terminology	Definition/Properties	Make an Example	Know It ✓
Equality	The property of two things being equal and symbolized by the equal sign (=).		
Equation	Quantities that are both equal.		
Equation of a line	Find the slope and y-intercept. Then the equation of the line can be written in slope-intercept form; y = mx + b.		
Equiangular Polygon	A polygon with all congruent angles.		
Equilateral Polygon	A polygon with all equal sides.		
Equilateral Triangle	A triangle with three equal angles that measure 60 degrees and three equal side lengths.		
Equivalence	States two quantities are equal in value.		
Evaluate	To replace variables of an expression with constants and then simplify them.		
Evaluate a Function	Insert a given x value, a number in the domain to see the result, which is a number in a range.		
Even Integer	An integer divisible by two with no remainder.		
Event	In statistics, the outcome of an experiment.		
Exclusive (numbers)	When either of two statements are true, but NOT BOTH.		
Expand	Use multiplication to eliminate the parentheses within an expression.		

Math Terminology	Definition/Properties	Make an Example	Know It ✓
Exponent	A shorthand notation used to indicate the number or value when a number (can be positive or negative) is multiplied by itself a certain number of times. E.g., $3 \times 3 \times 3 \times 3 \times 3 = 3^5$ For positive exponents, multiply the base by itself. For negative exponents, take reciprocal of the positive. For several exponents with identical bases, multiply by adding exponents and divide by subtracting them. Raise exponential expressions by multiplying them. Any number with exponent zero will equal one.		
Exponential Function	A function of form $y = b2$ where k and b are constants and $b \neq 0$ or $b \neq 1$.		
Exponential Term	A quantity that contains exponents.		
Exponential Growth	Growth whose rate becomes ever more rapid in proportion to the growing total number or size.		
Exterior Angle Theorem	Where the exterior angle of a triangle is equal to the sum of the two remote interior angles.		
Face	A two-dimensional planar surface that is part of a three-dimensional figure.		
Factor	A quantity that is a divisor of a larger number quantity without any remainders and when the positive integers are multiplied by each to achieve the number. E.g., 8 has the factors of 2 & 4 ($2 \times 4 = 8$), It also has the factors of 8 & 1 ($8 \times 1 = 8$).		
Factorial	If n is an integer greater than zero, the factorial of a positive integer n, denoted by $n!$, is the product of all positive integers less than or equal to n.		
Factoring Algebraic Expressions	Where an expression is broken down into two new expressions that, when multiplied together give the original expression.		

Math Terminology	Definition/Properties	Make an Example	Know It ✓
FOIL	(First, Outer, Inner, Last). Used to multiply two algebraic expressions. Multiply the **First** terms in each expression. Second, multiply the **Outer** expressions in the equation. Next, multiply the **Inner** terms. Lastly, multiply the **Last** terms.		
Formula	A mathematical sentence about relationships among certain quantities.		
Fraction	A ratio that indicates the division of two quantities. (**Multiply** them by numerator times numerator and denominator times denominator. **Divide** them by multiplying one fraction by the reciprocal of the other one.)		
Functional Notation	The use of letters and parentheses to indicate a functional relationship, such as $f(x) = 2x 2 + 3$.		
Geometric Notations	AB is the distance from A to B. AB◀▶ line goes through both points A and B (arrows indicate infinity). AB—— line segments w/ endpoints A and B. AB▶ ray w/endpoint A thru B and infinity. BA▶ ray w/endpoint B thru A and infinity. ∠ABC the angle B is the vertex and A and C points on each ray. m∠B is the measure of angle B. △ABC is a triangle with A, B, C as vertices. ▱ABCD quadrilateral with A, B, C, D as vertices. AB ⊥ BC line segments AB and BC are perpendicular.		
Geometric Sequence $an = a1 \times rn-1$	Each term after the first is formed by multiplying the previous term by same factor.		
Graph Direction	**Negative** correlation; **Positive** correlation.		

Math Terminology	Definition/Properties	Make an Example	Know It ✓
Graph Transformation 1.) Basic function 2.) $y = x3 + 5$ 3.) $y = x3 - 5$ 4.) $y = (x + 5)3$ 5.) $y = (x - 5)3$ 6.) $y = (-x)3$ 7.) $y = -x3$	$y + x$ graph shifted *up* five units graph shifted *down* five units graph shifted *left* five units graph shifted *right* five units graph reflected over *y-axis* graph reflected over *x-axis*		
Graph	The mark(s) made on a coordinate plane that indicate the location of a point or set of points.		
Greater Than	$>$		
Great Than or Equal To	$\geq$		
Greatest Common Factor (GFC)	The product of all prime factors common in every two or more items.		
Height	One dimension of a geometric figure.		
Hence	"From now"—e.g., "How old will Leah be 4 years hence?"		
Hexagon	A polygon with six sides and six vertices; to measure the sum of the angles (6 – 2) x 180, which totals a sum of 720º.		
Horizontal Distance	Distance measured only in the horizontal direction.		
Horizontal	A line on the xy plane that has zero slope.		
Hyperbola $\frac{(x-h)2}{a2} - \frac{(y-k)2}{b2} = 1$	The set of all points on a plane where the absolute value of the difference of the distances from two given points (foci) is constant.		
Hypotenuse	The side opposite the 90-degree angle in a right triangle (always the longest side in the triangle).		
Identity Function	A linear function such that $y = x$ or $f(x) = x$.		
Improper Fraction	A fraction with a numerator larger than the denominator.		
Inclusive	Includes the first and last elements.		

Math Terminology	Definition/Properties	Make an Example	Know It ✓
Inconsistent Equations	Equations with no common solution (like parallel lines).		
Increase from x to y	$y - x$		
Independent Events	In statistics, where the outcome of one event doesn't affect the probability of the occurrence of another event.		
Independent Probability	Separate probability questions that do not affect each other.		
Independent Variable	In a function, the variable whose value can be chosen.		
Index	The little number above and to the left of the radical sign that designates the root.		
Inequalities	Two values are not equal. To multiply or divide an inequality by a negative number changes the sign of the inequality.		
Inequality	The relationship between two expressions that states that one expression is greater than the other.		
Input	The value plugged into a function to yield an output.		
Inscribed Angle	An angle with its vertex "on" the circle, formed by two intersecting chords.		
Integer	Any number that can be expressed without a symbol, fraction bar or decimal point (whole number). An integer can be zero, odd or even. **Even**—divided by 2 and no remainder. **Odd**—divided by 2 with remainder of 1. Any integer can be written as a fraction over a 1.		
Integral	Referring to a number that's an integer.		
Intercept	The point where a line touches one of the coordinate axes on an xy plane.		
Interior Angle	The angle inside a polygon. The interior angles of a triangle add up to 180 degrees.		
Interior	A region enclosed by two or more geometric figures.		
Intersect	Having elements or points in common.		

Math Terminology	Definition/Properties	Make an Example	Know It ✔
Intersecting Lines	Where two lines meet.		
Intersection	Points that are common to two or more sets in a geometric figure.		
Intersection of Sets	When two or more sets have the same elements in common.		
Inverse Function [fog] (x) = [gof] (x) = x	Two polynomial functions, f and g, are inverse functions if and only if their compositions are identity functions.		
Inversely Proportional	When an increase in one quantity decreases the other member-objects in a set.		
Inverse Variation	A relationship between two variables such that their product is constant.		
Irrational Number	A real number that can't be written as the ratio of two integers.		
Irregular	A geometric region that can't be described in a normal way.		
Is, as, was, has, cost	= (equals)		
Isosceles Triangle	A triangle with two congruent (equal) sides and two congruent angles		
Isosceles Right Triangle	Having one right angle and two congruent legs. $x : x : \sqrt{2}x$ proportion		
It's divisible by 2 if…	It's an even number.		
It's divisible by 3 if…	The digits add up to a multiple of three. E.g., (**195**) 1 + 9 + 5 = 15		
It's divisible by 4 if…	The last two digits **form** a number divisible by 4. E.g., 6,316,832 (32 ÷ 4 = 8)		
It's divisible by 5 if…	It ends in a **5** or a **0**.		
It's divisible by 6 if…	It's divisible by 2 *and* 3. E.g., (**552**)		
It's divisible by 8 if…	The last three digits form a multiple of 8. E.g., (46,**352**) 352 ÷ 8 = 44		

Math Terminology	Definition/Properties	Make an Example	Know It ✔
It's divisible by 9 if…	Its digits add up to a multiple of 9. E.g., (**78,5214**) $7 + 8 + 5 + 2 + 1 + 4 = $ **27** $(9 \times 3 = 27)$		
It's divisible by 10 if…	It ends in **0**. E.g., (**6490**)		
Lead Coefficient	In a polynomial, the co-efficient of the term with the greatest exponent.		
Least Common Multiple	The smallest quantity that two numbers can be divided evenly.		
Leg	One of two smaller sides of a right triangle, but not the hypotenuse.		
Length	The distance from the endpoint of a segment to the other.		
Less Than (symbol)	$<$		
Less Than (word problem)	To the left on the real number line.		
Less Than or Equal To	$\leq$		
Like Terms	Monomials that differ from one another by their coefficients.		
Line	A geometric figure of two points and the union of all segments that contain the two points.		
Line Segments	A geometric figure of two endpoints and all the other points in between them.		
Line Formula	$y = mx + b$ (line has slope of m and a y-intercept of b). To figure out the y-coordinate multiply the slope by the point's x-coordinate and then add in the y-intercept.		
Linear Pair of Angles	Two angles that share a common side and whose unshared sides are collinear.		
Linear Equation	$ax + by + c = 0$, a first degree polynomial equation in one of more variables.		
Linear Function	$f(x) = mx + b$ where m and b are real numbers; to plot a point on a graph using (x, y), take x and separate it horizontally with the origin $(0,0)$ and vertically separate y from points (x, y) and $(0,0)$.		

Math Terminology	Definition/Properties	Make an Example	Know It ✓
Linear Growth	This occurs when the difference between quantities is constant over a period of time.		
Mass	The weight/amount of a 3D figure.		
Maximum	The largest possible quantity that satisfies a given set of conditions.		
Mean	The average of set of values.		
Median	Numbers ordered least to greatest with the middle exact number in an uneven set; if the set has an even amount of numbers, average the two numbers in the set that lie exactly in the middle.		
Midpoint	The point equidistant from both endpoints.		
Minimum	The smallest possible quantity that satisfies a given set of expressions.		
Mixed Numbers	A number that contains both an integer and a fraction.		
Mode	The elements/numbers that appear most often in a set.		
Monomial	A polynomial of one term.		
More (25 % **more**)	As many as, plus 25 % more.		
More Than	The number to the right on the real number line.		
Multi Variable Equation	An equation that contains more than one variable.		
Multiples	All numbers formed by the product of an integer and a given number. E.g., the multiples of 3 are 3, 6, 9, 12, 15, 18, 21, 24, 27…		
Multiplicative Inverse	For any number a if $a \neq 0$, $$a \times \frac{1}{a} = 1$$		
Multiplicative Identity	1 since $1 \times a = a$		

Math Terminology	Definition/Properties	Make an Example	Know It ✔
Multiplicative Property of Zero	Zero multiplied by any number is zero.		
n percent less than x	$x - (n/100)\ x$		
n percent greater than x	$x + (n/100)\ x$		
Natural Numbers	A set of numbers used to count things; also called *positive integers*.		
Negative	A quantity being less than zero.		
Negative Number	Is less than zero.		
Nested Functions	Functions within functions. The result returned from one function is used as the argument to another function.		
Non-Positive Number	Any negative number or zero.		
Nonzero Number	Any number besides zero.		
Null Set	The set with no members, denoted by the notation Ø.		
Numbers (Digits) Properties	**Places**: ones, tens, hundreds… **Distinct**: different, not identical **Consecutive**: in a row		
Number Sets	Numbers put in specified position.		
Number Line	A line of infinite length used to map the entire set of real numbers (both positive and negative) with a center of 0.		
Outliers	In a symmetrical distribution, if the average (mean) is equal to the median (middle) but contains values greatly smaller or larger, the average will go to the direction of the outliers and not the middle.		
Numerator	The dividend within a fraction.		
Obtuse Angle	Angles that measure more than 90 degrees and less than 180 degrees.		
Odd	An integer not evenly divided by two.		

Math Terminology	Definition/Properties	Make an Example	Know It ✓
Odds	The successful outcome of an event expressed as the ratio of the number of ways it can succeed to the number of ways it can fail.		
Of	Multiplied by		
Opposite	The side opposite the angle or side.		
Opposite Numbers	The same distance from zero on a number line, only in the other direction.		
Order of Operations PEMDAS	The order in which operations are performed on an algebraic expression. "Please Excuse My Dear Aunt Sally"—Parentheses, Exponents, Multiply, Divide, Add, Subtract.		
Ordered Pair	Numbers used to specify the position of a point on the xy-plane.		
Origin	A point on the xy-plane whose coordinates are (0,0).		
Outcome	A possible result in a probability problem.		
Parabola	The set of all points in a plane are equally distant from a given point and a given line not containing the point (quadratic graph).		
Parallel	Two lines with the same slope that lie on the same plane.		
Parallelogram	A quadrilateral with opposite sides parallel, two pairs of equal angles and four pairs of supplementary angles. All angles = 360°.		
Pattern	A repeated ordering of numbers or values.		
Parabola $y = a(x - h)^2 - k$	h, k is vertex of the formula I.e. vertex (h,k) $y = a(x - h)^2 + k$ (vertical shift) a is thinner if $a > 1$ a is wider if $0 < a < 1$ It becomes more open when a is positive and opens down when a is negative.		

Math Terminology	Definition/Properties	Make an Example	Know It ✔
Parallel Lines	Lines that do not intersect and are equal in slope.		
Pentagon	A special polygon with five sides. The sum of the angles = 540°.		
Percent	The percent number expressed as a fraction with 100 as the denominator (number of parts per hundred—take the proportion and divide the numerator by the denominator and multiply it by 100).		
Percentage	One number is compared to 100 by Direct Proportion; increasing both proportions equally.		
Percent Decrease	The amount of decrease divided by the original amount.		
Percent Increase from x to y ($y > x$)	$(y - x / x)$ 100		
Percent Increase	The amount of increase divided by the original amount.		
Perfect Cube	An integer equal to another integer raised to the third power.		
Perfect Square	An integer equal to another integer raised to the second power. (Watch out for hidden Perfect Squares)		
Perfect Square Trinomial	Is the expansion of a Binomial Squared. (binomial is a two–termed polynomial) and contains these characteristics: 1. First term is a positive perfect square 2. Last term is a positive perfect square 3. The middle term is twice the product of the square root of the first term and the square root of the third term.		
Perimeter	Measurement of the outside border of a shape achieved when all the sides added together.		
Permutation	To arrange things in a certain order; the "counting method," where if a choice can be made in a ways and a second choice can be made in b ways, then $a \times b$ will be the answer.		

Math Terminology	Definition/Properties	Make an Example	Know It ✓
Perpendicular	Two lines intersect and form a right angle. The slopes of two perpendicular lines have opposite reciprocals of each other.		
Place Value	Refers to the value of a digit in the base-10 number system.		
Pi ($\pi \approx 3.14$)	The ratio of the circumference to the diameter of that circle.		
Pie Chart	A circular chart divided into sectors, illustrating percentages. The arc length of each sector (its central angle and area) is proportional to the quantity it represents, and the sectors create a full disk.		
Pictograph	Represents statistical data using symbolic figures to match the frequencies of different kinds of data.		
Plane	A set of points spanned by two intersecting lines and all the points between them.		
Plotting Points	A rectangular coordinate system where a set of two intersecting and perpendicular axes form an xy plane. The horizontal axis is labeled the x axis, and the vertical axis is labeled the y axis. They divide the plane into four parts called *quadrants*. Any point on the plane corresponds to an ordered pair (x,y) of real numbers x and y. x represents the x-coordinate and y, the y-coordinate.		
Point (x,y)	The geometric figure formed at the intersection of two distinct lines.		
Polygon	A closed figure in a plane with three or more sides. To measure the sum of the angles, subtract 2 from the number of sides and multiply by 180. To find the perimeter, add all the lengths of the sides. To find the area (not a triangle or parallelogram), divide it into smaller polygons and proceed to find the area for each polygon.		

Math Terminology	Definition/Properties	Make an Example	Know It ✔
Polynomial	One term or a sum of individual terms, each having the form *ax*. *p(x)* indicates synthetic division. No exponents are found in a 1st degree polynomial which is normally used to divide a larger polynomial. This means there will be a remainder.		
Positive Number	A number greater than zero.		
Preceding	Coming immediately before.		
Progression	Arithmetic progression is a series of numbers in which each term progresses by adding a constant number to the previous term. (3, 7, 11, 15, 19) Geometric progression is a series of numbers where each term progresses by multiplying a constant number to the previous term. (4, 16, 64, 256)		
Prime Number	A positive integer whose factors are one and the number itself. It's always positive; 2 is the only even prime number; 1 is not prime because it has only 1 factor.		
Prime Number Ratio	A relationship expressed with a colon between the numbers. E.g., 3:1.		
Prime Factors	Factors that are prime numbers.		
Probability/Chance	Probability = ratio of number of desired outcomes and total number of outcomes in the sample space. Chance = number of times a certain thing could happen or number of times any of the things could happen.		
Product	The result when two or more numbers/quantities are multiplied together.		
Profit	The difference between income and expenses.		
Proportion	Equality between two ratios (written as a fraction 4/3).		
Pythagorean Theorem $a^2 + b^2 = c^2$	The addition of the squares of the two legs of a right triangle adds to equal the square of the hypotenuse		

Math Terminology	Definition/Properties	Make an Example	Know It ✔
Pythagorean Theorem 3D	The same triangle facing a different way, but 3D! If we call the sides x, y and z instead of a, b and c, we get: $x2 + y2 + z2 = distance2$ Measure the x-coordinate [left/right distance], the y-coordinate [front/back distance], and the z-coordinate [up/down distance]. And now we can find the 3D distance to a point given its coordinates!		
Pythagorean Triple Special Right Triangles	Consists of three numbers that can all be the lengths of the sides of a right triangle. Example: {3, 4, 5} is the same as $3^2 + 4^2 = 5^2$ {1, 1, $\sqrt{2}$} is the same as $1^2 + 1^2 = \sqrt{2}^2$ {1, $\sqrt{3}$, 2} is the same as $1^2 + \sqrt{3}^2 = 2^2$ {5, 12, 13} is the same as $5^2 + 12^2 = 13^2$ To get another Pythagorean triple, multiply the same number by each side. E.g., {9, 12, 15} is simply {3, 4, 5} multiplied by 3.		
Quadrant	One of the four regions in the xy-plane that form the xy-axis.		
Quadratic Equation	Involves three terms. In an equation in the form of $ax + bx + c = 0$, one unknown has the number 2 as the highest power of the variable; one term is a variable not raised to any power; one term is a regular number with no variable. E.g., $x^2 + 5x = 20$; solved by factoring.		
Quadratic Formula $x = \frac{-b \pm \sqrt{b2 - 4ac}}{2a}$	That **amazing** formula for finding all values of x that satisfy the equation $ax2 + bx + c = 0$. Works even if you can't factor the left-hand side.		
Quadrilateral	A four-sided polygon with four angles. The five most common types are parallelogram, rectangle, square, trapezoid and rhombus.		
Quarter Circle	Part of a circle that is one-fourth the area of a circle.		
Quotient	The number of times a divisor will completely divide into a given quantity.		

Math Terminology	Definition/Properties	Make an Example	Know It ✔
Radians	A unit of angle, equal to an angle at the center of a circle whose arc is equal in length to the radius and can also express angle measures.		
Radical Expression	An expression that involves a root.		
Radical Sign	A symbol that denotes a root.		
Radicand	A number underneath the radical sign.		
Radius	A segment extending from the edge point on the perimeter of a circle to the center of the circle. The radii of a circle have the same length.		
Remainders	The number left over when you divide one number by another, and it doesn't come out even.		
Range (of function)	Set of numbers where $f(x)$ comes out equal. E.g., $f(x) = x3 + 6$ has range of both negative and positive infinity. The function $f(x) = \sqrt{x}$ only has range of non-negative numbers.		
Range	The difference between the greatest and least values in a set of data.		
Rate	Distance or jobs divided by time, or price per item.		
Ratio	The comparison of two numbers expressed by dividing one by the other (another name for a *fraction*). E.g., 3:1.		
Ratio of Sides	Right Triangle: determined by comparing the lengths of two sides (Opposite side divided by adjacent side).		
Rational Number	Any number that can be written as the quotient of integers (division by zero excluded).		
Rational Expression	An algebraic expression written in the form of a fraction.		
Rational Equation	An equation that contains one or more rational expressions.		
Rationalizing	The process whereby radicals are eliminated from the denominators.		
Real Number	Any number that can be found on the number line.		

Math Terminology	Definition/Properties	Make an Example	Know It ✓
Reciprocal (Law of)	The product of a number and its reciprocal is always one (opposite number where numerator and denominator swap places). E.g. $\dfrac{xy}{z} = \dfrac{1}{\dfrac{z}{xy}}$		
Rectangle	A four-sided figure with four interior right angles—they are parallelograms with all angles measuring 90°.		
Recursive Notation	To find the next term in a progressive series other than multiplying or adding. E.g. $t_1, t_2, t_3, t_4, t_5, t_6...$ Each t represents a term in the progression and the subscript tells us the order of the terms.		
Rectangular Box or Solid	A three-dimensional object with six sides, all of which are rectangles.		
Reflection Line	A line that acts as a mirror in the form of a perpendicular bisector so that corresponding points are the same distance from the mirror.		
Reflexive Property	For any number a, $a = a$.		
Regular Polygon	A closed geometric figure with at least three sides, where the interior angles and sides are congruent.		
Relation	A set of ordered pairs.		
Remainder	The fractional part that remains after dividing.		
Respectively	In the same order; e.g., Dustin, Derek and Drake are 5, 3, and 2, respectively.		
Right Triangle	A triangle with one interior angle measuring 90°.		
Rise	A vertical change from any one point to another.		
Run	A horizontal change from any one point to another.		

Math Terminology	Definition/Properties	Make an Example	Know It ✔
Scalene Triangle	A triangle that has no sides of equal length.		
Scatter Plot	A diagram using Cartesian coordinates to display values for two variables for a set of data. It's displayed as a collection of points, each has the value of one variable which determines the position on the horizontal axis and the value of the other variable determines the position on the vertical axis.		
Scientific Notations	A number in the form of $a \times 10n$, where $1 \leq a < 10$, and n is an integer.		
Second Degree Equation	Any equation with terms having 2 as its highest exponent.		
Sector	A region of a circle bounded by an arc and a central angle.		
Segment	A line segment.		
Semicircle	Half a circle.		
Sequence/Series	A set of numbers in a specified order; they can stop at a point or go on to infinity. Some sequences follow a pattern of addition or multiplication.		
Set	A collection of numbers or objects; things in a set are called members or elements.		
Set Notation	A method of designing a set by enclosing the numbers of the set within brackets.		
Side	A segment that makes up one part of a figure in a plane.		
Similar Triangle Rule	The smaller triangle is similar to the larger triangle if the bases are parallel: their relationship is the same between any two corresponding sides, which are also proportional.		
Similar	Having the same shape but not the same size.		
Simple Interest	$A = P(1 + rt)$ where P is the Principal amount of money to be invested at an Interest Rate R% per period for t Number of Time Periods.		

Math Terminology	Definition/Properties	Make an Example	Know It ✓
Simplifying	Addition, subtraction, multiplication and division in an expression by combining like-terms.		
Slope	The ratio of the rise to the run between two points on the line. (Intercept form: $y = mx + b$)		
Solids	A geometric figure having three dimensions.		
Square	1) The result when a number is multiplied by itself. 2) A rectangle which has four equal sides.		
Square Root	A number that when squared, yields x. $(\sqrt{x})2 = x$		
Squared Quantity	A quantity within an expression which is raised to the second power.		
Standard Deviation	A measure of how far the difference in values in a data set is from the average of the data set.		
Standard Form	A linear equation in the form of $ax + by = c$ where a, b and c are real and a and b are not both zero.		
Straight Angle	An angle that measures 180° (Straight line).		
Subscripted Variable	A variable with a subscript—a little letter slightly below and to the right of the variable.		
Substitution	Expresses a variable, expression or constant which has the same value.		
Successive	Directly following.		
Sum	The result of addition.		
Supplementary Angles	Two angles that measure 180°.		
Surface Area	The total area of all the faces or surfaces of a three-dimensional figure.		
Surface Area of Cube	$6l2$, where l = the length of side.		
Surface Area of Prism	Rectangle: $2(wh + lw + lh)$ Triangle: 2(Area of the base) + (Perimeter of the base) (Altitude)		

Math Terminology	Definition/Properties	Make an Example	Know It ✓
Synthetic Division	A shortcut method used to divide polynomials by binomials.		
System	A collection of two or more equations or inequalities.		
Systems of Equations and Inequalities	Two or more mathematical statements considered at the same time.		
Tangent to a Circle	A line that touches the circle at one point; a tangent line is perpendicular to the radius at the point shared by the tangent and the circle.		
Tenths	The first decimal place to the right of the decimal point.		
Term	A number and/or one or more variables multiplied together.		
Thousandths	The third decimal place to the right of the decimal point.		
Time	A variable related to distance and time by the equation: rate • time = distance		
Transitive Property	For all numbers a, b and c, if $a = b$ and $b = c$ then $a = c$.		
Translation of Function	A graph of a function can be moved up, down, left or right by adding (moves it up) or subtracting (moves it down) from the output or the input.		
Transposition	Changing sides and changing signs.		
Transversal Line	A line that cuts across two or more (usually parallel) lines.		
Trapezoid	A quadrilateral with one pair of parallel sides.		
Triangle	A three-sided polygon (The sum of the angles is the same as a straight line—180 degrees. Longest side is opposite biggest angle. Shortest side is opposite smallest angle.) **The length of each side must be less than the length of the total sum of the other two sides.** (If not, the triangle could not "close.")		
Triangular Inequality Theorem	The sum of any two sides of a triangle that is greater than the third side.		

Math Terminology	Definition/Properties	Make an Example	Know It ✓
Trigonometry Terms	Sine: the ratio of the leg opposite an acute angle and the hypotenuse of a right triangle. Cosine: the ratio of the leg adjacent to an acute angle and the hypotenuse of a right triangle. Tangent: the ratio of the leg opposite an acute angle and the leg adjacent to the angle in a right triangle. Radian: the measure of an angle formed by 2 radii of a circle so that the intercepted arc has a length equal to the radius of the circle.		
Trinomial	A polynomial of three terms.		
Union	A set consisting of all members of set A and set B.		
Unit's Digit	The number that's farthest to the right, or the first digit to the left of the decimal point. E.g., in 34,672, the unit's or one's digit is "2."		
Value (Fair Market)	Fair market value is an amount considered to be fair and reasonable, given its accurate representation to a buyer.		
Variable	A quantity represented by a letter whose value may vary.		
Venn Diagram	Made up of two or more overlapping circles. It's often used in mathematics to show all hypothetically possible logical relations between a finite collection of sets.		
Vertex Angle	The angle formed by two equal sides in an isosceles triangle. The angle located opposite the base is called the vertex.		
Vertex	The point where two sides of an angle or polygon, intersect.		

Math Terminology	Definition/Properties	Make an Example	Know It ✔
Vertex Form Converted to Standard Form	$y = (x-1)^2 - 12$ (Vertex Form) $y = (x-1)(x-1) - 12$ (Perfect Square) $y = (x^2 - 2x + 1) - 12$ $y = x^2 - 2x - 11$ (Standard Form)		
Vertical	The direction of the y-axis.		
Vertical Distant	The distance between two points on the xy-plane represented by the change in the y-coordinates.		
Vertical Line Test	A test used to determine if a relation is a function. A relation is a function if there are no vertical lines that intersect the graph at more than one point.		
Vertical Angles	Non-adjacent angles formed when two lines intersect.		
Volume	The measurement of how much space a figure takes up. Custom volume is when a 3D picture is not a rectangular, cylinder, pyramid, sphere or cone then you would find the area of one face and multiply it by its height.		
Volume of Cube	Cube the length of an edge of the cube.		
Volume of Prism	The area of the base times the altitude.		
Whole Number	A non-negative number that has no fractional or decimal part.		
Width	One of the measurements used to calculate the area of a rectangle, or the volume of a rectangular box.		
x older than y	$x + y$		
x younger than y	$y - x$		
x and y	$x + y$		
x-coordinate	One of the coordinates to specify a point on the xy-axis.		
y years from now	$+ y$		
y years ago	$- y$		
y-coordinate	One of the coordinates to specify a point on the xy-axis.		

Math Terminology	Definition/Properties	Make an Example	Know It ✔
Zero (of a function)	The zero of a function is any replacement for the variable that will produce an answer of zero. Represented graphically, the real zero of a function is where the graph of the function crosses the x-axis (where the zero of a function is the x-intercept/s of the graph of the function).		
Zero Product Property	For any numbers a and b, if $ab = 0$ then $a = 0$ and $b = 0$.		
Zero Exponent	x 0 = 1 where x ≠ 0		

APPENDIX C:

My Motivation Test

MY MOTIVATION TEST

WE ARE ALL MOTIVATED by something, but we are not all motivated by the same thing(s). Your job is to figure out what will be the catalyst to drive you to set a strong unwavering priority to study for the *SAT* and PSAT—consistently. Below is a fun quiz for you to fill out that will help you identify your prime motivators. It is a guideline to help you set test-prep goals you can readily achieve.

Read each line below and choose the statement that best suits you. If both descriptions apply, pick the one which has been more dominate in your life until now.

In most questionnaires you may perceive a pattern. You may also be more inclined to choose the response that applies to the person you want to be, the ideal version of yourself, or what you think should be the right answer, instead of what you really think and feel. Do your best to reflect the real you.

Next, score your answers. Use the first letter of each section to create your motivational trait. Then, find the title that best depicts your motivational style.

Finally, using the suggested questions, create a game plan that will help you chart your course to stay on track and reach your test-score goals.

MY MOTIVATIONAL TRAIT

Circle the letter that best represents you:

I am a loyal person and I have a few intimate friends.   **(A)**
I strive for goals and want to reach the top by surpassing others.   B

Others may see me as insecure at times.   **(A)**
My confidence can sometimes overwhelm others.   B

I usually like being the leader.   **(A)**
Usually I prefer others to take the lead.   B

For the most part, I am congenial and very laid-back.   **(A)**
For the most part, I am intensely ambitious, positive and self-assured.   B

I am a planner.   A
I just let things happen.   **(B)**

Basically, I'd rather conform and fit in.   A
Basically, I'd rather stand out from the crowd.   **(B)**

I like to pacify people and keep the status quo.   A
It's a test to me to question the existing state of affairs.   **(B)**

TOTAL

A	B
4	3

Count the number of As and Bs. Which column is higher?
If A is higher, you are a Supervisor. (S)
If B is higher, you are an Associate. (A)

My title is _____Supervisor_____ and the first letter (S or A) is _S_

I can be bold and impulsive.   (C)
I like to analyze and calculate the situation.   D

I enjoy being rewarded for my accomplishments.   C
I make contributions that are significant to me.   (D)

I am invigorated and determined and I like to be stimulated.   (C)
I seek to keep the peace and maintain a steady pace in my life.   D

I am constantly thinking of new and exciting ideas and
I love to include others in the process.   (C)
Follow-through and making sure the job is done right,
is very important to me.   D

I like to be innovative and deal with problems on the spur of the moment. (C)
Being attentive and planning for the future is a
major strength of mine.   D

I lean toward spontaneity and risk-taking.   (C)
I lean toward being orderly, concentrated, and disciplined.   D

Details bore me and I don't like them.   C
I like dealing with details.   (D)

I thrive on challenges and discovering new things first-hand. Ⓒ
I like to keep the peace and maintain a stable environment. D

Changer (C)
Balancer (B)

TOTAL

C	D
6	2

Count the number of Cs and Ds. Which column is higher?
If C is higher, you are a Changer. (C)
If D is higher, you are a Balancer (B)

My title is ___Changer___ and the first letter (B or C) is _C_

Personal recognition and financial success are important to me. E
Making an important difference means more to me than financial gain. Ⓕ

I like it when I am recognized publicly. E
I would prefer to be recognized privately. Ⓕ

Obtaining material possessions is very important to me. E
Obtaining material possessions is not very important to me. Ⓕ

Gaining my own fortune is important to me. E
I want to be known for my legacy of contribution to the world. Ⓕ

I am mainly interested in salary and benefits when it comes to
looking for a job.   (E)

I desire to hold a job that gives me personal pleasure
more than the pay and perks.   F

I am a people-pleaser and am concerned with what others think of me.   E
I don't care what people think of me.   (F)

Outside (O)
Inside (I)

TOTAL

E	F
1	5

Count the number of E's and F's. Which column is higher?
If E is higher, your motivation comes from Outside. (O)
If F is higher, your motivation comes from Inside. (I)

My title is ___Inside___ and the first letter (O or I) is _I_

Take the first letter of each title/trait and write it here:

S	C	i

Dreamer

Below you'll find each possible 3-letter combination. Match your letters
to the motivation-guides below.

(SBI) MANAGER

Managers tend to be:

- Very responsible
- Detailed problem-solvers
- Organized and structured
- Practical
- Positive contributors
- Strategic thinker
- Time-managers
- Goal-oriented

Design a test-prep plan to maintain consistency and accountability with clear goals outlined for success. Track your progress daily with a steady routine and use charts and spreadsheets. Work toward specific goals for improvement by marking dates on your calendar. Start a competition that makes the reward benefit yourself as well as others when you have reached your goal. You could, for example, have others pledge money to your favorite charity or help others who are less fortunate with their prep goals, when you reach a goal.**Checklist for Reaching Test-Score Goals:**

☐ What is my test-prep goal?
☐ Make a <u>daily</u> spreadsheet/chart with specific goals
☐ Mark calendar with goal deadlines
☐ Accountability Partner _____
☐ Start a competition
        How will it benefit me? _____
        How will it benefit others? _____
☐ Like-minded friends to team up with:

_____
_____
_____
_____

☐ My reward for reaching my goal(s) _____

_____

(SCI) DREAMER

Dreamers tend to be:

- Visionary
- Confident
- Multi-tasker
- Creative
- Imaginative
- Energetic
- Original Thinker
- Innovator
- Persistent

Create an inspiring practice time with original ideas for achieving test-prep goals. Make a list of several ways to reach higher scores. Make the goals enjoyable and exciting and change them up daily (or weekly). Stick only to the ones that work for you. Record why this is important to you and review your motivation daily. Write down the consequences if you don't reach your goal. How will this goal benefit you as well as others?

Checklist For Reaching Test-Score Goals:

☐ What is my test-prep goal?
☐ Make a list of ideas to reach goals (fun and exciting)

1. _____

2._____

3._____

4._____

5._____

☐ Why is this goal important to me?_____

☐ Consequences of not reaching my goal._____

☐ How will this goal benefit me?_____
_____

☐ How will this goal benefit others?_____

_____

☐ Friends that can help lead me to success

_____

_____

_____

_____

_____

☐ My reward for reaching my goal(s) _____

_____

(SBO) LEADER

Leaders tend to be:

- Independent
- Determined
- Strong-minded
- Quick-decision makers
- Methodical
- Organized
- Planner

Create a consistent plan to work a little bit each day on your goals in small manageable pieces with a set deadline. Your goals need a specific objective. Work in some public recognition for your accomplishments. Plan to reward yourself along the way each time a goal is reached. Make sure the reward is tangible and something you really want.

Checklist for Reaching Test-Score Goals:

☐ What is my test-prep goal?

☐ Specific Daily Goals

       Daily _____

       Weekly _____

       Monthly _____

       Yearly _____

☐ Deadline to reach goal _____

☐ My Incremental Reward (for achievements toward my goal) Daily

Daily _____

Weekly _____

Monthly _____

Yearly _____

(SCO) CHALLENGER

The Challenger tends to be:

- Charismatic
- Engaging
- Negotiators
- Risk-takers
- Popular
- Fun-loving
- Fighter
- Enthusiastic

Create a plan that fits into your busy schedule. Block off specific time to work on your goals and be flexible to make sure it gets done. Discipline yourself to be consistent and avoid busy-work. Start a challenging competition that ends with an equally rewarding prize. Find like-minded achievers to join in on the contest. Make sure the process is fun and enjoyable.

Checklist for Reaching Test-Score Goals:

☐ What is my test-prep goal? _____

☐ How can I make studying enjoyable?_____

☐ How much time will I spend daily?_____

☐ What time of day? (If I miss it, what are my back-up plans?)

       Plan A _____

       Plan B _____

       Plan C _____

☐ Start a competition. _____

☐ Friends I will involve in the competition:

_____

_____

_____

_____

☐ My reward for reaching my goal(s) _____

_____

(ABI) SUPERVISOR

Supervisors tend to be:

- Loyal
- Dependable
- Detail-oriented
- Methodical
- Caring
- Supportive
- Conscientious
- Practical

Create a realistic goal you can achieve in a reasonable timeframe. Don't be hard on yourself to be perfect. Find others who are as equally committed to test-success. Use teamwork to work toward individual and team goals. Find a support group to cheer you on. Reward yourself by celebrating success privately with a few close people.

Checklist for Reaching Test-Score Goals:

☐ What is my individual test-prep goal? _____

☐ When can I expect to accomplish my goal? _____

☐ Friends to team up with:

_____
_____
_____
_____
_____

☐ What are my team test-prep (score) goals? _____

☐ Resources I will use _____

☐ My support group _____

☐ My reward for reaching my goal(s) _____

_____

(ACI) CONNECTOR

- Outgoing
- Friendly
- Creative
- Caring
- Resourceful
- Adventurous
- Loyal
- Dependable

Create a test-prep plan that works together with a partner or a group of like-minded people with the same goal. Accountability is very important to make sure you follow through with your plan. Work daily on your goal, even if only for a short time, because even small steps move you closer to your goal. Don't isolate yourself—don't do this on your own. Refer back to your goals, daily, to reinforce its importance to you. Post it in clear site.

☐ What is my test-prep goal? _____

☐ Why is it important to me? _____

(Look at the above reasons each day to remind you to do something every day to work toward your goal.)

☐ My partner or the group who I will work with: _____

☐ My support group for accountability _____

☐ My reward for reaching my goal(s) _____

(ABO) POLISHER

- Disciplined
- Focused
- Systematic Thinker
- Conscientious
- Diligent
- Deliberate
- Dependable
- Analytical

Create the best possible way for you to reach your goal and research the ideal way to achieve it. Maybe seek to be coached by a mentor. Research all the facts; find others who have already accomplished your dream and ask them for assistance. Make sure you set back a significant portion of money you have allotted to splurge on yourself when you have met your desired goal each week.

Checklist for Reaching Test-Score Goals:

☐ What is my test-prep goal? _____

☐ What is the best way to reach my goal? _____

_____

☐ Who can mentor me? _____

☐ People I know who have achieved the same goal:

_____
_____
_____
_____
_____

☐ Money I will set aside each week to splurge _____

☐ My reward for reaching my goal(s) _____

_____

(ACO) INVESTIGATOR

- Adventurous
- Considerate
- Thoughtful
- Insightful
- Perceptive
- Impulsive
- Energetic
- Creative

Create a goal that involves others you can encourage along the way. Work together with others to help you stay excited about your goals and make the studying process fun. List all the ways that have helped others reach the same goal and work on those. Learn a new strategy each week. Reward yourself with something small at every stage and when you have completed your goal, give yourself a big reward.

Checklist for Reaching Test-Score Goals:

☐ What is my test-prep goal? _____
—

☐ What are some different ways to reach my goal? _____

_____

_____

☐ Who can I involve so that we can reach this common goal:

_____

_____

_____

_____

_____

☐ My reward for reaching my daily goal _____

_____

☐ My reward for reaching my weekly goal _____

_____

☐ My reward for reaching my monthly goal _____

_____

☐ My BIG reward for reaching my final goal _____

_____